Labov

GUIDES FOR THE PERPLEXED

Guides for the Perplexed are clear, concise, and accessible introductions to thinkers, writers, and subjects that students and readers can find especially challenging. Concentrating specifically on what it is that makes the subject difficult to grasp, these books explain and explore key themes and ideas, guiding the reader toward a thorough understanding of demanding material.

Guides for the Perplexed available from Bloomsbury:

PRAISE FOR *LABOV:*
A GUIDE FOR THE PERPLEXED

" Yes, William Labov really did establish a whole new academic field when he was a graduate student. And he has remained at the forefront of that field to this day. Matthew Gordon describes how, why, when and where this happened, and explains with great clarity the importance and excitement of it all. It's a remarkable story, and Gordon has really done it justice.

PETER TRUDGILL, *University of Agder, Norway*

" Gordon has written a mesmerizing narrative of one of the greatest linguists in the history of the profession, capturing the historical, social, and theoretical significance of Labov's pioneering studies of language in its social context. It is an invaluable, timeless contribution to understanding the modern development of our discipline.

WALT WOLFRAM, *North Carolina State University, USA*

" For linguists and science historians, Gordon paints a contextually rich picture of William Labov's scholarship. Gordon provides extensive explanation of Labov's many milestones from the 1960s to 2010 and also contextualizes the development of linguistic and sociolinguistic fields over this time. This book would be helpful for any student of sociolinguistics.

KIRK HAZEN, *Department of English, West Virginia University, USA*

" Gordon's book is an amazingly comprehensive yet brilliantly clear presentation of the frameworks and contributions of William Labov, the founding figure in modern sociolinguistics and indeed one of the defining figures in linguistics more generally. With his characteristic lucidity, wit and personal touch, Gordon offers a presentation of the origin, growth and continuing development of Labov's thoughts and works, and Labovian sociolinguistics, that will prove to be indispensable reading for introductory students as well as an invaluable and engaging reference for even the most established scholars in the field. If a sociolinguistic were stranded on a desert island (or an island like Martha's Vineyard), and could choose one book for company, this essential distillation of the "Best of Labov" would truly be it.

NATALIE SCHILLING, *Associate Professor of Linguistics,*
Georgetown University, USA

Labov

MATTHEW J. GORDON

B L O O M S B U R Y

LONDON • NEW DELHI • NEW YORK • SYDNEY

Bloomsbury Academic

An imprint of Bloomsbury Publishing Plc

50 Bedford Square	175 Fifth Avenue
London	New York
WC1B 3DP	NY 10010
UK	USA

www.bloomsbury.com

First published 2013

British Library Cataloguing-in-Publication Data
A catalogue record for this book is available from the British Library.
ISBN: HB: 978-1-4411-9250-9
PB: 978-1-4411-5852-9

Library of Congress Cataloging-in-Publication Data
Gordon, Matthew J.
Labov: a guide for the perplexed/Matthew J. Gordon.
p. cm. – (Guides for the perplexed)
Includes bibliographical references and index.
ISBN 978-1-4411-9250-9 – ISBN 978-1-4411-5852-9 (pbk.)
– ISBN 978-1-4411-8600-3 (ebook (pdf)) – ISBN 978-1-4411-9508-1 (ebook (epub))
1. Labov, William. 2. Sociolinguistics. I. Title.
P85.L33G67 2013
306.44092–dc23

2012029263

Typeset by Deanta Global Publishing Services, Chennai, India
Printed and bound in India

CONTENTS

ACKNOWLEDGMENTS

I first met William Labov at an academic conference in 1995. I was a novice graduate student nervous to be speaking with the leading voice in my chosen field of study. He graciously answered my questions and asked me about the project I was beginning for my dissertation. Later that day, my heart nearly stopped when Labov mentioned me and my research during a presentation before the entire conference. The fact that this eminent scholar even bothered to remember my name, let alone speak positively about my work, was a powerful source of encouragement. Since that time, Labov and I have spoken on several occasions, and I continue to take encouragement and inspiration from our conversations. Moreover, like most sociolinguists, I recognize that almost all the work I do bears Labov's influence. His research gave birth to the field and continues to shape the discussions that take place in it. Thus, through his published research as well as through our interactions, Labov has enriched my career immeasurably, and I take this opportunity to express my gratitude.

I gratefully acknowledge the encouragement and support of my family, especially my wife, Lesley, whose design skills have also been invaluable to me. My colleagues at the University of Missouri have been tremendously supportive as well. I am especially grateful to Vicki Carstens and Michael Marlo for guidance through the largely foreign (to me) territory of mainstream grammatical theory. I am also grateful to the many linguists and others I have engaged with in the "Twitterverse," the user community for the social networking service Twitter. I posted numerous queries – questions about technical matters in sociolinguistics, requests for help with sources, even questions about whether particular expressions would be understood by readers outside the United States – and was consistently surprised and delighted to receive helpful responses within minutes. Outside of Twitter, I received helpful comments and suggestions from Maciej Baranowski, Natalie Schilling, and Walt Wolfram.

Finally, I note that this book was the brainchild of Gurdeep Mattu at Bloomsbury. He recognized the value of adding a volume on Labov to the series of *Guides for the Perplexed*. I thank him for his encouragement and patience in working with me to see this project through, and I thank his editorial team, especially Laura Murray, for their hard work throughout the process.

LIST OF FIGURES

CHAPTER ONE

The challenges of Labov

Who is William Labov? What is the significance of his work? When I pose these questions to students in my linguistics classes, I get a range of responses along the lines of:

- He studied how fishermen talk on some island.

- He showed that people who work in department stores try to sound like their customers.

- He proved that nonstandard dialects were just as logical as any other.

- He found that women tend to be innovative in their speech while men are more stuck in their ways.

- He wrote an atlas that maps dialect differences across the continent.

- He invaded England in 1066 and introduced Norman French as the language of power.

The responses hint at the breadth of Labov's impact on the field, well, except for the final response, which hints at the student's poor study habits.

William Labov is an American scholar who pioneered the field of "variationist sociolinguistics." Labov's work illustrates a particular approach to the study of language in its social context, one that focuses on the everyday speech of people from a range of backgrounds and that draws on quantitative methods to reveal patterns amid the apparent chaos of socially complex communities. This approach has been enormously influential. Labov is commonly cited by scholars from a range of disciplines including sociology, anthropology, and education as well as by linguists from a range of subfields including phonology, discourse analysis, and historical linguistics. Labov's approach has become virtually synonymous with sociolinguistics, at least in the US and UK. If an introductory student learns about sociolinguistics – that is, if the instructor includes such a section – then that student almost certainly learns about Labov's work since it is mentioned in practically all entry-level textbooks.

In that last sentence lies an important caveat to this consideration of Labov's impact. It is not inconceivable for an introductory linguistics course to omit any discussion of sociolinguistics, Labovian or otherwise, from its syllabus. This is not to say that such omissions are the norm; I suspect that most courses do cover sociolinguistics, though typically this is a relatively short unit late in the term. To use a food metaphor, at the banquet of Linguistics 101, sociolinguistics is not usually served as an entrée but rather as something between a condiment and a tasty side dish.

In this way the standard introductory syllabus reflects the field at large. The priorities of linguistics as a discipline may strike outsiders as strange. Many nonlinguists think of communication as the *raison d'être* of language, and thus might imagine that the social functions of language (as a medium of interpersonal communication) would be of central concern to linguists. Quite the opposite has traditionally been the case. In linguistics, talk of the social dimensions of language has generally not dominated the scholarly conversation. Moreover, when it comes to the language material (the data) examined by linguists, relatively little of this represents language produced in a genuine social context. So, here we find one of the challenges of this chapter's title. In emphasizing language as a fundamentally social phenomenon, Labov represents a challenge to mainstream thought and practice in linguistics.

To readers interested in or even sympathetic to his emphasis on the interplay of language and society, Labov presents a different kind of challenge: How does one get a handle on his vast body of work? With a dozen or so books and well over a hundred articles in print, Labov has been a remarkably prolific scholar. Moreover, his publications reflect his diverse research interests and span a range of topics from general theories of linguistic change, to questions of how children's dialects affect their learning to read, to the rules for ritual insults in African American vernacular culture. Even fellow researchers trained in sociolinguistics find it difficult to keep up with the breadth of Labov's work. For readers outside sociolinguistics, and doubly so for those outside linguistics altogether, the challenge is heightened by the fact that Labov mainly writes for an audience of specialists. Without some familiarity with the theoretical context in which he writes, someone approaching Labov's work for the first time may fail to grasp its full significance. Actually, when we consider the technical jargon and formalisms (including phonetic symbols) that Labov and other linguists use in describing language, we might wonder whether nonspecialists will grasp any of the significance of this work.

Labov recognizes this issue himself. When we spoke for an interview in 2006, he raised this concern with regard to his *Atlas of North American English* (Labov et al., 2006), which maps dialect patterns across the continent:

> [T]here's been an enormous amount of publicity about the *Atlas*; I've spent a lot of time talking with reporters and participating in talk shows. People have told me all kinds of fascinating and interesting things about the history of certain areas, and I'm benefitting from it. But the *Atlas* is not readable by the average citizen who's so passionately interested in these dialect differences because it's full of measurements and discussions of chain shifts among front vowels, back vowels, rounding and so on, and without a course in linguistics, the book itself is not readable. (Gordon, 2006, p. 349)

Labov is certainly correct about the opacity of this particular work, but it would be unfair to suggest that he has spent his life in an ivory tower. Throughout his career he has sought to apply insights from his research to broader societal issues. We see the clearest evidence of this in his work on African American English as discussed in Chapter Eight. He has reached out to educators, speech pathologists, and the general public with the message that nonstandard dialects are not degenerate versions of "Proper English," but rather follow rules as systematic as those governing prestigious dialects.

Still, as in the case of the dialect patterns of the *Atlas of North American English*, much of Labov's scholarship remains inaccessible to readers outside the field. I hope that this book can bridge some of that gap. My primary goal is to introduce several of the main currents of Labov's research to readers who have not yet had the pleasure of studying linguistics. At the same time, I believe the book also has value for those readers with experience in the field. Linguists of various specializations will find here a convenient overview of ideas and approaches developed by Labov over the course of his career. Even those who work in sociolinguistics might appreciate this discussion as a kind of "Best of Labov" collection.

What makes Labov perplexing certainly varies based on the background of the reader. In general, however, it's fair to say that the challenge comes more from accessing his work than from the impenetrability of the ideas themselves. By this, I certainly don't wish to imply that Labov's ideas are facile; instead, what I mean is that Labov's thinking generally offers plenty of points of connection. His research engages questions that specialists and nonspecialists alike can grasp, and his arguments are grounded in the evidence of real speech. Once accessed, then, his ideas resonate in ways that much of the abstract theorizing in other branches of linguistics doesn't.

A brief biography

Born on December 4, 1927, Labov spent his childhood in New Jersey. Early on he lived in Rutherford, which was then a small town about ten miles from New York City and just beyond the boundaries of the city's traditional dialect area. At the age of twelve, his family moved to Fort Lee, just across the Hudson River from Manhattan. As Labov described this area:

> That's well within the New York City dialect area, where people don't pronounce their *r*'s except when they think about it, and don't like the way they say *mad* and *more*. They also don't like kids with a big mouth from Rutherford, New Jersey, and my high school years were full of conflict (fights, which I usually lost; arguments which I usually won). A lot of these characters were pretty rough, and I grew up believing that most of the local families were on better than speaking terms with the Mafia. (1997a)

Labov attended college at Harvard University, graduating in 1948 with a degree in English and Philosophy. After Harvard he took various jobs as a writer over the course of a year or so but did not find much success in this line. Eventually he found his way into work as an industrial chemist, formulating inks for various commercial applications. He worked in a laboratory at his family's business, Union Ink Company of Ridgefield, New Jersey, and spent his days with people from a range of backgrounds. Speaking of this experience, Labov wryly notes that he gained "a firm belief in the existence of the real world" (1997a). Among other things, this job gave him extensive practice in research, and his research had observable consequences: he could see whether the inks he designed served their purpose or failed.

Labov left one world of ink for another when he entered graduate school in 1961. He studied linguistics at Columbia University, in New York City, under the direction of Uriel Weinreich, a scholar of diverse interests who is probably best known for his work on how languages in contact influence one another.[1] By today's standards, Labov proceeded rapidly through his graduate studies. He completed an MA in 1963 and a PhD in 1964. His Master's thesis was a study of sound changes in the dialect of Martha's Vineyard, an island off the coast of Massachusetts. This became Labov's first major publication when it appeared in the journal *Word* in 1963. For his dissertation project he took on the speech of New York City, concentrating again on particular sounds and exploring how their pronunciation varied across different social categories of speakers and across different situations of speaking. This study was published as a book by the Center for Applied Linguistics in 1966.

Labov taught at Columbia for several years after completing his PhD. During this time he directed a collaborative project that explored African American speech patterns. The project involved extensive fieldwork in the New York City neighborhood of Harlem. The full report appeared as Labov et al. (1968), and many of the key insights were discussed in Labov's *Language in the Inner City* (1972a).

In 1970, Labov moved to the University of Pennsylvania in Philadelphia, which has remained his academic home ever since. Much of his research attention has been focused on the speech of Philadelphia. He developed the Project on Linguistic Change and Variation which researched a wide range of features of the

Philadelphia dialect, making it the most extensively studied regional variety of American English. In the 1990s, Labov directed a project with the ambitious goal of surveying varieties of English across all of North America. The data were collected over the telephone and the results appeared in the *Atlas of North American English* (Labov et al., 2006). Through projects like these, Labov has trained dozens of graduate students, many of whom have become leading figures in the field including John Baugh, Penelope Eckert, Gregory Guy, Shana Poplack, John Rickford, among others.

Over the course of his distinguished career Labov has received many honors. He was elected to the American Academy of Arts and Sciences in 1976 and the National Academy of Sciences in 1993. In 1979, he served as president of the Linguistic Society of America, the field's major professional organization in the US. He has been the most frequently cited sociolinguist for at least the past forty years, and his influence has been acknowledged in footnotes and prefaces to no doubt hundreds of scholarly articles and books. What Chambers, Trudgill, and Schilling-Estes wrote about their *Handbook of Language Variation and Change* (2002) applies in many ways to the field more generally as they dedicated their collection to Labov "whose work is referred to in every chapter and whose ideas imbue every page" (p. v).

Labov in perspective

I imagine that Labov has attended his fair share of cocktail parties, coffee breaks, and similar gatherings over the past fifty years where someone has asked him about his work and his responses have varied according to who's asking. In the context of meeting with fellow academics or the general public, he might describe himself as a linguist, while among linguists he might identify himself as a sociolinguist, and among sociolinguists as a variationist. Actually, considering his renown in the field, it seems highly unlikely to me that he has had to identify himself or his work in any gathering of linguists for a very long time. Still, my point is that Labov can be described with increasing specificity as a linguist, a sociolinguist, and a variationist sociolinguist. To appreciate Labov's contributions we need to see him from a broader scholarly perspective. This means we need to understand how sociolinguistics differs from linguistics in general, and how the variationist approach differs from others in sociolinguistics.

Sociolinguistics within linguistics

The label "sociolinguistics" clearly advertises the field's primary address at the intersection of society and language. Sociolinguists explore this territory in various ways but generally assert the value of considering language within its social context. As noted above, this approach runs contrary to the dominant thinking within linguistics. For the last century or more the discipline has focused its attention on questions of language structure rather than language use. After all, language is a complex system with many component parts (e.g. sounds, words), and linguists have generally sought to understand the principles that govern how these components operate and how they interact. For the most part they have pursued this goal by voluntarily donning blinders that restrict their view to matters internal to language structure. In this way, questions about what people do with language or how language shapes and is shaped by social settings have been seen as outside the purview of linguistics. Insights into linguistic structure were thought to come only from abstracting language away from the realities of its use by actual people.

The most influential embodiment of this position has been Noam Chomsky, whose theories of grammar and language more generally have dominated the field for over half a century. Chomsky operates within a tradition that views language as a fundamentally psychological phenomenon. What is of interest to researchers in this tradition are linguistic rules internalized in the minds of speakers and what those rules might tell us about the human language faculty more generally. To be sure, this is a perfectly legitimate, worthwhile scholarly pursuit. Nevertheless, research in this vein operates under certain assumptions about the nature of language and the appropriate ways of investigating language. Chapter Two explores this issue more fully, but we can preview that discussion with a glimpse at Chomsky's statement of what matters to the field:

Linguistic theory is concerned primarily with an ideal speaker-listener, in a completely homogeneous speech-community, who knows its language perfectly and is unaffected by such grammatically irrelevant conditions as memory limitations, distractions, shifts of attention and interest, and errors (random or characteristic) in applying his knowledge of the language in actual performance. (1965, p. 3)

This passage, which is almost certainly quoted more often by sociolinguists than by authors who accept Chomsky's premise, clearly differentiates "knowledge of language" from the implementation of that knowledge. Chomsky labeled the former "competence" and the latter "performance." As his statement indicates, competence is what linguists should really be after, and performance can only muddy the waters of this investigation. One of the methodological implications of this position, explored further in Chapter Four, is that speakers' intuitions about what is grammatically possible in their native languages constitute the appropriate data for analysis and that examining actual speech produced in real social settings is likely to be unproductive.

One of the reasons that investigating language in the wild was thought to be unproductive was the "problem" of variation. Notice that Chomsky's idealization proposes "a completely homogeneous speech-community." Real communities always display some degree of linguistic variation; but, according to the dominant paradigm, this diversity masks the fundamental unity of the underlying linguistic system. This view reflects what J. K. Chambers calls the "axiom of categoricity," described in more detail in the next chapter. The basic assumption here maintains that language structure depends on perfect regularity to function properly, and so a linguist's description of that structure should rely on rules that apply categorically. Whatever differences are observed within an individual speaker's usage or across two or more individuals are of little consequence in terms of language structure.

In sum, mainstream linguistics has focused its attention on questions of language structure, which is assumed to be fundamentally homogeneous, and has pursued these questions by abstracting language away from its social context. Since his entry into the field in the 1960s, Labov has challenged this dominant narrative, but he was by no means the first linguist to recognize the value of studying language in its social context. For example, Labov took inspiration from Antoine Meillet, a giant in the field in the early twentieth century, who acknowledged the value of studying language "from a purely linguistic point of view" but also noted:

> [F]rom the fact that language is a social institution, it follows that linguistics is a social science, and the only variable to which we can turn to account for linguistic change is social change, of which linguistic variations are only consequences. We must determine which social structure corresponds to a given linguistic structure, and how, in a general manner, changes in social structure are translated into changes in linguistic structure. (Meillet, 1921, quoted by Labov, 2006, pp. 11–12)

Even earlier William Dwight Whitney (1867) maintained, "Speech is not a personal possession, but a social; it belongs, not to the individual, but to the member of society" (quoted in Koerner, 1991, p. 59). Similarly, Hugo Schuchardt (1885) observed, "Nowadays we see linguistics as a human science, belonging to the humanities, and we no longer see language as a natural organism, but as a social product" (quoted in Seuren, 1998, p. 97).

It is also worth noting that variation in language did not escape the notice of linguists before Labov's variationist approach was born. Indeed it was commonplace for researchers to acknowledge differences of speech. For example, in his enormously popular introduction to the field of 1921, the preeminent American linguist Edward Sapir wrote:

> Everyone knows that language is variable. Two individuals of the same generation and locality, speaking precisely the same dialect and moving in the same social circles, are never absolutely at one in their speech habits. A minute investigation of the speech of each individual would reveal countless differences of detail – in choice of words, in sentence structure, in the relative frequency with which particular forms or combinations of words are used, in the pronunciation of particular vowels and consonants and of combinations of vowels and consonants, in all those features, such as speed, stress, and tone, that give life to spoken language. (1921, p. 147)

Relative to his contemporaries, Sapir was exceptionally attentive to the issue of variation and its theoretical implications (see Chapter Two). Nevertheless, as J. K. Chambers observes, "Even Sapir, in practice, was unprepared to incorporate insights about variability into his linguistic analysis" (2008, p. 11).

In the area of methodology, we can also find precedents for the concerns raised by Labov and other sociolinguists. For example, in the nineteenth century Karl Brugmann and Hermann Osthoff stressed the importance of studying language as it is spoken today instead of only as it has been documented in the historical records:

> Only those comparative linguists who manage to leave the hypothesis-laden atmosphere of the workshop . . . and enter the clear air of tangible actual reality so as to gain insight into things that grey theory will never show . . . only those can achieve an adequate picture of how linguistic forms live and change . . . (Brugmann and Osthoff, 1878, quoted in Seuren, 1998, p. 91)

As it happens, the field generally did not take up this challenge and many researchers continue to practice armchair linguistics.

I have presented this assortment of quotations from various linguists as a way of contextualizing Labov's work and sociolinguistics more generally within the wider field of linguistics. While much of what Labov and others undertook in the 1960s was new, many of the fundamental tenets of the field that emerged had precedents. Indeed, not only had views about the social functioning of language been previously expressed, but they had been held by prominent linguists like Meillet and Sapir, among others. These were not voices in the wilderness. Nevertheless, no school of thought, no subfield of linguistic study coalesced around these views until the 1960s.

To be fair, there is one tradition that might qualify as an exception to this rule: dialect geography. This subfield, described in more detail in Chapter Two, arose in the late nineteenth century in response to the kinds of issues highlighted by Brugmann and Osthoff in the passage cited above. With regional speech patterns as its object of study, it not only acknowledges but embraces wholeheartedly the variable nature of language. Dialectologists pursued the living language as it existed in places far removed from the normative pressures of national, literary standards. In this sense they certainly concerned themselves with the social context of language. Still, when it came to examining how social factors shape speech patterns, their focus was squarely on geographic issues (e.g. topography, settlement history, etc.). They generally did not attempt to paint a complete picture of the social dimensions of language.

The field(s) of sociolinguistics

As we've just seen, a variety of linguists over the course of the nineteenth and twentieth centuries had addressed questions that we might characterize as sociolinguistic in nature. Moreover, the term "sociolinguistics" (or "socio-linguistics") first appeared, according to the *Oxford English Dictionary*, in a 1939 journal article by Thomas C. Hodson, and was later re-coined, apparently independently, by Eugene Nida in 1949 and Haver C. Currie in 1952. Still, as a proper field of study, sociolinguistics didn't coalesce until the 1960s. It was during this era that scholars from various institutions and research backgrounds began a conversation about the relationship between language and society.

In reviewing the history of American sociolinguistics, Roger Shuy highlights 1964 as a particular watershed year. In May of that year several researchers came together for a conference on sociolinguistics hosted by UCLA at Lake Arrowhead, California. The attendees included scholars who were or would later become standard-bearers of the field such as Charles Ferguson, Harold Garfinkel, John Gumperz, Einar Haugen, Dell Hymes, and Labov, who was then still a PhD student. Many of these scholars reunited weeks later at the Linguistic Society of America's Summer Institute, an annual (now biennial) summer school for advanced students, held that year at Indiana University. The Institute featured a course titled "Sociolinguistics" taught by Ferguson and another titled "Language and Society" taught by Gumperz. In addition to the regular curriculum, a special seminar on "Social Dialects and Language Learning" was organized, and prominent researchers from sociology, psychology, and education joined with linguists, including Labov.

In underscoring the events of 1964, Shuy is quick to clarify that he does not intend "to pinpoint the creation of modern sociolinguistics" (1990/2003, p. 11). Interest in the social dimensions of language was taking hold in many corners of linguistics and related disciplines.

In fact, Shuy suggests this trend was part of a broader *Zeitgeist* inspired by President Kennedy and his emphasis on community service and meeting the needs of the disadvantaged. Still, the meetings in 1964 provided a key stimulus for the field for, "It is often the coming together of a nucleus of scholars with the same growing concerns that frees it and lets new ideas bloom" (Shuy, 1990/2003, p. 11).

Sociolinguistics as a field certainly did bloom in the following years. A flurry of publications soon followed, including several collections of papers from meetings like the Lake Arrowhead conference (see Bright, 1966) and the seminar on social dialects held at Indiana (see Shuy, 1965). Courses in sociolinguistics began to appear as part of the regular curriculum at universities around the country. Over time, annual conferences and new journals dedicated to sociolinguistic research were launched.

As is perhaps inevitable, the growth of the field eventually led to fragmentation. The range of approaches to the study of language and society is no longer circumscribed by the heading of "sociolinguistics." In fact that heading never adequately represented the totality of approaches, and debates about what to call this field have raged from the beginning. In origin and orientation, the field is an interdisciplinary one; an important part of what happened in the 1960s was that a variety of scholars from linguistics and neighboring disciplines came together to discuss their shared interest in the relationship of language and society. A good deal of fruitful cross-pollination of ideas resulted, but disciplinary boundaries shaped the trajectories that research has taken. In order to appreciate Labov's position in the spectrum of "sociolinguistic" approaches, it's useful to briefly survey some of the alternative trajectories.[2] This includes work done within linguistics proper as well as within neighboring disciplines such as sociology and anthropology.

Based on the name alone, one might suppose that sociolinguistics involved substantial disciplinary overlap with sociology. In actuality, the relationship between the fields has historically been rather distant. Nevertheless, one tradition that bridges at least part of the gap between these fields is the "Sociology of Language." Joshua Fishman, an attendee of the 1964 Summer Institute, has been a leading voice in this field. As a label, "Sociology of Language" stresses the emphasis on exploring social issues related to language; to be sure this is an approach to sociology that examines language and not an approach to linguistics that examines society. One general topic that has been fruitfully pursued under this banner is language relations in multilingual societies. For example, what do the choices about where and when particular languages are used tell us about the social dynamics of a given community? Often research in this area explores language from a fairly global perspective rather than engaging in fine-grained analyses of linguistic structures. For this reason the term "macro-sociolinguistics" is sometimes applied to research in this vein.

Anthropology is a field that has historically had even stronger ties to sociolinguistics than has sociology.[3] Indeed, the traditional model of the discipline in the US held linguistics (all of linguistics, not just sociolinguistics) as one of the four core fields along with cultural anthropology, physical anthropology, and archeology. In American anthropology the strong connection to linguistics was certainly due to early scholars' interest in American Indians. Over the years, various labels have been applied to sociolinguistic research within anthropology including "linguistic ethnology," "ethnolinguistics," and "anthropological linguistics." The preferred usage today, at least in the US, seems to be "linguistic anthropology." Just as "sociology of language" is a way of doing sociology, "linguistic anthropology" is a way of doing anthropology. As Alessandro Duranti described it, linguistic anthropology is "dedicated to the study of the role of languages (and the language faculty) in [the various] activities that make up the social life of individuals and communities" (2001, p. 1), or more simply it is "the study of language as a cultural resource and speaking as a cultural practice" (1997, p. 2). In other words it is the social world that is the primary target of understanding and language serves as a point of entry to that world. Research in linguistic anthropology often involves quite sophisticated analyses of language data, but these serve to illuminate broader questions about society or culture.

Within linguistic anthropology one program that merits special mention is "Ethnography of Communication" (also known as "Ethnography of Speaking"), which was championed by Dell Hymes. The terminological choice of "ethnography" implies a particular methodological perspective, one grounded in direct observation, often over a long term, and seeking a holistic understanding of the social or cultural context of the observed behavior, practices, and so forth. Hymes explained the reasoning behind the label in an early essay that introduced a special issue of *American Anthropologist* he edited with John Gumperz:

> In short, "ethnography of communication" implies two charac-
> teristics that an adequate approach to the problems of language
> which engage anthropologists must have. Firstly, such an
> approach cannot simply take separate results from linguistics,
> psychology, sociology, ethnology, as given, and seek to correlate
> them, however partially useful such work is. It must call attention
> to the need for fresh kinds of data, to the need to investigate
> directly the use of language in contexts of situation so as to
> discern patterns proper to speech activity, patterns which escape
> separate studies of grammar, of personality, of religion, of kinship
> and the like, each abstracting from the patterning of speech
> activity as such into some other frame of reference. Secondly,
> such an approach cannot take linguistic form, a given code, or
> speech itself, as frame of reference. It must take as context a
> community, investigating its communicative habits as a whole,
> so that any given use of channel and code takes its place as but
> part of the resources upon which the members of the community
> draw. (1964, pp. 2–3)

This approach takes a much more holistic approach to language than is typical, certainly within linguistics. The principal unit of analysis is the "communicative event" which entails attending to much more than simply the evidence of language used. Hymes laid out a detailed model of the scope of "what has to be inventoried and related" in an ethnography of communication including the participants in communicative events, the settings, the available channels of communication (e.g. writing, singing, speaking), the genres employed, and so on. (Hymes, 1964, p. 13).[4]

Hymes's work has certainly shaped generations of research within anthropology, but his influence has also been felt in linguistics. Perhaps the clearest example of this appears in the work of John Gumperz, who might rightly be called a co-developer of the Ethnography of Communication.[5] Gumperz shares with Hymes a wide-net approach that explores language within a broader context of communicative events. Much of Gumperz's research has examined conversational exchanges between people and how such interactions shine a light on higher-level social processes. Thus, his approach is known as "Interactional Sociolinguistics." It typically involves an ethnographic methodology but also delves into detailed analysis of linguistic features. In a recent survey of this research, Cynthia Gordon describes the key contributions of Interactional Sociolinguistics as explaining:

> how speakers use signalling mechanisms, or 'contextualization cues,' often prosodic (like intonation, stress, pitch register) or paralinguistic (like tempo, pausing, hesitation) in nature, to indicate how they mean what they say, and how listeners, through a nuanced, context-bound process Gumperz calls 'conversational inference,' recognize and interpret contextualization cues through their own culturally-shaped background knowledge. (2011, p. 67)

As this description makes clear, for Gumperz and others working in this paradigm, the study of language takes in much more than sounds and words and sentences. What this line of research has demonstrated is that valuable insights into social dynamics can be drawn from even brief interactions when researchers attend to a broad range of the components of communication.

Work in Interactional Sociolinguistics and Ethnography of Communication highlights how very limited the perspective on language promoted in mainstream linguistic theory is. We can see this clearly by considering the notion of "communicative competence" developed by Hymes. Here Hymes is responding directly to Chomsky, who used "competence" to describe the internalized knowledge people have about their native languages. For Chomsky, the only knowledge that's interesting is the grammar, the rules that allow a person to understand and generate sentences. Hymes points out that there is far more to being a competent speaker of a language than this. After all, a person who goes around producing grammatical sentences without regard to context is "likely to be institutionalized." Knowing a language involves recognizing what's appropriate as well as what's grammatical, knowing when to talk and when to be silent, as well as what to talk about and how, where, when, and with whom (Hymes, 1972, p. 277). Communicative competence describes this broader knowledge.

Labovian sociolinguistics

The preceding discussion has sketched some of the range of approaches to the study of language in its social context and underscored the fact that all such approaches have generally occupied a minor position on the agenda of linguistics as a whole. As we turn to consider how Labov fits into the larger picture, two things should be clear already:

1 Labov did not invent sociolinguistics.

2 Labov's way of doing sociolinguistics is one of several practiced in linguistics and adjacent disciplines.

So, how should we characterize Labov's contribution? What distinguishes his approach from others? Of course, this entire book is meant as a response to these questions, but some brief consideration here will serve as orientation.

First and foremost is the fact that Labov is a linguist. He is neither a sociologist nor an anthropologist who mines linguistic material for insights into social processes. His primary objective is to contribute to our knowledge about language. Early in his career he noted, "Each time that we search for a piece of information, even if it is the most technical kind of sociolinguistic detail, I think we should be fairly clear, as linguists, on its relevance to the problems of linguistic theory" (1966a, p. 104). In keeping with this focus, his research has addressed questions of long-standing interest within linguistics. Thus, he described his work as generally "concerned with the forms of linguistic rules, their combination into systems, the coexistence of several systems, and the evolution of these rules and systems with time" (1972b, p. 184). In other words, Labov is concerned with those matters that concern all linguists.

With his stated emphasis on language as the object of study, Labov separates himself from scholars such as Fishman, Hymes, and Gumperz for whom studying language stands as more of a means to an end. Labov's methods present a further point of contrast. For one thing, the linguistic units that Labov studies are generally of a traditional sort. They include consonants and vowels as well as grammatical forms like verbal suffixes that very much represent the kinds of things studied by other linguists, even those who work outside the sociolinguistics framework. In this way they differ from many of the "contextualization cues" examined in Interactional Sociolinguistics as well as from other elements of communicative events considered in Ethnography of Communication. It is also significant that Labov relies on quantitative analysis: many of his observations come from statistical comparisons in which linguistic usages correlate with social variables like age or social class. This approach relies on the analysis of group behavior; in fact, Labov maintains that individual speakers cannot be fruitfully studied in isolation and their speech behavior only makes sense when viewed from the perspective of the wider community (see Chapter Four). Again, the contrast with other sociolinguistic approaches is striking. Gumperz, for example, often relies on qualitative analyses of illustrative cases.

Understanding Labov's methodology and the theory that undergirds it is crucial to appreciating his contributions to linguistics. On the one hand there is the simple fact of his insistence on considering social factors in the investigation of language. Labov, like others involved in promoting this position in the 1960s, clearly saw the field as desperately needing reform on this count. As he reflected on that early period, "I have resisted the term *sociolinguistics* for many years, since it implies that there can be a successful linguistic theory or practice which is not social" (1972b, p. xiii). Hymes illustrates a similar sentiment when he proclaims, "The final goal of sociolinguistics, I think, must be to preside over its own liquidation" (1974, p. 206). Several decades later, sociolinguistics remains a separate subfield, and many linguists continue to engage in asocial theories and practices. Nevertheless, Labov and others succeeded in carving out a place for sociolinguistic work to thrive within and across the borders of linguistics.

It is important to recognize that Labov's challenge to the field involves more than simply shining a light on the importance of considering the social dimensions of language. As discussed in more detail in Chapters Three and Four, he entered linguistics with unusually clear sense of what he hoped to accomplish, and part of his goal was to put linguistics on a firmer empirical footing. This entailed studying the everyday speech of a diverse range of people in ordinary social contexts. In this way he sought "to avoid the inevitable obscurity of texts, the self-consciousness of formal elicitations, and the self-deception of introspection" (1972b, p. xiii).

Making linguistic theory accountable to actually occurring speech data would also introduce a higher standard of proof. From Labov's perspective in the early sixties, "I first saw this field of linguistics as an assemblage of young people with all kinds of exciting ideas arguing vigorously with one another, but they didn't quite have an idea of how to prove whether they were right or wrong" (quoted in Gordon, 2006, p. 333). Testing hypotheses against real data would help settle such debates, or so Labov imagined. In some early work, Labov described his approach as "secular linguistics." It appears that he meant this in reference to the focus on the language of ordinary "lay" people as opposed to the literary standards. Still, I suspect that Labov also wanted to play off this term's theological connotations and have it serve as a jab at the mysticism that he saw as dominating mainstream linguistic theory.[6]

These days the most common term for Labov's approach is "variationist sociolinguistics," or simply, "variationism." The name reflects the field's traditional focus on describing and explaining linguistic variation within and across speech communities. Of course, most approaches to sociolinguistics involve the study of variable use of language as they explore how people use linguistic resources to effect social actions. But, for Labov, variation truly plays a central role. His work is premised on the fact that variation is not only a normal aspect of every living language but that it is actually fundamental to a language's smooth functioning. Moreover, variation is not random or chaotic but rather patterned (see Chapter Four). Labov's methodology, particularly his quantitative analysis, offers a way of detecting order within the linguistic heterogeneity found in all real speech communities. It is this analytical approach, grounded in a variationist theory, that distinguishes Labov's work from others in sociolinguistics and linguistics more generally.

Overview of *Labov: A Guide for the Perplexed*

My goal for this book is to offer an overview of the framework that Labov operates in as well as to survey his contributions in several particular areas of research. The first part of the book addresses the former objective. In Chapter Two, I build on themes introduced above by describing how linguists before Labov generally dealt with variation in theory and practice. I also present a general review of key concepts in linguistics for readers new to the field. Chapter Three discusses Labov's first forays into linguistic research: his Master's thesis study of a sound change active on Martha's Vineyard and his doctoral dissertation on the social stratification of New York City speech. These projects illustrate what was new about Labov's approach and highlight themes that he has continued to pursue throughout his career. Stepping back from the details of particular projects, Chapter Four presents a general characterization of Labov's variationist approach. Elaborating on issues sketched above, I hope to make clear how this approach differs from others and to detail the theory that informs Labov's work.

Labov's contributions to the field have come in a range of areas, and the second half of the book explores several components of Labov's research agenda. Chapter Five examines his work on stylistic variation – how and why we adjust our usage according to situation – and discourse analysis. In Chapter Six we turn our attention to "social factors," a topic that in a real sense permeates all of Labov's work. Here, though, we focus on his theorizing on the role that factors like social class and gender play in shaping linguistic variation. Chapter Seven looks at Labov's contributions to the study of language change. This topic has been central to his research agenda since his graduate studies, and it offers many excellent examples of how Labov's approach can shine fresh light on questions of long-standing interest to linguists of various stripes. In Chapter Eight, which examines Labov's work on African American English, we see how Labov's influence extends beyond the field of linguistics. While the study of African American English touches on a great many issues of theoretical interest to specialists, Labov and others were drawn to this research by social justice concerns including a desire to challenge harmful attitudes toward nonstandard dialects. Labov's advocacy on these issues certainly represents a legacy as valuable as any of his insights within linguistics proper. The book concludes with a look at where the field that Labov founded stands today, some fifty years later. We explore how generations of researchers have built upon Labov's pioneering efforts as well as how critical consideration of aspects of Labov's work has opened new avenues of research.

No discussion can claim to fully represent the wealth of Labov's scholarly contributions. There is no substitute for exploring Labov through his own words. My hope is that the present book will inspire the reader to do just that. Ideally it will live up to its title and serve as a guide by providing the tools necessary for a fruitful navigation of Labov's body of work.

Notes

1   Uriel Weinreich was the son of Max Weinreich, a scholar of Yiddish. The elder Weinreich popularized the quip "A language is a dialect with an army and a navy" as a comment on the fact that whether we label a speech code a "language" or a "dialect" is a matter of politics, not linguistics.

2   I don't pretend to offer a comprehensive overview of the range of approaches to the study of language and society. Fuller treatments are available from Trudgill (1978) and Lavandera (1988). Also, Wodak et al.'s (2011) collection includes excellent chapters reviewing the work of major figures such as Fishman, Hymes, Gumperz, and Labov.

3   More details on the anthropological ancestry of sociolinguistics are provided by Shuy (1990/2003), on whom my brief discussion draws.

4   In early versions of the model, Hymes identified seven components of communicative events (this was later expanded to sixteen). Hymes suggested the acronym SPEAKING as a helpful mnemonic for his model: Situation, Participants, Ends, Act sequences, Key, Instrumentalities, Norms, Genre (Duranti, 1997, p. 288).

5   Gumperz collaborated with Hymes on landmark works in the formation of this program including the special issue of *American Anthropologist* in 1964 and the collection *Directions in Sociolinguistics: The Ethnography of Communication* (Gumperz and Hymes, 1972).

6   Apparently I'm not alone in this suspicion. Nikolas Coupland explains "secular linguistics" as presenting a challenge to "what we might think of as the high priesthood of theoretical linguistics and its reliance on idealised linguistic data" (2007, p. 4).

CHAPTER TWO

Linguistics and sociolinguistics before Labov

As a student, I once had a conversation with a linguistics professor who had recommended some anthropological studies to me. I noted that even though these were current studies, the authors all cited work by Franz Boas and other luminaries from the early days of American anthropology. My professor explained, "Anthropology is a field that practices ancestor worship." While he was poking fun at one of our closest academic neighbors, the joke cuts both ways. It is probably true that anthropologists pay more attention to the history of ideas in their field than linguists do. We tend to be more focused on the state of the art at present and less interested in how the art got to this state. This is unfortunate because understanding our academic ancestors – worshiping them is not required – provides a crucial perspective on current trends.

In this chapter I hope to offer perspective of this sort. When Labov entered linguistics in the 1960s, he was joining an established field. While some aspects of his work can be fairly deemed revolutionary, others were more evolutionary. In order to fully appreciate his contribution, we need to put it in some historical context. Later in this chapter we consider how some of the issues Labov took up had been approached previously. Before that discussion, however, we turn to a more general orientation to linguistics. This section is intended to give readers new to the field the background information necessary to understand Labov's role. Readers with linguistics training may wish to skip ahead.

Linguistics as the "science of language"

If "linguistics" were a crossword answer, the clue might be "the science of language," or at least that phrase commonly serves as a shorthand definition of the field. What is implied by this label? In what sense are linguists scientists? Can language be studied unscientifically?

On the one hand, calling linguistics a "science" distinguishes the field from others interested in the study of language. Literary scholars, for example, might describe themselves as students of language since that is the vehicle in which literature travels. Also, poets, novelists, and other creative writers attend carefully to language as if their careers depended on it, which they do. Still, these would not be called scientific approaches to language.

What distinguishes the linguist's study of language as scientific boils down to a matter of the assumptions we make about the nature of language and the attitudes we adopt in approaching it. On both scores, linguistics promotes an approach to language that differs not only from those practiced in other academic fields, but from popular conceptions as well.

Descriptivism

One way in which the linguist's approach to language might be characterized as scientific relates to our stance toward our subject. Linguists seek to describe language as it exists, to observe the ways in which people use language and develop theories to account for those observations. This attitude stands in contrast to many popular notions about language. Most nonlinguists view language through an evaluative lens. This is especially evident in discussions of usages associated with regional and social dialects, which are the focus of Labov's research.

The contrast is often framed as pitting the "descriptive" approach of the linguists against the "prescriptive" approach of, well, everyone else. Linguists describe how language is used while others prescribe how language should be used. Linguists encounter a phenomenon like "copula deletion" in which the verb *be* is omitted (e.g. *The coffee cold*; *She running*) and try to document the circumstances that permit such deletion, the factors that determine how likely the verb will be deleted in a given situation, and the history of this grammatical feature. A prescriptivist encountering this same phenomenon would dismiss it as "bad" grammar and likely the product of laziness. The fact that copula deletion is rule-governed and even conveys shades of meaning distinct from comparable mainstream usages is irrelevant to a prescriptivist, who simply views it as a problem to be fixed.

Prescriptivism reigns as the dominant view in the US, UK, and other societies with an acknowledged standard language. The educational system, the media, and other institutions in these societies promulgate the idea that the variety known as the standard is superior to others. This standard is perceived as more logical, more precise, clearer, and even more beautiful than nonstandard dialects.

The prescriptivist attitude is obviously something that linguists must contend with. This is especially true for a linguist like Labov who focuses on varieties of English that are considered nonstandard. As we'll see in the next chapter and elsewhere, Labov developed techniques for exploring popular attitudes about language directly and for managing the effects of such attitudes on the speech data he was seeking.

The structure of language

Another reason for considering linguistics a science relates to the systematicity of our investigation of language. To get a sense of how a linguist differs from others on this score we can consider an automotive analogy. In the US and other industrialized nations, many people use a car on a daily basis. They drive wherever they need to go and rarely, if ever, think about what's going on under the hood (or bonnet). They don't need to understand, and probably have little interest in, the complex mechanical operations and chemical reactions that make the car function. If we liken language to the car, we see illustrated here how most people deal with language: they use it successfully everyday but with limited understanding of how it works.

A linguist, to play out the analogy, approaches language more like a mechanic approaches a car. We spend our lives under the hood, trying to learn more about how everything works. Actually the analogy really falls short here since a mechanic typically becomes involved only when something is broken or improvements are needed. Languages don't break, and linguists are not in the business of making improvements to them. A linguist is more like a mechanic who is driven by intellectual curiosity to examine the inner workings of cars and to share the resulting insights by publishing detailed descriptions and developing automotive theories. Is there a name for that?

To a linguist, language is a highly structured system, a kind of network of connections that link forms (sounds and words) with meanings. Moreover, the system as a whole is dependent on several subsystems. A typical list of these would include:

- phonology: the inventory and operations of sounds
- morphology: the structure of words
- semantics: the domain of meaning
- syntax: the ways that words are organized into phrases and sentences

Each of these components of language is systematic in the sense that rules govern what is and what isn't possible at every level. To nonlinguists, talk of language rules usually brings to mind grammatical issues such as subject-verb agreement, but it is important to realize that there are semantic and phonological rules as well. Unfortunately, the powerful influence of prescriptivism means that many popular discussions of language focus on "rules" that don't really describe the way that people actually speak, but rather how someone believes they should speak. A rule like "A sentence can't end in a preposition" clearly represents wishful thinking more than grammatical reality.

The kinds of rules that linguists have traditionally focused their attention on operate below the level of consciousness. They represent fundamental patterns that native speakers of a language follow without thinking. They are rules that we know but that we don't know we know. As a simple example, consider the pronunciation of the English past-tense suffix *–ed*. In some cases, such as *walked, laughed, ripped*, the suffix is pronounced as a "t," while in other cases, such as *logged, paved, towed*, it is pronounced as a "d," and in still others, such as *waited* and *aided*, it appears as a whole syllable "id." The rule has a phonological basis; the final sound of the verb root determines how the suffix is pronounced though the details need not concern us here. Speakers of English follow this rule consistently, and yet none of us has ever been taught it. Like most linguistic rules, this is one that native speakers acquire without explicit instruction.

By studying rules such as this, linguists have uncovered countless patterns that constitute language structure. Patterning is, of course, crucial to language's ability to function in communication. A language without rules would not be a language, and having a shared set of linguistic rules is what allows two people to communicate through language. Fair enough, but it's easy to see how this common sense belief can lead one to conclude that languages depend on absolute consistency in order to operate. Logically, the most efficient communication system would be one for which the rules were not only shared across a community, but were also applied without exception. If the rules of language were more like the laws of nature, communication might never fail. If combining sounds into words or words into sentences were like combining atoms into molecules, messages could be sent and received with perfect consistency. Linguistic rules, however, are not like chemical reactions. Nevertheless, a good deal of linguistic analysis has operated as if this were the case, as if rules applied categorically. We return to this issue below in discussing traditional approaches to linguistic variation.

More about sounds

The study of sounds within linguistics is one area that often doesn't translate well for nonspecialists. Whereas most educated people receive some exposure to basic grammatical concepts (e.g. parts of speech), they typically have little to no experience with phonology. For the most part, the terminology and theoretical apparatus for describing sounds remain unknown outside the field. Since many of Labov's most significant contributions to linguistics have come in the area of phonology, it's useful to give an overview of key concepts.

Linguists divide the turf of the sound realm into two related pursuits. Phonetics explores the physical properties of sounds, while phonology covers the systematic relations among sounds in a language. Thus, understanding how the vocal tract produces sounds and the articulatory differences between two sounds are phonetic concerns. Determining the rules governing which combinations of sounds can occur at the beginning or end of a word in English, or some other language, falls under the purview of phonology.

Phonetics

Phonetics provides a systematic method for describing and representing sounds. We need a special set of characters to represent sounds (a phonetic alphabet) in order to avoid the ambiguities of regular English orthography. In this book I have adopted a modified version of the International Phonetic Alphabet (IPA).

When it comes to describing sounds, phoneticians make a primary distinction between consonants, which are produced by restricting or blocking air flow at some point along the vocal tract, and vowels, which involve freer flow of air. The large class of consonants includes sounds articulated in different ways and at different points in the vocal tract. For example, consonants like [t] and [n], the final sounds in *beat* and *bean*, involve placing the tip of the tongue on gum line behind the upper front teeth, a location linguists call the "alveolar ridge." By contrast, with consonants like [k] and [ŋ], the final sounds in *luck* and *lung*, the back of the tongue is called into action and raised to the back of the roof of the mouth, which linguists call the "velum" (and we call sounds produced there "velar"). Even though consonants like [t] and [n] or [k] and [ŋ] take place in the same part of the mouth, the members of each pair differ in terms of how the sound in produced. For [t] and [k], the flow of air is completely blocked off in the mouth, and linguists label these "stop consonants." By contrast, the air continues to flow with [n] and [ŋ], and this is because the passageway to the nasal cavity is open with these sounds. Thus, these consonants are called "nasals."

A completely different kind of consonant, a fricative, is produced by creating a narrow gap somewhere in the vocal tract. This results in turbulence as air is forced through that narrow spot as with [s] (the final sound in *hiss*). We have here just a small sampling of the various types of consonants in English. A fuller discussion is available in introductory textbooks like Curzan and Adams (2011) or Finegan (2011).

Vowels differ primarily in terms of the position of the tongue during their production. For some vowels, such as the [i] of *beet*, the tongue is pushed toward the front of the mouth, while for others, such as the [o] of *boat*, the tongue is held in the back of the mouth. Vowels vary in the vertical dimension as well. The [i] of *beet* requires a high tongue position, while the tongue is much lower in pronouncing the [æ] of *bat*. This dimension of height is sometimes termed a matter of openness since it relies on raising and lowering the jaw to produce a more closed or open mouth. These positional differences are usually visualized in terms of a two-dimensional vowel space, as indicated in Figure 2.1. This chart plots the vowel symbols in terms of height and frontness. I provide guide words to illustrate each vowel's pronunciation in American English, the variety Labov works with most.

	FRONT	CENTRAL	BACK
HIGH			
TENSE	i (*beat*)		u (*boot*)
LAX	ɪ (*bit*)		ʊ (*book*)
MID			
TENSE	e (*bait*)		o (*boat*)
LAX	ɛ (*bet*)	ə ʌ (*but*)	ɔ (*bought*)
LOW	æ (*bat*)	a	ɑ (*box*)

FIGURE 2.1 *Vowels of American English. The schwa,* [ə], *represents the unstressed vowel in words like* above *and* sofa. *The low central* [a] *is not a distinctive sound (phoneme) in most American dialects, but it does form the first part of the diphthongs* /ai/ *and* /au/ *of* bite *and* bout.

In addition to their position in space, two other parameters are relevant to describing English vowels:

- Lip rounding: In producing some vowels, such as [u] in *boot* and [o] in *boat*, the lips are rounded, while for others, such as the [i] of *beet* and the [e] of *bait*, the lips are spread apart.

- Tenseness: The muscles in the jaw are tensed when producing some vowels and lax for others. You can feel this by placing your fingers under your jaw while you alternate between the tense [i] of *beet* and the lax [ɪ] of *bit*. This tense/lax distinction also corresponds to slight positional differences as well. Tense vowels tend to be higher and more peripheral (fronter for front vowels and backer for back vowels) than their lax counterparts, as suggested by Figure 2.1.

There are vowel sounds of English not represented in the above chart because they involve a more dynamic articulation. These vowels are called diphthongs, and the tongue travels across vowel space during their articulation. For example, the [ai] of *hide* is a diphthong that starts in the low central region and raises to the high front region. Other diphthongs in American English include the [au] of *loud* and the [oi] of *boy*. Actually, some or all of the tense vowels in Figure 2.1 are pronounced as diphthongs in most modern dialects of English. So, to be precise, we might transcribe the vowels of *bait* and *boat* as [eɪ] and [oʊ].

Phonology

Every language has rules that govern which sounds are used and how those sounds are deployed. Phonology is the field devoted to studying this "grammar" of sound. For example, phonologists look for patterns in where a given sound may occur and how the pronunciation of that sound may be affected by occurring in different locations.

One of the fundamental challenges of phonology is accounting for the mismatch between the physical properties of sounds and how sounds are processed (organized, perceived, etc.) in speakers' minds. When I introduce this issue in my classes, I begin by pronouncing a simple word like *book* several times, sometimes at a normal pace and sometimes a bit more slowly. I have two or three students say *book* as well. Then I ask the class what they heard. The response is, of course, several repetitions of *book*. But, I push, how can this be? Every time they heard the word, it was produced differently, at different speeds or by different vocal tracts and possibly with different accents. From a strictly phonetic perspective no two of those (or any) renditions of *book* are the same. Why do we hear them as the same?

The answer lies in the fact that we pay attention to some differences of sound but ignore many others. We somehow factor in things like speaking rate and differences between people's voices in our perception of language. This process is called "normalization" by phoneticians. Speakers of any language learn that many auditory differences don't matter for decoding the meaning of words in their language. That decoding of meaning relies not on specific auditory inputs, but rather on abstract categories of sounds. For every sound of our language, we have an idea in our heads of the various ways it can be pronounced, and when we hear someone talking we categorize each sound by type.

The concept of the "phoneme" is used to describe this kind of abstract category of sound. It is defined as a distinctive or contrastive category of sound in a given language. When we think about the sounds of our language, we normally think in terms of phonemes. If asked how many sounds there are in the word *pipe*, for example, most English speakers would say there are three: a [p], a vowel, and another [p]. As noted above, that vowel is actually a diphthong, a combination of two vowel sounds, but we think of it as a single sound because the /ai/ functions as a single phoneme in English. Moreover, by perceiving the [p] at the beginning of *pipe* as the same sound as the [p] at the end of *pipe*, we ignore a clear physical difference between those sounds. The initial [p] is produced with aspiration – a slight puff of air accompanies the release of the [p], which you can see by holding up a piece of paper to your mouth as you say the word. The [p] at the end of *pipe* doesn't have this aspiration. So, these are not the same sound from a phonetic perspective: one is aspirated, which phoneticians denote with a superscript *h* ([pʰ]), and the other is unaspirated (just [p]).

However, English speakers perceive them as the same sound because they're counted as types of the /p/ phoneme. These phonetically different variants of a phoneme category are called "allophones." To signal this status, we use square brackets when referring to allophones or actual phonetic sounds (e.g. [p], [pʰ]) and slashes when referring to phonemes (e.g. /p/).

Many times allophones of a given phoneme follow particular rules that govern when each variant can occur. This makes their distribution predictable. For example, the aspirated [pʰ] only occurs as the first sound in a stressed syllable, and the unaspirated [p] never occurs in this phonological context. This kind of pattern is called "complementary distribution."

Traditional approaches to phonology also recognize a different kind of relationship in which allophones are more interchangeable. Rather than one variant appearing in one context and another in a different context, both variants can appear in the same context. A classic example is the final sound of *pipe* which can be pronounced as a regular [p] or as an unreleased stop, which means the lips don't open (immediately) to release the sound. Whether the released or unreleased form is used has no effect on the meaning of the word, and the choice is not predictable by a phonological rule. Thus, this pattern is known as "free variation." As it happens, most of the variation studied by Labov falls under this category, though his work shows that cases of "free variation" are not as unpatterned as that label implies.

Approaches to variation before Labov

Even the casual observer knows that variation is an inescapable fact of linguistic life. In most languages there are recognized dialects that distinguish speakers from different regions and/or different social groups. We also know that different contexts demand different forms of language; indeed modifying one's usage to fit the situation is part of being a competent speaker of a language. The study of these kinds of variation became the focus of the branch of linguistics founded by Labov, but, as discussed in Chapter One, Labov was not the first researcher to take note of linguistic variation. The realities of dialects and other types of variation had long been recognized among linguists. Still, the mainstream of the field saw such diversity as presenting a challenge to be overcome rather than a resource to draw on.

To begin to sketch the picture of how the field conceived of variation before Labov arrived on the scene we can look to Leonard Bloomfield, one of the giants of American linguistics in the first half of the twentieth century. In his influential synthesis of the field, simply titled *Language* (1933/1984), Bloomfield spelled out his conception of a "speech-community," which he initially defines as "a group of people who use the same system of speech-signals" (p. 29). By this definition, all speakers of a given language constitute a speech community, and indeed Bloomfield endorses that interpretation as he describes a community of "all English-speaking people" consisting of two main divisions: the United States and the British Empire (p. 42).

All the same, Bloomfield seems cognizant of the difficulties in identifying all English speakers as users of the same linguistic system. He writes of the challenge of "determining in each case exactly what people belong to the same speech-community" given the ubiquity of variation: "If we observed closely enough, we should find that no two persons – or rather, perhaps, no one person at different times – spoke exactly alike" (p. 45). He offers a rich account of the factors that contribute to the diversity within any speech community, including social class, gender, and, of course, geographic separation. Bloomfield acknowledges the significance of these differences for the linguist seeking to describe a language, but in his view they stand as a methodological hindrance:

> These differences play a very important part in the history of languages; the linguist is forced to consider them carefully, even though in some of his work he is forced provisionally to ignore them. When he does this, he is merely employing the method of abstraction, a method essential to scientific investigation. (p. 45)

In other words, yes, every speech community teems with linguistic variation, but we must proceed as if homogeneity was the rule. Bloomfield's view survives to this day in many approaches within the field. The statement is reminiscent of Chomsky's position quoted in Chapter One that "Linguistic theory is concerned primarily with an ideal speaker-listener, in a completely homogeneous speech-community" (1965, p. 3). In fact, Chomsky intended his claim as a statement of an idealization that he felt was necessary for getting to the heart of the matter: an understanding of the core properties of language (or, more precisely, of the language faculty of the human mind).

As a methodological convenience, ignoring linguistic variation may be defensible, but it's clear that for many linguists this approach is much more than simply a strategy for sorting through complicated data. The idealized homogeneity is frequently interpreted as a fundamental property of linguistic structure; it's taken to represent how languages work rather than how linguists work. J. K. Chambers labels this position "the axiom of categoricity," since it treats the basic units of language as "invariant, discrete, and qualitative" (2008, p. 25).

As an illustration of the axiom of categoricity, we can consider how phonological rules are handled in this paradigm. One feature that distinguishes varieties of English around the world is rhoticity: whether or not /r/ is pronounced. In nonrhotic (or r-less) dialects /r/ is not pronounced when it appears before a consonant or at the end of a word before a pause. So in a phrase like "Park the red car" the /r/'s in *park* and *car* are dropped but the one in *red* remains.[1] This pattern can be described by a relatively straightforward phonological rule that states that /r/ is pronounced in some contexts (i.e. before a vowel) and deleted in others. The application of this rule is taken to be categorical so that every /r/ before a vowel will be pronounced and every /r/ before a consonant (or before a pause) will not. What we should not expect to find is the /r/ in *park* sometimes being deleted and sometimes being pronounced.

The trouble is that sometimes examinations of real speech communities uncover cases where rules do not apply categorically. If a researcher finds differences across members of that community – some people say "pahk" and some say "park" – then the solution is simple: these people represent different dialects with different rules. What does the researcher do, however, when the variability is found within a single speaker? It turns out this situation, too, was typically interpreted as a case of dueling dialects. Someone who sometimes says "pahk" and sometimes "park" is treated as mixing two dialects, each with its own categorical rules.

The basic assumptions underpinning the axiom of categoricity and advice for dealing with problematic cases were discussed by Zellig Harris in his influential guide to research, *Structural Linguistics*

(1951). After noting that the target of the researcher's investigation is "a single language or dialect," Harris suggests that usually "the whole speech of the person or community shows dialectal consistency," but that in some instances "we find the single person or the community using various forms which are not dialectally consistent with each other" (p. 9). In these cases Harris recommends that the analysis make a clear distinction between the competing dialects: "the material of one dialect can be marked so as to distinguish it from the material of the other" (p. 10). He suggests the same technique can be used to distinguish differences of speaking style, such as "be seeing you" versus "be seein' ya."

Harris's straightforward advice belies an enormous methodological challenge. How is the researcher to know which forms belong to which dialects or which styles? Harris suggests that dialect differences can be sorted out by surveying several communities. This presumes, of course, that such a survey would record the full range of variants so that whenever an unusual form (a word, pronunciation, etc.) is heard in one location, it could be traced to its source in another location. Stylistic variation, Harris acknowledges, presents a greater challenge and requires such detailed study that it is best for the researcher to assume "that all styles within a dialect may be roughly described by a single structural system" (1951, p. 11). As Labov found when he carried out the required detailed study, this assumption turns out to be a valid one in many cases. Still, it offers little guidance for the researcher trying to sort through variation in the recorded speech data. When one encounters alternative forms, how does one know whether they operate as part of a single structural system (stylistic variation) or as part of different systems (dialect variation)?

Dialect geography

While the axiom of categoricity has held sway in most areas of linguistic research, an important exception to this pattern is seen in dialect geography. This is the field of study devoted to uncovering how a language varies from region to region. Such an endeavor obviously implies a belief not only that variation is a normal feature of every language, but also that embracing such variation, rather than ignoring it, leads to insights about the nature of language more generally. This way of thinking is very much shared by Labov. Indeed, he owes a lot to this tradition and has frequently acknowledged this debt in his writings. Still, despite some clear similarities between them, Labov represents a break with that tradition in terms of the questions he pursued and the methods he employed in that pursuit.

The stock-in-trade of dialect geography is the map. A basic map plots the variant forms of a particular feature as recorded over some area. An example of this is seen in Figure 2.2, which illustrates the distribution of various words for "dragon fly" in the eastern US. This map is based on research carried out for the Linguistic Atlas of the United States and Canada (LAUSC) project directed by Hans Kurath. It shows that, traditionally speaking, people from the Northeast called dragon flies *darning needles*, while those in the South tended to use the term *mosquito hawk* and those in the middle part of the country preferred *snake feeder* or *snake doctor*. It's important to characterize these usages as "traditional" because the data plotted in this map were collected in the 1930s and 1940s, mainly from speakers who were fairly old at the time.

A map like the one in Figure 2.2 serves as a starting point for determining dialect divisions. From the raw data of this map, the researcher moves to determining the boundaries of the variants or their "isoglosses." An isogloss is essentially a line on the map that marks the geographical extent of a given form. For example, the isogloss for *darning needle* would be drawn across northern Pennsylvania and curve down into New Jersey. An individual isogloss is only as interesting to the researcher as the usage it demarcates, but often several isoglosses follow roughly the same distribution. This is known as an "isogloss bundle," and it provides evidence to the more general issue of dialect divisions. As it happens the isogloss for *darning needle* forms part of a bundle that corresponds to one of the major regional divisions in American English, separating the North from the Midland. On the basis of these kinds of data, Kurath proposed a view of American dialects represented in Figure 2.3. This view posits a three-way main division separating the North, Midland, and South. Within each of these broad regions, smaller groups of isoglosses form subregions, labeled with numbers in Kurath's map.

Kurath's research represents a tradition that arose in Europe in the late nineteenth century. The origins of dialect study are closely

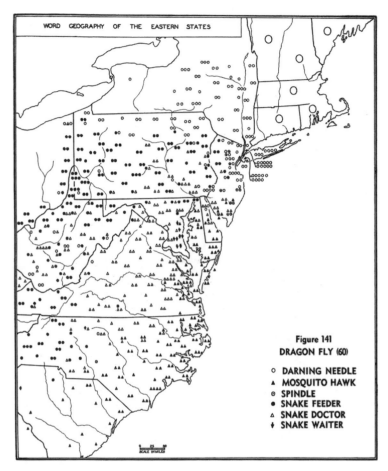

FIGURE 2.2 *Regional variation in terms for "dragon fly" in the Eastern US (from Kurath, 1949, Figure 141; reprinted by permission of University of Michigan Press).*

tied to concerns in historical linguistics of the time. Chambers and Trudgill (1998) discuss the early relationship between dialectology and philology, the branch of language study focused on tracing historical connections among related languages. They note, for example, how dialectological evidence was brought to bear on claims about the nature of sound change made by scholars like the Neogrammarians (see Chapter Seven).

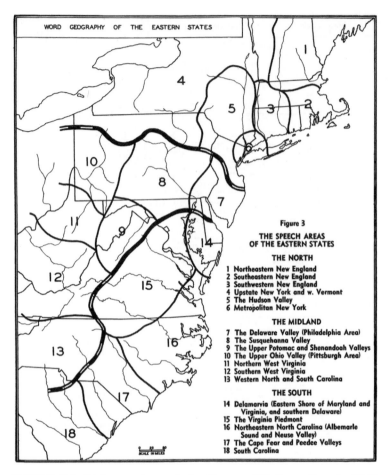

FIGURE 2.3 *Dialect regions of the Eastern US (from Kurath, 1949, Figure 3; reprinted by permission of University of Michigan Press).*

As it developed in the early twentieth century, dialect geography maintained its retrospective focus. To a large extent the field was involved in documenting the survival of traditional features. This objective is reflected well in their methods. Chambers and Trudgill coined the memorable acronym NORMs to describe the ideal subjects for dialectological research: Non-mobile Older Rural Males (1998, p. 29). Dialect geographers targeted this demographic because they felt it would produce a linguistically conservative sample. They wanted to capture the usage of people whose dialect would be untainted by recent trends or by the normative influence of standard dialects. People who had lived their entire lives in the same rural area were ideal in this respect, especially if they had little formal education. As for the gender bias, men were thought to maintain traditional speech forms better than women, a prediction that gained empirical support in later sociolinguistic research (see Chapter Six).

Data collection in dialect geography involved fieldwork in which researchers would travel across an area, interviewing a few subjects in each of several locations. Thus, they prioritized broad geographical coverage over in-depth examination of particular locales. As suggested by the narrow demographic focus of their subject population, they weren't much interested in exploring social diversity within speech communities. It's worth noting, however, that the LAUSC project under Kurath's direction was somewhat exceptional in this regard. While the emphasis on NORMs remains evident in the sample, Kurath did survey some middle-aged people and some people with college educations as well.

The fieldwork interviews mostly followed the pattern of an oral questionnaire. The fieldworker would pose a question of the type "What do you call X?" and the subject would respond. These questions generally call for a single response and reflect the assumption that a given person in a given location uses one linguistic form consistently to describe X. With lexical variables (vocabulary) this assumption may generally hold.[2] Thus, to use another example from LAUSC, people generally carry water in either a "pail" or a "bucket" but not both. For some phonological variables, however, such categoricity doesn't hold. Consider, for example, the pronunciation of the suffix –ing (e.g. walking). In most varieties of English this suffix is sometimes heard with a velar nasal [ɪŋ] and sometimes with an alveolar nasal [ɪn], known popularly as "g-dropping" and represented as –in' (e.g. walkin'). This variable shows interesting social patterning, with the alveolar form being more common in certain regions and among certain social groups, but, crucially, all speakers use both variants. What distinguishes people is not whether they say walking or walkin', but rather how frequently they use one form or the other.

This kind of variation cannot be explored using the traditional questionnaire approach because a single response is meaningless.

Imagine that the fieldworker constructed a question to test for the
–ing variable like a fill-in-the-blank item, "When someone is happy,
you might say he or she is _____ on air." Depending on the
response, the subject will be categorized as either a user of *–ing* or
of *–in'* when the reality is that he or she uses both forms. What are
needed in order to produce a meaningful assessment of this feature
are several examples of *–ing* words and a count of how often each
variant is pronounced in these words. This kind of quantitative
measure was not employed, at least not widely, in dialect geography
(or elsewhere) until Labov demonstrated its value in the 1960s.

We do find a precursor to Labov's quantitative approach outside
dialect geography in a study conducted by anthropologist John
Fischer in 1958. Fischer examined the familiar variation between
–ing and *–in'* in the speech of 24 New England children. Reflecting
the same frustration with the dominant linguistic theory that
eventually fueled Labov's work, Fischer notes that the alternation
he's studying would ordinarily be dismissed as a case of free
variation since the choice between *–ing* and *–in'* has no effect on
meaning and both forms exist on an equal footing in terms of the
structure of English. But, Fischer continues,

> "Free variation" is of course a label, not an explanation. It does
> not tell us where the variants came from nor why the speakers
> use them in differing proportions, but is rather a way of
> excluding such questions from the scope of immediate inquiry.
> (1958, p. 48)

Fischer's inquiry led him to record the children in various speaking
tasks. He then listened to several tokens of *–ing* words (apparently
around 50 examples in each of three contexts) and counted the
number of times each child used the *–ing* and the *-in'* forms. He
analyzed his results in various ways, but the study is best known for
his findings related to gender. Fischer suggested that the *–ing* form
was preferred by girls while the *–in'* form was preferred by boys.
What is especially relevant for us is how he reaches this conclusion.
He divides the children into two groups – those who favor *–ing* and
those who favor *–in'* – based on which variant each child used more
of. Then he examines the gender split across these categories and
finds that seven out of twelve of the boys used *–in'* more than *–ing*
while ten out of twelve of the girls used *–ing* more than *–in'*.

Fischer's study certainly deserves its reputation as a landmark in language and gender research and in the use of quantitative methods in exploring social variation. Still, his statistical analysis is remarkably simplistic. Particularly striking is the decision to categorize the speakers binarily as favoring *-ing* or *-in'*. In some ways this offers little improvement over the hypothetical approach of the dialect geographer described above who would categorize a subject on the basis of a single example of an *-ing* word. Given the way Fischer analyzed the data, it's surprising that he didn't compare the children in terms of percentage use of each variant. Such an approach would have better reflected the continuous nature of the variation. On the other hand, there's no reason to suspect that a more sensitive quantitative measure would have led to different conclusions. In fact, subsequent analyses of this variable and of gendered variation more generally have been consistent with Fischer's research.

Before concluding this examination of how variation was traditionally explored in linguistics, we consider a trend that gained momentum in the mid-twentieth century, just before and during the time when Labov was finding his way in the field. At this time several dialect geographers turned their attention to the cities and pursued what came be known as "urban dialectology." This work offers a valuable perspective on what makes Labov's approach distinctive because it represents an attempt to take traditional dialectology in new directions, and in doing so, reveals the limitations of the existing paradigm.

Concentrating on rural speech reflected the original motivation of dialect geography to document conservative patterns as a window into language history. Cities, with their turbulent social dynamics and mixing of people from various backgrounds, were felt to be breeding grounds for new speechways. Nevertheless, in the middle of the last century some dialectologists began to question the traditional neglect of urban speech. Actually, Kurath had already taken a step in this direction in the 1930s when he decided to survey cities as well as rural areas for the Linguistic Atlas of the United States and Canada. Still, the city folk surveyed tended to fit the usual demographic profile, and only minor adjustments were made in terms of sampling rates to reflect the population size. For example, in most rural areas and small towns LAUSC interviewed two people. In New York City, which had a population of around 7.5 million in 1940, they interviewed thirteen people from Manhattan and another twelve from the other boroughs. In Philadelphia, a city of nearly two million in 1940, they surveyed only eight people.[3]

As it happens, the LAUSC sampling was generally more thorough than some studies that specifically targeted urban dialects. Chambers and Trudgill (1998 p. 46) review this literature including a 1960 study of Cockney speech, the dialect of the working class in London's East End, by Eva Sivertsen. Her analysis of the dialect was based mainly on data from four women over the age of 60. In 1966, Wolfgang Viereck published a study of the dialect of Gateshead, a small city in northeast England. The data for this work came from twelve mostly elderly men. In these examples we find the assumptions of traditional dialectology have simply been carried over to the examination of urban speech. Using a small number of speakers cut from the same demographic cloth is justified by these researchers because they seek to describe not the full range of speech in the urban community, but rather only the "pure" dialect, by which they seem to mean the variety untouched by outside influences. This approach begs the question of whether such dialect purity even exists. Is there any variety of English or any other language that has remained unaffected by contact with others?

While some dialect geographers made only minimal adjustments to their protocols for the study of urban speech, others embraced the challenge of accounting for the social diversity of the city. Lee Pederson stands as an example of the latter for his study *The Pronunciation of English in Metropolitan Chicago*, which appeared in 1965. Pederson's analysis was based on a sample of 136 Chicagoans. At the core of this sample were the 38 "primary informants" who completed the full 700-item questionnaire (based on standard LAUSC protocols).[4] This pool was supplemented by 66 "subsidiary informants" who completed a shorter checklist of major dialect features. With his sample of primary informants, Pederson sought to represent a range of ethnic groups (including African Americans), and "within each ethnic group, pronunciation was investigated among members of as many different age groups, educational types, and social classes as were available for interview" (1965, pp. 6–7). Pederson succeeded in constructing a diverse sample, though it should be noted his technique was more informal than one might find in social science research of the time. He did not attempt to produce a sample that strictly paralleled the city's demographics, nor did he choose subjects through random sampling.

Pederson's inclusive approach positioned him to offer a more representative account of Chicago speech than one associates with traditional dialectology. Moreover, Pederson used a tape recorder for the interviews which gave him access to a wider range of speech since he recorded conversational speech as well as the briefer responses to questionnaire items. However, Pederson's analysis fails to take full advantage of this unusually rich dataset. Despite his methodological innovations, he can't seem to escape the limitations of the tradition he was trained in.

The bulk of Pederson's analysis consists of detailing the range of pronunciations recorded for all the vowel and consonant phonemes of the Chicago dialect. Following the usual LAUSC protocols, each of the phonemes is examined in a particular set of words. For example, /æ/ is represented by *ashes, bag, raspberries, January, vacuum,* and so on, all of which Pederson elicited through direct or indirect questioning (e.g. What do you call the small red fruit that grows on thorny bushes? Please list the months of the year.). Pederson lists the "free variants" he observed in the target words and offers summary statements characterizing the overall variation. Thus, for /æ/ he notes the phoneme "is usually [æ]" but that certain diphthongal allophones are frequently heard before velar consonants in the words *bag* and *vacuum*. He also indicates that a nasalized allophone occurs apparently as a "socially restricted" variant since it was heard from seven informants, six of whom represent the lower middle to working classes (1965, p. 30). This characterization illustrates the typical pattern of Pederson's sociolinguistic analysis: he notes a variant, lists the speakers who used that variant, and comments on the social distribution of those speakers. The discussion is full of statements of the form "Of the X number of people who used A, Y shared a certain demographic identity."

For reasons that should become clearer in the light of Labov's work described in the next chapter, Pederson manages to sketch only a faint picture of the sociolinguistic complexities of Chicago. His statements on the social distribution of particular allophones don't usually establish a firm correlation between a given usage and a demographic category. Knowing that some of the speakers who used some form fit a certain social profile may be suggestive of such a correlation, but it's difficult to assess without a count of how many other speakers with that profile didn't use the form at issue.

A much more significant shortcoming stems from the practice of treating phonemes as components of particular words rather than as elements in a phonological structure. This criticism can be fairly leveled at many studies in the dialect geography tradition.[5] One aspect of the problem is the potential confusion of lexical effects with more general patterns. If your analysis is based on particular words, you may not be able to distinguish whether the variation you observe is conditioned by those words or by some phonological factors. Suppose, for example, that you're examining /æ/ in words such as *bag*, and you find that some people use a raised variant so that *bag* sounds like *beg*. Is this raising of the vowel a property of the word *bag* or is it a broader pattern that applies whenever /æ/ occurs in the relevant context such as before a /g/? Unless your analysis considers a wider range of /æ/ examples, you cannot address this question.

In Pederson's case it seems his intense focus on the lexical trees led him to miss the phonological forest at least with respect to a major accent feature of the area he was researching. Chicago lies in the heart of a region participating in a fascinating series of vowel changes known as the Northern Cities Shift, described in more detail in Chapter Seven. With these changes, the /æ/ of *bat* raises to a mid or even high position, making *bat* sound like *bet* or *bit*. Also the /ɑ/ of *box* comes forward so that *box* may sound closer to *backs*. The changes of the Northern Cities Shift – I have only described two of the six vowels involved – are not restricted to particular words, but rather operate across the board, potentially shifting all occurrences of the phonemes. We know that the Shift was active in Chicago in the 1960s when Pederson conducted his study, and yet apparently he did not notice it. His accounts of the relevant phonemes suggest that he recorded some shifted forms (e.g. a slightly raised /æ/, a slightly fronted /ɑ/), but he makes no mention of a broader pattern. Perhaps if his methods had encouraged him to explore relations among the phonemes in the phonological system, Pederson might have recognized how the Northern Cities Shift was rearranging the Chicago vowels.

More broadly, Pederson's study reflects the limiting effects of the axiom of categoricity. In opening this section, I framed the work of dialect geography as an exception to the dominant influence of this axiom. That's certainly true in the sense that dialectologists made variation the target of their work rather than something to drive past on the way to that work. Still, traces of categorical thinking continued to guide their approach. We see this in the assumption that a small group of words could be used to uncover the range of phonetic variation for a given phoneme, and especially in the assumption that a single elicitation of each of these words from each speaker could give a complete picture of that speaker's usage. This method presupposes that the researcher knows beforehand which words will reveal the patterns of variation and that a speaker uses a particular variant in a particular word categorically. Here, we arrive again at the problem outlined earlier with respect to the *–ing/in'* variation. For many interesting linguistic variables, especially phonological ones, the population of speakers does not divide neatly into two groups: those who use form A and those who use form B. Rather, it's often the case that every speaker draws on both forms in varying degrees.

The methodology of dialect geography, though immensely productive in the study of many types of linguistic variation, was too deeply rooted in traditional concepts like the phoneme to come to grips with the full spectrum of speech differences. What was required was a definitive rejection of the axiom of categoricity, as a methodologically motivated idealization and especially as a statement of how language actually works. A strong movement away from the traditional view came in the 1960s under Labov's leadership. At the heart of this revolution was the concept of the linguistic variable, an idea operationalized by Labov in the research he did in graduate school and developed further in subsequent work. We begin to explore what set this new approach to linguistic variation apart in the next chapter as we look at Labov's initial forays in the field.

Notes

1 This description of the how r-lessness works holds for many varieties of English, but the patterns differ in certain cases. Also, phonetically the /r/ may be completely deleted or it may be pronounced as a vowel like [ə] or as something in between.

2 The LAUSC fieldworkers actually dug a little deeper to record alternative forms. After the initial answer, they might ask if the subject had ever heard other words for the concept and sometimes even asked about particular forms (e.g. Have you ever heard anyone call that a Y?).

3 The LAUSC information comes from Kretzschmar et al. 1994.

4 The standard questionnaire requires a substantial time commitment on the part of the subject. Pederson notes that the shortest interview with a primary informant lasted four hours while the longest lasted fifteen hours and was carried out over several sessions (p. 20).

5 See, for example, Chambers and Trudgill 1998, p. 34.

CHAPTER THREE

How to establish a field as a graduate student

When I began work on my PhD dissertation, I entertained thoughts of how innovative my project was and how it would really shake things up in my field. I was going to challenge existing paradigms and bring fresh insights to linguistics. Over the year or so I spent working on my dissertation I adjusted my expectations downward and hoped that I would be able to shine new light on the particular phenomenon I was examining, the vowel changes of the Northern Cities Shift mentioned in the previous chapter. I figured that my study would add to the ongoing scholarly conversation about those changes but not change the topic of that conversation.

From speaking to colleagues, I find that my experience is a common one. Many students embark on their graduate studies with dreams of revolutionizing their fields. Eventually they realize either (a) the field is not as messed up as they believed, or (b) it's hard for a graduate student to spark a revolution. After all, graduate school usually functions as an apprenticeship program, and the dissertation is meant to demonstrate that one is capable of performing the work of the masters under whom one studies. The hierarchical structure of the academy makes it difficult for young scholars to have an immediate impact.

Labov stands as a dramatic exception to this rule. As a graduate student under the direction of Uriel Weinreich at Columbia University, Labov completed two studies that brought fresh approaches to traditional problems and eventually gave birth to the new subfield of sociolinguistics. It seems that someone forgot to tell him that graduate students aren't meant to be revolutionaries.

This chapter describes the work that Labov did for his Master's thesis, a study of sound change on Martha's Vineyard, and for his PhD dissertation, an exploration of sociolinguistic variation in New York City. In these projects Labov blazed new methodological trails and introduced ideas that have shaped the conversation in sociolinguistics ever since. The dimensions of that conversation are explored more fully in later chapters. My focus here is on describing the Martha's Vineyard and New York City studies, which continue to rank among Labov's most commonly cited works.

The Martha's Vineyard study

After several years working as an industrial chemist for an ink company, Labov returned to school in 1961. He had long been interested in language and had recently heard about the field of linguistics. In the late 1950s the field was abuzz with controversy in the wake of Noam Chomsky's introduction of transformational grammar and his challenge to B. F. Skinner's theories on language learning. As Labov notes in a biographical essay (1997a), he imagined the field of linguistics to be "an exciting one, consisting mostly of young people with strong opinions who spent most of their time arguing with each other."[1] Labov had majored in English and philosophy as an undergraduate and was no stranger to arguments. Also, he grew up in New Jersey, where arguing is known as "conversation."

Still, Labov did not get into linguistics solely for the love of scholarly debate; he felt he had something valuable to offer the field: a more scientifically grounded approach to language. As he notes in reference to the debates involving Chomsky and other theoretical linguists: "When I found that they were also drawing most of their data out of their heads, I thought that I could do better" (1997a). His idea of better was an empirical approach, one based on how people actually speak and verified by careful experimental techniques.

The initial steps on Labov's path toward an empirical linguistics were taken on Martha's Vineyard, an island off the coast of Massachusetts. In the fall and winter of 1961–62, Labov visited the island to conduct fieldwork for his Master's thesis. This choice of a research site was perhaps influenced by traditional concerns of dialect geography, a field Labov had certainly been trained in by his mentor, Uriel Weinreich.

Islands hold a special place in the dialectologist's heart because they represent examples *par excellence* of isolated speech communities. As described in the previous chapter, traditional dialectology sought "pure" dialects, those that had not been corrupted by mixing with standard varieties or other regional forms. The physical isolation of island communities from the mainland often results in unique linguistic developments that mark island dialects as distinctive from nearby varieties. Island dialects also often preserve features that have been changed in mainland varieties. This is yet another reason why they traditionally caught the dialectologist's eye, which was so often focused on the retention of archaic features.

Beyond the choice of locales, however, Labov's study has little in common with the research tradition in dialect geography. He makes this immediately apparent by framing his work as a study of how the dialect of Martha's Vineyard was changing at the time. Here he departs not just from dialectology, but from mainstream linguistics, where language changes were studied only after the fact. Indeed, conventional wisdom within linguistics held that language change could not be directly observed. This point is discussed in more detail in Chapter Seven, but the argument centers on the claim that the change process is a chaotic one. A sound change, for example, involves a competition between a conservative pronunciation and an innovative one, with the latter gradually taking the place of the former. The researcher observing this process might note the fluctuations between the two forms but wouldn't know whether such alternations were due to a change or just the normal variation in speech. Thus, it was claimed that changes could only be detected after the dust had settled and the innovative form had won out. On this point Labov cites prominent linguists like Leonard Bloomfield and Charles Hockett. He remains, however, undaunted by the skepticism of these scholarly icons and proceeds to make his case.

Labov's argument lays the groundwork for a fresh approach not only to linguistic change, but to language in general. Is it true that speech is highly variable? Absolutely. The same phoneme may be pronounced in slightly different ways by different people and even by the same person from one moment to the next. But are these fluctuations in speech chaotic? Absolutely not. The variation heard between speakers and within an individual's speech is not random but instead reflects patterns shaped by linguistic and social factors. These views form the central tenets of what came to be called "variationist sociolinguistics." The broader theoretical significance of this approach is explored further in Chapter Four. For now, we focus on how Labov challenges mainstream thinking about variation in speech.

Labov's key innovation here is methodological. He develops a way of deciphering patterns amid the apparent chaos, and he does this by embracing the variation rather than by trying to eliminate it from consideration. Only by sampling a wide range of speech from a wide range of speakers can the patterns be detected. In order to construct that sample, Labov must take into account the social landscape of the community.

In the case of Martha's Vineyard, a key aspect of the cultural geography was the division between up-island and down-island. Down-island referred to the part where most of the population lived in small towns like Vineyard Haven. Up-island, by contrast, was a mostly rural area with villages of a few hundred people, farmland, and uninhabited marshes and forests.

At the time of Labov's study, Martha's Vineyard had a population of around 6,000 year-round residents. Many of these represented the descendants of the English settlers who came to the island in the seventeenth and eighteenth centuries. There was also a substantial number of Vineyarders of Portuguese descent, and a smaller group of Wampanoag Indians, descendants of the original inhabitants of the island.

As Labov discovered in his fieldwork, these cultural distinctions (e.g. up- vs. down-island, English vs. Portuguese) played an important role in the social dynamics of island life. But, over the course of the twentieth century, life on Martha's Vineyard had also been shaped by a powerful outside force: the influx of summer visitors. The Vineyard was (and remains today) a popular vacation spot. By the 1960s over 40,000 people flocked to the island from June to August. This incursion of vacationers helped to throw the up-island/down-island distinction into greater relief. Most of the visitors stayed down-island, and the economy of those communities catered to their needs, while up-island Vineyarders typically clung to traditional ways of life such as farming and fishing.

In order to learn about the dialect of a particular place you need to speak with locals. It's almost always impractical to speak with every member of a community, and so a sample of people must be taken. The choices that researchers make about whose speech they sample say a lot about their goals. Certainly this is the case with dialect geographers as noted in the previous chapter. As it happens, Martha's Vineyard was surveyed for the *Linguistic Atlas of New England* in the 1930s. That project drew its picture of Vineyard speech on the evidence of just four people, all over the age of 55 and all representing the old-stock "Yankee" segment of the population. Choosing mostly older rural speakers for their sample fit well with their interest in traditional dialect forms.

Labov, however, was interested in social variation within the community and so needed a sample that represented significant divisions within the society. He surveyed Vineyard speech by interviewing 69 natives. His sample represented a cross-section of island society and included both men and women, both down-islanders and up-islanders, and representatives of various professions and of each of the three main ethnic categories (English, Portuguese, Indian).

Labov's approach to data collection also reflects his preference for casting a wide net. As described in Chapter Two, interviews in the linguistic atlas tradition were highly structured events. The fieldworker asked a series of questions about language (e.g. What do you call a heavy rain storm that appears suddenly and lasts a short while?), and the interviewee gave brief responses. This format produces examples of relatively careful speech, which may be far removed from the person's usage in less controlled settings. Labov sought a broader slice of the spectrum, and he designed an interview protocol that produced casual conversation as well as formal speech.

One of the upsides of using open-ended interviews to study speech is the sheer volume of data they produce. This is especially true in the study of phonological variation. A one-hour interview will typically result in dozens of examples of almost every sound the researcher might be interested in. Labov focused his investigation on the pronunciation of two diphthongs, the /ai/ of *right, prize, high*, and so on, and the /au/ of *out, loud, cow*, and so forth. He noticed that Vineyarders varied their pronunciation of these vowels by using different starting points for the first part of the diphthong, called the "nucleus" in phonology. In many dialects of American English the nucleus of both of these diphthongs is a low central vowel, [a]. Vineyarders, however, sometimes pronounced these sounds with a higher nucleus closer to the vowel of *cut*. If you have access to a Canadian, you can get a sense of how these raised variants sound by having your Canadian say *light, price, house,* and *about*, since a similar pronunciation is common in Canadian English.

The variation demonstrated by the /ai/ and /au/ diphthongs presented Labov with significant analytical challenges. In order to appreciate these challenges, let's consider a comparatively straightforward example of phonological variation. The word *creek* varies in pronunciation across American dialects. Some speakers pronounce *creek* with the /i/ vowel of *leak* while other pronounce it with the /ɪ/ vowel of *lick*. For the most part, people use either one or the other vowel, and they do so consistently. If you wanted to study this variable, you could simply record various people saying *creek* and note which pronunciation they use. Your classification would involve two groups: those who rhyme *creek* with *leak* and those who rhyme *creek* with *lick*.

On Martha's Vineyard, /ai/ and /au/ behaved quite differently as phonological variables. For one thing, the vowel sometimes began with a low [a] and sometimes with a "centralized" [ə] (as in *cut*) and sometimes with a starting point somewhere in between these two. Thus, the variation was along a continuum rather than among discrete categories. Moreover, the full range of this continuum might be used by any given speaker. It is not the case that an individual consistently used the low variant or the centralized variant or any intermediate variant. Rather the typical Vineyarder might pronounce some instances of the diphthongs with a low nucleus and others with a nucleus that is centralized to some degree. It is not a matter of whether one uses centralized diphthongs or not, but rather it is a matter of degree: how high does the speaker raise the vowel and how frequently does the speaker produce raised variants? Getting a handle on such variation is much more complicated than in the *creek* case. How can the researcher categorize an individual's usage of /ai/ and /au/ and compare that person with others?

To address these challenges Labov turns to quantitative analysis. He tackles the problem of continuous variation by breaking the continuum up into a series of discrete steps. He categorized pronunciations along a four-point scale of height differences for the nucleus of the diphthongs with the low [a] on one end and the centralized [ə] on the other end. The scale was used to transcribe the recorded interviews. The basic procedure involved listening to each interview for examples of /ai/ and /au/ and classifying the interviewee's pronunciation of each word containing an /ai/ or an /au/ in terms of the four categories on the scale.[2]

The transcription of the speech data documented the variants used by each person, but the problem of how to compare individuals remained. To address this issue Labov devised a "centralization index," which measured the degree of raising of each diphthong. Separate indexes were calculated for each diphthong for each speaker. This was done by converting the transcribed vowels to numbers: a token (example) of the diphthong with a low nucleus was assigned a 0 and a token with the maximally centralized [ə] was assigned a 3, with 1 and 2 assigned to the intermediate steps in the four-point scale. The index for each person was calculated by averaging values from several examples of each diphthong. For /ai/ Labov counted about 50 tokens per speaker on average, and for the less frequent /au/ he counted about 20 tokens per speaker. In this way the centralization index represents how frequently and how extremely a person raises the nucleus of the diphthong. A centralization index near 0 characterizes someone who doesn't raise the vowel much beyond [a] and uses any raised variants infrequently. An index near 3 would characterize someone who consistently produced extremely raised variants.

The centralization indexes provide a means of comparing individuals, but Labov is interested in the social dimensions of the variation. To examine the role of social factors, he groups speakers by relevant categories (e.g. up-island vs. down-island) and calculates mean index scores for the member of each category. In this way he has a simple numerical method of comparing the degree of centralization among members of various social groups.

This detailed review of Labov's methods highlights the many ways in which the Martha's Vineyard study breaks new ground. But, this project would not have been as influential as it was had it not been for the results that those methods produced. Labov's analysis revealed fascinating complexities in how the centralization of the /ai/ and /au/ diphthongs was embedded in the social structure of the island, and the picture that emerged posed new ways of thinking about the forces of language change.

As discussed earlier, Labov frames his project as a study of sound change, but conventional wisdom in linguistics maintained that change could not be observed directly. How does a linguist show that a language change is underway? There are two basic approaches. One way is to compare the current linguistic situation with one from an earlier time period as described in some previous study. This is called a "real-time" study since it compares the language at two actual times. The real-time method is the norm in historical linguistics. Those studies, however, explore completed changes and usually compare two time periods in the past.

The other approach to demonstrating that a language change is taking place draws on "apparent-time" reasoning. Here, changes across time are inferred from a comparison of people of different ages. The thinking is that the speech of a 70-year-old represents an earlier form of the language than the speech of a teenager, and so by comparing the usage across generations of speakers, we can observe changes. This approach relies on the assumption that people's speech does not change significantly over the course of their lives, at least after they enter adulthood. Empirical tests of this assumption have generally supported its validity (see the discussion in Chapter Seven).

In the Martha's Vineyard study Labov draws on both kinds of evidence to support his claim that a sound change is underway. On the real-time side, he had access to the records of the *Linguistic Atlas of New England* from roughly 30 years prior. These data show only moderate degrees of centralization of the /ai/ diphthong among the four speakers recorded and virtually no centralization of the /au/ diphthong. The fact that Labov found higher rates of centralization for both sounds in his study supports the claim that Vineyard speech had experienced change.

The evidence of change is even clearer in the apparent-time picture, which Labov paints by calculating the mean centralization indexes for each of five groups of Vineyarders arranged by age. The pattern is clear:

Age	/ai/	/au/	
over 75	0.25	0.22	
61–75	0.35	0.37	
46–60	0.62	0.44	
31–45	0.81	0.88	
14–30	0.37	0.46	(Labov, 1963, p. 291)

With both diphthongs we see a clear rise in the centralization indexes as we go from the oldest generation (those over 75 years) down. In the youngest generation (those aged 14–30) there appears to be a reversal of the trend toward centralization, and we'll return to this finding later.

These results are exactly what we should expect to see in a situation of ongoing language change. The pattern is so perfect that it's worth recalling how it was uncovered. Labov listened to some 3,500 instances of /ai/ and some 1,500 instances of /au/ in various words pronounced by 69 speakers. He assigned a code to each of these instances based on the height of the vowel as he heard it. He used these codes to calculate an index that represented the degree of raising of each diphthong for each of the 69 people. He then grouped these people by age and calculated the averages for each group.

When I consider this process, I find the regularity of the results all the more impressive and surprising. Things could have gone differently at any stage and produced a less clear picture. For example, /ai/ and /au/ are separate phonemes, and there's no necessity for them to pattern as similarly as they do here. Also, the age breakdown needn't have worked out so perfectly with a regular increase in each group except the youngest. In many studies of this type, the apparent-time views are much messier and the researcher might adjust the age grouping to arrive at a consistent trend in the data.

Reviewing Labov's analytical process also highlights how his approach effectively countered the argument that language change could not be directly observed. Grounding this position was the claim that the change process introduced a fog of variation into a speech community that thwarted the researcher's ability to detect diachronic patterns. What Labov's work demonstrated was that such detection was possible if one's method for sorting through the variation was sophisticated enough. Developing a means of precisely quantifying speech behavior proved key to this method. A casual observer of the Martha's Vineyard dialect might notice that locals sometimes pronounce /ai/ and /au/ with low nuclei and sometimes with raised nuclei, and that the raised variants were used more often by some people than by others. Such variation might seem random or even chaotic. It's only after some counting and systematic comparison that the patterns may emerge. Labov was not the first linguist to apply such techniques in the examination of language change, but his approach was more sophisticated than earlier studies and served as a model for a new "sociolinguistic" study of change.

Having demonstrated the operation of a sound change in Vineyard speech, Labov set out to address the much more difficult issue of the motivation for that change. As a rule, linguists are much better at answering the "what" and "how" of language change, but we have less satisfying responses to the "why." The latter presents a notorious challenge when posed as "why does a particular change happen in a particular place at a particular time?"[3]

The title of Labov's article, "The social motivation of a sound change," tells us where he seeks an explanation. As it happens, Labov's focus on social factors as a cause of language change set him apart from mainstream linguistics, where such issues have generally received less attention than "internal" motivations. The latter refers to factors related to the language system itself. This includes the articulatory properties of sounds (i.e. how they're produced) as well as more abstract structural properties. Exploring language-internal factors is crucial to understanding how and why sounds change, but Labov makes a strong case for looking beyond the realm of linguistic structure.

Labov grounds his argument in the recent history of Martha's Vineyard and the attitudes of the residents. His search for an explanation for the rise in centralization begins by digging further into the data. He compares the average centralization indexes across key social groupings. For example, he divides his sample by occupation and again by ethnicity and yet again by the geographical difference between up-islanders and down-islanders. In this way he seeks to draw a social profile of the change, to understand which groups are driving it. He finds, for example, that centralization is much more advanced among up-islanders than down-islanders. Moreover, fishermen tend have higher centralization indexes than farmers or other professions. The data related to ethnicity reveal a more complex pattern: while those of English descent appear to lead the centralization of /ai/, the Portuguese and especially the Indians show enthusiastic participation in the centralization of /au/. To clarify, the apparent-time evidence indicates that all three groups are moving in the same direction with both vowels; what differs is which group leads the change for each diphthong.

The social analysis suggests that the change is led by those Vineyarders who represent the most traditional lifestyles on the island.

Why should these people, who are in many ways icons of conservatism, emerge as linguistic innovators? The answer lies in the uprooting of traditional life on the island that came about as a result of the summer trade. The Vineyard's economy had become dependent on tourism. Moreover, wealthy mainlanders were increasingly buying up property on the island. As Labov notes, many native Vineyarders saw these trends "as a threat to their personal independence" (1963, p. 297). These feelings are strongest among the up-island people who have striven to resist the incursion of the summer visitors. Centralization of the diphthongs acts as a symbol of their resistance. Whenever a Vineyarder speaks a word with /ai/ or /au/, he or she has an opportunity to mark a stance on this issue, though it's worth noting this pattern operates below the level of conscious awareness.

Labov fleshes out his argument by drawing on the qualitative evidence he recorded in his interviews with Vineyarders. In another break with dialectological tradition, Labov designed his Martha's Vineyard interviews to gather insight into the local beliefs and attitudes. He included questions about "value judgments" and the interviewee's "social orientation" (1963, p. 283). He also probed "insider" knowledge with questions such as "Where on the island would a typical old Yankee be most apt to live?" (1963, p. 298).

This kind of evidence clarified the social dynamics of island life and helped Labov gauge each interviewee's orientation to recent developments and to the island more generally. As he often does in his writing, Labov points out individual cases as a way of illustrating broader trends. He describes the two speakers with the highest indexes of /ai/ centralization. One is a 60-year-old Chilmark (up-island) lobsterman, and the other is his 31-year-old son. The father's usage makes perfect sense in light of the social profile of centralization, but the case of the son is more intriguing. As a young man, he left the island and went to college. After graduation he lived and worked in a mainland city but found that he "didn't care for it" and returned to Martha's Vineyard. As a college graduate who had experienced city life as well as city accents, this man no doubt had a wider dialect repertoire on which he might have drawn, but he chose to hold close to his roots. In this way, the example suggests the power of linguistic forms, such as a way of pronouncing vowels, to mark social attitudes.

As it happens, Labov had a conversation with the mother of the 31-year-old enthusiastic centralizer, and she remarked on how his speech had changed. She indicated that he "didn't always speak that way" and that since returning after college he seemed to want to sound more like the local fishermen. This comment leads us to return to the apparently anomalous behavior of the youngest generation as seen earlier in the apparent-time data. The generation is the only one that shows lower centralization scores than the generation before it. One interpretation of this finding might be that the trend toward centralization is undergoing a reversal. Labov, however, points to a different explanation. This age group contains many high school students, which is relevant because children typically have no control over where they live. While most adult residents of the Vineyard have in some sense chosen to live there, the children are there because of their parents' choice. Martha's Vineyard is like many small towns in that the local school population can be divided into two groups: (1) those who want to spend their lives on the island (or in that small town), and (2) those who plan to leave after finishing school and never move back. These two groups clearly represent distinct orientations to island life, and yet they were counted together in the apparent-time analysis. When the groups are treated separately – since Labov asked about each student's plans during the interviews, he could carry out this analysis – a "marked contrast" was found. Those students who planned to leave the island had very low rates of centralization while those who planned to stay had very high rates. Thus, it appears that the change was not experiencing a reversal in the youngest generation and that centralization will continue among "true" Vineyarders.

Weaving various strands of evidence together, Labov posits a social history of centralization on Martha's Vineyard.[4] Some degree of centralization for /ai/ has been part of the traditional dialect for at least the last century, judging from the real-time evidence of the *Linguistic Atlas of New England*. With the incursion of summer people in recent decades, centralization became one way of marking nativity. As Labov observes, "When a man says [*right* or *house* with raised vowels], he is unconsciously establishing the fact that he belongs to the island: that he is one of the natives to whom the island really belongs" (1963, p. 304). In each generation, those seeking to maintain the traditional ways of life on the island, such as fishing, look to the old-timers as their reference group, including in language. In this way the phonetic trend toward centralized diphthongs is advanced and concentrated since those who have no interest in island life leave for the mainland.

At some point /au/ is brought aboard the centralization train. This is a relatively new development, one not seen in the real-time data from the 1930s. On linguistic grounds, it's not surprising to see /ai/ and /au/ acting in concert. They are structurally similar vowels and connected as members of the historical class of long vowels. Still it's interesting that /au/ centralization attains a slightly different social profile as its most advanced forms are heard among the Portuguese and Indian Vineyarders rather than the English. Nevertheless, the change seems to serve the same social function of asserting one's rights as a native of the island.

Ideally this discussion has made clear why the Martha's Vineyard study has achieved the legendary status it occupies. It introduced innovative methods for sorting through linguistic variation and presented an elegant account of a surprisingly complex sociolinguistic environment. It also told a good story.

The New York City study

In the final section of his Martha's Vineyard paper, Labov observes several limitations of his study. He notes, for example, that his sampling methods were rather informal and that he couldn't explore subjective reactions because the variable pronunciations of /ai/ and /au/ lacked salience among Vineyarders. He wanted to apply his methods and theories to the investigation of a more complex speech community, one with greater cultural diversity and one where a wider range of linguistic features might be studied. As a student at Columbia, he only had to step outside (and catch a downtown-bound subway train) to find such a research site. New York City presented him with the perfect laboratory.

Labov carried out the New York study for his PhD dissertation, which was completed in 1964. The work was published by the Center for Applied Linguistics in 1966 as *The Social Stratification of English in New York City*. The book quickly drew attention and circulated widely despite certain presentational shortcomings. It was produced by photographing the typed pages of the original dissertation with typos and other editorial oversights preserved. It also stretched to over 650 pages but lacked an index and even a detailed table of contents and lists of figures and tables. Fortunately, Cambridge University Press persuaded Labov to produce a second edition of the work to mark its fortieth anniversary in 2006. This version not only reflects modern publication standards, but also includes new commentary from the author. As he noted in an interview with me around the time of the new publication, "At each point, Labov 2006 is looking over the shoulder of Labov 1966 and commenting on what's happened since, and what the significance of this and that was" (Gordon, 2006, p. 332). Because it is more widely available than the original, I will use page references from the 2006 edition throughout this discussion.

By any measure, but certainly by the standards of dissertation projects, Labov's study stands as exceptionally ambitious and wide-ranging in scope. He approached his subject from various angles and used a remarkable variety of techniques in pursuit of his goals. Before diving into the details of how Labov carried out his research, it's important to appreciate the principles that guided his investigation. Topping that list is the belief that linguistic variation is structured, not random, a theme developed in his Martha's Vineyard research. In the case of New York City, the research literature included several attempts to describe the dialect, and while these studies identified many important language features, they failed to come to terms with the variable use of those features. Labov cites an exasperated Alan Hubbell, who published *The Pronunciation of English in New York City* in 1950:

> The pronunciation of a very large number of New Yorkers exhibits a pattern in [words containing /r/] that might most accurately be described as the complete absence of any pattern. Such speakers sometimes pronounce /r/ before a consonant or a pause and sometimes omit it, in a thoroughly haphazard fashion. (p. 48, cited in Labov, 2006, p. 23)

Such thinking represented the consensus of linguistic thought at the time as discussed in Chapter Two. Phonological rules such as when to pronounce /r/ and when to omit it were understood to be governed by linguistic conditions, such as whether a sound preceded a consonant or a vowel, and normally they operated on a categorical basis. When people's speech behavior did not conform to this model, the usual assumption was that they exhibited dialect mixing.

Labov took on this view of linguistic variation in general, and in the particular case before him, he set out to demonstrate that

"New York City is a single speech community, and not a collection of speakers living side by side, borrowing occasionally from each other's dialects" (2006, p. 6). There are significant differences in how New Yorkers of different backgrounds speak, but, Labov claims, they all participate in a "consistent and coherent structure" (2006, p. 7). As he showed in the Martha's Vineyard case, however, the outlines of such a structure may only become apparent in the light of a "socially realistic description" (2006, p. 7); that is, one that surveys the distribution of speech differences across the social categories that constitute the community.

The social structure of New York City is far more complex than that of Martha's Vineyard, and so a socially realistic account demands methods that are sensitive to that complexity. The main part of Labov's study was a survey of a neighborhood on the Lower East Side of Manhattan. The Lower East Side contains a fair cross-section of New Yorkers in terms of socioeconomic status, ethnicity, and so on. It also served traditionally as a port of entry for immigrants including Irish, Italians, Jews, and Eastern Europeans. The diversity and social dynamics of the Lower East Side made it a microcosm of New York and an ideal site for Labov's study.

For his Martha's Vineyard study Labov constructed a "judgment sample," which means he relied on his own sense of the relevant dimensions of variation in the community and sought out subjects to represent that variation. Given the social complexities of a speech community like New York City, Labov pursued an approach less subject to bias. A statistically random sample fit that bill. With a random sample, the selection of participants is not left up to the researchers, rather the participants are chosen according to predetermined protocols. The guiding principle of such a sample is that everyone in the population has an equal chance of being selected.

Random samples represent the gold standard in many types of sociological research, but they require a lot of time and effort to construct. Labov was fortunate to be able to bypass much of the legwork demanded in building a random sample by coordinating his efforts with an existing project. As it happened, a group of researchers from the New York School of Social Work at Columbia University had conducted a comprehensive survey of the Lower East Side in 1961. Their survey was for a project called the Mobilization for Youth Program, which targeted juvenile delinquency, and they had constructed a random sample of households in the area. The Mobilization for Youth team conducted interviews with 988 people in these households and collected valuable demographic and other data. Labov was given access to these research materials and thereby saved many months of work in preparing his own study.

It would have been impractical, and arguably unnecessary, for Labov to collect speech data from all 988 of the Mobilization for Youth participants. He therefore pared down the original random sample to a more manageable number, in essence taking a sample of the sample. Labov followed the usual procedures for a random sample in contacting potential subjects. Working from the list based on the original Mobilization for Youth sample, he attempted to reach each target household. If he wasn't able to make contact, he went down the list. The number of households that he was not able to make contact with was sizable, and, of course, not every person he contacted agreed to participate in his study. This led Labov to an ingenious but ethically problematic follow-up technique. He contacted the people with whom he had not been able to secure a regular interview and posed as someone taking a survey about the television reception in their building. He asked a series of questions about picture quality and related matters in an effort to elicit the pronunciation of particular words of interest. Most of these interviews were conducted over the telephone and were recorded without the subject's knowledge. The consensus in linguistics today holds that this technique, while legal in some jurisdictions, crosses an ethical line, and certainly no graduate student would be permitted to adopt such an approach in his or her dissertation research today.

In the end Labov collected data from 158 people. There were 122 who completed the standard interview and 33 were sampled through the television interview.[5] Still, the first group included several who had moved to New York City from other places. While this material offered a useful perspective, Labov concentrated his analysis on 81 native New Yorkers, a category defined as having lived there since the age of eight or younger. He carried out most of the data collection himself, but a research assistant, Michael Kac, conducted some of the interviews.

Labov's primary interest with regard to the stratification he was investigating lay with socioeconomic status (i.e. class). The Mobilization for Youth project had developed a multidimensional index of social class based on objective criteria including occupation, income, and education. This index categorized subjects on a ten-point scale. Labov borrowed this classification, but because his sample was smaller than in the sociological study, he tended to group several categories together in his analysis. For convenience we can refer to these groups by familiar labels such as lower, working, and middle class. On the Lower East Side that's as high as the scale goes; members of the upper class do not live in this part of New York City.

As noted earlier, the way that Labov collected data in the Martha's Vineyard study captured a wider range of speech than the traditional dialectological interview. During an open-ended interview, people vary their usage significantly across different conditions such as answering direct questions versus conversing casually. Sociolinguists use "style" to describe this intra-speaker variation. While it did not receive much attention in the Martha's Vineyard study, style played a much larger role here. To examine stylistic variation, Labov refined his earlier approach into a multistage protocol that has come to be known as the "sociolinguistic interview" (see Chapter Five).

The main Lower East Side interviews included a wide range of questions. Some required one-word answers while others were more open-ended. Also, some attempted to elicit particular linguistic forms such as words that characterized the traditional New York dialect according to linguistic atlas studies (e.g. *cruller* and *pot cheese*).[6] After 30–45 minutes of questions and answers, the interviewees were asked to read some prepared materials aloud. These included two prose passages written as stories, a list of a few dozen words containing target vowels, and a series of minimal pairs, which are two words that differ in terms of a single sound. More accurately, the words in a minimal pair differ for some speakers but are pronounced identically by others. For example, Labov's list included *source* and *sauce,* which are homophones for nonrhotic (r-less) speakers. The interview protocol also involved tasks designed to investigate subjects' attitudes and reactions to their own speech and the speech of other New Yorkers.

Labov's approach to recording each interviewee's speech across a range of styles was based on an "attention-to-speech" model. We explore this model in more detail in Chapter Five, but the basic idea is that a person's speech varies partly due to how much attention they're paying to the way they're speaking as opposed to what they're saying. Interviewees monitor their speech less closely when giving unscripted responses to questions than when reading prepared materials, and presumably pay the most careful attention to their pronunciation when reading words in isolation and minimal pairs.

Even within the unscripted parts of the interview people vary the attention they pay to their speech. Labov differentiated "careful" from "casual" speech. The former applies to the bulk of the talk produced during an interview, where the subject gives answers "which are formally recognized as 'part of the interview'" (2006, p. 59). Casual speech describes the type used in informal contexts such as conversations between friends. Because an interview conducted by a stranger is by definition not an informal context, casual speech would not ordinarily be generated in this setting. Still, Labov identified some opportunities for recording casual speech even in the context of an interview. For example, sometimes the one-on-one interview is interrupted by a third person, such as a family member of the interviewee. During one of Labov's interviews, the subject got a telephone call from a cousin, and Labov left the recorder running to capture twenty minutes of casual speech. There are also times where the usual back-and-forth of the interview is suspended for a while. This was the case in another of Labov's interviews when the subject interrupted the proceedings to hand Labov a beer and offered a minute or two of commentary on the challenge of opening it.

Such glimpses into the realm of casual speech are valuable, but of course the researcher can't rely on these kinds of chance events happening in every interview. The remedy to this problem has been to try to steer the interview conversation toward topics that would promote the interviewees' dropping their guard. Labov pioneered this strategy by pursuing a line of questions about childhood, including asking subjects to repeat rhymes from games. He also introduced the well-known "danger of death" question:

Have you ever been in a situation where you thought there was a serious danger of your being killed? That you thought to yourself, "This is it"? (2006, p. 70)

This question seeks to prompt a retelling of the near-death experience. During this narrative the interviewee may become emotionally involved as he or she re-lives the frightening experience. The result for Labov was often a good sample of casual speech.

In selecting linguistic variables to analyze, Labov sought pronunciation features that would reveal interesting patterns of variation in both the social and stylistic dimensions. He chose five variables to focus his analysis on:

(r)[7] Presence or absence of the consonant /r/ when it appears before another consonant or as the last sound in a word (e.g. *card*, *car*). When /r/ comes before a vowel, it is normally pronounced (e.g. *red*, *marry*, *four o'clock*).

(th) Whether the voiceless[8] interdental fricative /θ/ is pronounced as a fricative or as a stop [t] (e.g. "ting" for *thing*) or as something in between (e.g. [tθ]).

(dh) Whether the voiced interdental fricative /ð/ is pronounced as a fricative or as a stop [d] (e.g. "dat" for *that*) or as something in between (e.g. [dð]).

(æh) The height of the vowel in words such as *ask*, *bag*, *dance*, and so on, which varies from a low [æ] to a high [ɪ]. In New York City and elsewhere in the Mid-Atlantic region, the class of words historically pronounced with "short a" has split into two groups, and the raising is heard with only one group.[9]

(oh) The height of the vowel in words such as *caught*, *coffee*, *dog*, and so forth, which varies from mid [ɔ] to the high [ʊ].

Usage of three consonantal variables was measured as a choice between two or three forms. The /r/ was either pronounced or not; (th) and (dh) were either pronounced as fricatives, stops, or the intermediate affricates. The two vowel variables were measured on multipoint scales similar to those used in the case of the centralization of /ai/ and /au/ on Martha's Vineyard. These techniques allowed Labov to quantify each person's usage of each of the five variables in an index score.

The main part of Labov's analysis follows the pattern he pioneered in his Master's thesis: he looks for correlations between linguistic variation and assorted social factors by comparing groups of speakers in terms of average indexes for each of the five phonological variables. There is, however, an important added wrinkle in the New York City study, and that's the consideration of stylistic variation. As we'll see, this adds a crucial perspective.

Anyone seeking insight into the dynamics of New York City speech has much to gain from Labov's study; however, since this book is not meant to be a description of New York City speech, I make no attempt to offer a full account of Labov's findings. Instead I will highlight some of the results that have been influential in guiding the line of research Labov founded.

If we imagine ourselves in the position of a linguist in 1966 who was familiar with the research literature before Labov's study, what would we find most remarkable? Certainly the fact that New Yorkers of different social classes spoke differently would come as no surprise. The significance of such social divisions in shaping linguistic choices had long been recognized by dialectologists and other linguists as well as by just about anyone with ears. No, the striking aspect of Labov's study was not the demonstration that social differences had linguistic correlates, but rather that these correlations were so overwhelmingly regular. Contrary to the perceived randomness described by Alan Hubbell and others who had attempted to crack New York City speech using traditional approaches, patterns jump from every table and graph in Labov's work. Labov explores correlations across several social factors and all five phonological variables, but it seems no matter what lens Labov uses to examine the data, he finds structure.

Some of the best examples of this structure are seen in the parallels between stylistic and class stratification. In case after case we find that usage across different contexts from casual speech to careful speech to reading tasks follows the same trajectory as usage across class groups from the upper middle class to working and lower classes. Figure 3.1 illustrates this pattern for the (th) variable. For this diagram Labov arranged the ten class categories – SEC stands for socioeconomic class – into five groups and calculated mean indexes for each group across four contexts: casual speech, careful speech, reading passage, and word list. The Y-axis measures the usage of the stop variant of (th) instead of the fricative (i.e. [t] against [θ]).

Figure 3.1 reveals a clear pattern of class stratification for (th) with the use of the stop variant decreasing as we move up the social ladder. Crucially, the differences among the classes are quantitative not qualitative. Members of every social class use both the stop and

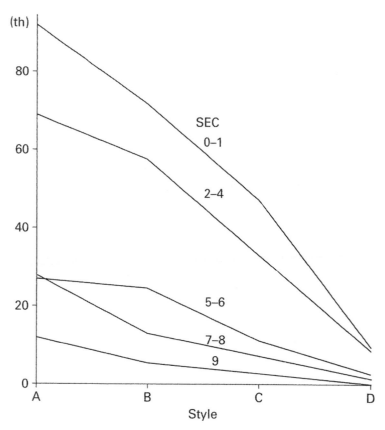

FIGURE 3.1 *Distribution of* (th) *by social class (SEC) and contextual style in the Lower East Side study (from Labov, 2006, p. 167. Copyright © 2006 William Labov. Reprinted with the permission of Cambridge University Press).*

the fricative variant. What distinguishes them is the relative mix of these two variants, how often they use one or the other. Still, there is a fairly wide gap between the lower two groups (0–1 and 2–4) and the others. This pattern of "sharp stratification" between the working/ lower class and middle class groups was found for some variables while others show a "fine stratification" with less of a gap.

The stylistic pattern is equally clear: use of the stop variant is most common in casual speech (Style A) and decreases in careful speech (Style B) and again when reading story passages (Style C) and yet again when reading words in isolation (Style D). Notice that this trajectory applies to every SEC group. They may start in different places, but they all move in the same direction. This finding, which illustrates a pattern seen with many linguistic variables, served as critical evidence in Labov's argument that New York City constitutes a speech community. Labov's definition of a speech community does not require that everyone in the community talk in the same way, but rather that they participate in a shared set of norms about speech. Thus, members of the New York City speech community vary tremendously in terms of the absolute rates of usage for (th), but they all agree in using the stop variant [t] more frequently in casual speech than in more formal contexts.

The same coordination of stylistic and class-based variation is evident with the (r) variable. Figure 3.2 presents those findings. Here the classes have been grouped somewhat differently, and on the style axis we have an additional point (D') for the minimal pairs (e.g. *source ~ sauce*). The Y-axis marks the (r) index scores which are essentially percentages of how often the consonant was pronounced.

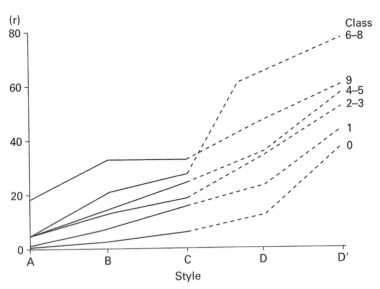

FIGURE 3.2 *Distribution of* (r) *by social class and contextual style in the Lower East Side study (from Labov, 2006, p. 152. Copyright © 2006 William Labov. Reprinted with the permission of Cambridge University Press).*

The class differences for (r) show more continuity than was the case for (th). Thus, we have an example of "fine stratification" noted above. There is, in fact, very little separation among the classes in Style A (casual speech) with the exception of the upper middle class (group 9). However, as we move rightward across the graph, the stratification increases. Notice too that we see similar trajectories for each class group, indicating a shared norm that the more formal the speech context, the more [r] should be pronounced.

There is one obvious break in the overall pattern. The regular class distribution is interrupted by the behavior of the lower middle class (groups 6–8) in the word list (D) and minimal pair (D') styles. Rather than scoring between the groups above or below them on the social ladder, as they did in the other stylistic contexts, their usage shoots up, and they pronounce [r] at higher rates than even the upper middle class. Why should this "crossover" appear only for Styles D and D'? These are, of course, the contexts in which we expect that people attend most to their pronunciation. Labov describes this behavior as "hypercorrection," a statistical overshooting of the mark perhaps motivated by concerns about sounding "proper" (see Chapter Six).

The crossover pattern of Figure 3.2 also signals that (r) is undergoing change, as the behavior of the lower middle class represents a reaction to a new norm. New York City has traditionally been a nonrhotic (r-less) region, but over the course of the twentieth century r-fulness was on the rise. As he did in his Martha's Vineyard study, Labov cites both real-time and apparent-time evidence to show this change. The implementation of the change, however, seems to proceed very differently from the earlier case. The class breakdown of the apparent-time data shows the expected pattern of increasing rates of r-fulness only among the highest group (SEC 9). Thus, the upper middle class has always pronounced /r/ at higher rates than other groups, and now those rates are increasing with each generation. Labov labels this pattern "change from above," which he distinguishes from "change from below." The terminology is potentially confusing.[10] His "above" and "below" refer to the salience of the linguistic feature: Does it operate above or below the level of conscious awareness? Typically, change from above involves the introduction of a feature that carries prestige as more "proper" or "standard" than the alternatives, and the case of (r) fits this description since it appears to represent a change toward the unmarked, standard pronunciation in American English.

The two vowel features Labov studied illustrate the case of change from below. For both (æh) and (oh), the apparent-time data suggest that the vowels are increasingly raised. Moreover, this trend is fairly consistent across the class spectrum; everyone appears to be moving in the same direction. Nevertheless, social distinctions do still have a role to play in driving the changes, but here it appears that ethnic differences take on that function. Labov suggests that the raising of (æh) is a change led by Italians, while the raising of (oh) is lead by Jews. This kind of differentiation appears to be central to the process. As Labov notes, "the social significance of most changes from below is a form of self-identification, of group membership, which establishes the speaker as an authentic representative of a sub-group within the community" (2006, p. 231).

The distinction between changes from below and changes from above acknowledges the fact that linguistic features differ in terms of their social salience. Labov designed the interviews with the inclusion of reading tasks along with opportunities for free-flowing conversation in order to examine these kinds of issues as a reflection of attitudes and opinions about speech. His methods also involved a more direct approach to such questions. He included a series of questions and tasks designed to probe the social evaluation of New York City speech by New Yorkers themselves. These methods included:

- A subjective reaction test in which recordings were played for interviewees, who rated the suitability of each voice they heard for various types of jobs.

- A self-evaluation test in which Labov pronounced seven words in three or four different ways, illustrating a range of variants heard in New York City. The interviewees were asked to indicate which of those variants they used in their own speech.

- An index of linguistic insecurity which was calculated by having interviewees listen to two alternate pronunciations of 18 different words and indicate: (a) which pronunciation they considered correct, and (b) which pronunciation they actually used. These words represented a range of phonological differences, most of which were relevant well beyond New York City (e.g. *vase* with /e/ vs. /ɑ/).

The index is simply the number of discrepancies between the two judgments (i.e. the number of cases for which the interviewee notes using an incorrect form).

- A series of questions about the interviewee's own speech and about New York City speech in general. These questions explored attitudes (e.g. What do you think of your own speech?) as well as personal experiences (e.g. Have you been recognized as a New Yorker by your speech?).

In designing these protocols, Labov was hoping to shed new light on the social dynamics of speech. He recognized that most New Yorkers felt that some forms of speech were superior to others – his style-shifting results offered evidence of this view – and he wanted to document the influence of such attitudes with the same precision he brought to the rest of his study. His quantitative approach here allowed him to examine the effects of particular linguistic variables on how speakers are judged and to compare interviewees' perceptions of their own speech with how they actually spoke earlier in the interview, to name just a couple of examples of Labov's analysis of these materials.

One of the lessons learned from this exploration of the social evaluations of speech is that people are generally poor judges of their own usage, at least with regard to the kinds of features that linguists are typically interested in. For example, when asked whether they normally pronounced *cards* with [r] or without [r], 61 percent of the New Yorkers identified their own pronunciation as r-ful. You need only compare this number to the results in Figure 3.2 above to see how unrealistic this self-assessment was. Labov recounts an especially poignant case of this phenomenon. He interviewed a middle class mother and her daughter who offered strong opinions about many of the phonological variables and ridiculed speakers from the subjective reaction test, including one who dropped an [r] in one word. They insisted that their own speech was impeccably r-ful. Labov "unwisely" played back part of their interview to demonstrate that they regularly dropped [r] too. This left them "disheartened in a way that was painful to see" (2006, p. 314).

What such examples illustrate is the unreliability of self-reports as a means of determining how people speak. Of course, this is not how Labov was using these techniques. He had that picture in his findings

of stylistic and social stratification of the linguistic variables. He turned
to the social evaluation data for a complementary perspective, and
this is certainly what he got. These materials contributed supporting
evidence for key concepts arising elsewhere in the study such as the
notion of linguistic insecurity and the distinction between change
from above and change from below.

The department store study

When students hear about Labov's New York City research in their
introductory courses, the focus is often not the material reviewed
above. Rather, many textbooks concentrate on what amounts to
a side project: "The social stratification of (r) in New York City
department stores." This memorable sub-study appeared as a
chapter in Labov's dissertation and was reprinted in the landmark
Sociolinguistic Patterns in 1972b. The work deserves the attention it
has received, but the imbalance is somewhat ironic since, as Labov
noted, "Of the year and a half spent studying New York City, a day
and a half was spent in the three department stores" (2006, p. 40).

The department store survey, like the main study, was designed
to explore the linguistic correlates of social stratification. In
particular, Labov set out to test the hypothesis that a ranking of
New Yorkers along a class scale would parallel their ranking in
terms of (r) usage. The Lower East Side survey provided clear
evidence in support of this hypothesis, but Labov held that "the
differential use of (r) pervades New York City so thoroughly, that
fine social differences will be reflected in the index as well as gross
ones" (2006, p. 41). So, he constructed "a very severe test" by
examining a kind of reflective class stratification among people
with the same occupation:

> If we select three large department stores, from the top, middle,
> and bottom of the price and fashion scale, we can expect that the
> customers will be socially stratified. Would we expect the sales
> people to show a comparable stratification? (2006, p. 41)

To explore this question, Labov pioneered a technique known as
the "rapid and anonymous survey." First, he selected three stores to
represent different strata of retail prestige. On the basis of several

criteria, he chose Saks Fifth Avenue to represent the highest level, Macy's to represent the middle level, and S. Klein to represent the lowest level.

Labov developed an ingenious method for collecting data from workers in the three stores. Posing as a customer, he approached an employee and asked where he could find a certain department that he knew to be on the fourth floor. The employee would usually respond "Fourth floor," to which Labov would say, "Excuse me?" in order to prompt a repetition. Then, he would move along and, when out of the employee's view, jot down notes on the exchange. The linguistic data included whether the employee pronounced the /r/ in *fourth* and *floor* the first time and when repeated. Labov also recorded demographic information about the employee, including race, sex, and estimated age. Using this method, he gathered data from a total of 264 people at the three stores in a period of six and half hours.

The main advantage of this approach, in addition to its efficiency, lies in the naturalness of the speech event. The research subjects (employees) are not aware that they are part of a speech study. From their perspective, the "interview" is an everyday exchange with a customer. However, this naturalness comes at a cost for the researcher. Labov was limited in the information he could glean from the exchange, especially with regard to the employee's background. Age, for example, had to be estimated. In recording the linguistic variation too, Labov had to rely on his ability to hear which variant the person used (in each of four examples) and remember that until he could enter it into his notes.

Labov's elegantly simple protocol produced data bearing on not only the social stratification of (r), his main concern, but also the linguistic conditioning of this feature and even its stylistic variation. By eliciting the phrase "fourth floor," he collected examples of (r) in two phonological contexts: before a consonant (*fourth*) and at the end of the word (*floor*). In this way he could explore which context was more favorable to deletion of the /r/. Insight into the stylistic variation of (r) came from the repetition of the phrase. We might predict a more careful pronunciation when the speaker repeats him/herself for the customer who appears to have not heard the initial answer.

Figure 3.3 summarizes Labov's main findings. This graph shows the percentages of employees at each store who pronounced the

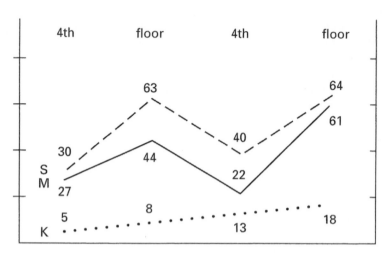

FIGURE 3.3 *Rates of* [r]-*pronunciation in New York City department stores: S=Saks, M=Macy's, and K=Kleins (from Labov, 2006, p. 48. Copyright © 2006 William Labov. Reprinted with the permission of Cambridge University Press).*

/r/ in each of the four contexts (in *fourth* and in *floor*, initially and in repeating the phrase). The social stratification fits Labov's expectations perfectly. Saks employees pronounce /r/ at higher rates than Macy's employees, who in turn pronounce it more than S. Klein employees. The phonological pattern also holds across all three stores: /r/ is more often deleted when it appears before a consonant (in *fourth*) than when it stands as the final sound (in *floor*). The predicted pattern of style shifting also mostly holds. The rates of pronouncing /r/ are greater during the repetitions with the one exception of *fourth* in the Macy's results (27 percent r-ful initially vs. 22 percent when repeated).

We have only scratched the surface of Labov's analysis here, but the broader significance of the study is clear. Labov demonstrates how deeply the social stratification of (r) has penetrated the speech community of New York City. It has become thoroughly integrated into the sociolinguistic structure of the city. Differential use of (r) by class appears not only among representatives of different socioeconomic groups, but also among members of the same group (department store employees) who differ in status only by association with others (clientele of the stores).

The study is also valuable as an illustration of what can be gained through a rapid and anonymous survey. Labov demonstrated that a systematic examination of speech could be accomplished outside the confines of "the formal linguistic interview" (2006, p. 56). In the years since Labov's study, this style of survey has been adopted in a range of other communities (see, e.g. Labov, 1984, pp. 49–50).

Conclusion

In 1961, Labov left his job as an inkmaker for graduate study in linguistics, a field he had little formal training in. He embarked on his graduate career with an exceptionally clear vision of what he hoped to contribute. He wanted to raise the standards for empirical research into language and make linguistics accountable to the ways that people actually spoke.

A Master's thesis, a dissertation, and three years later Labov had made enormous progress toward his goal. Did his approach immediately supplant the dominant paradigm within the field? No it didn't, nor has it done so even 50 years later. What Labov did accomplish in his graduate work was to prove his point that linguists can learn much about language by examining everyday speech. His thesis and especially his dissertation served as models for other scholars.[11] In this way Labov planted the seeds for a new study of language: variationist sociolinguistics.

Many of the ideas that Labov wrestled with in his graduate work eventually became central tenets of this new brand of sociolinguistics. These include:

- Language change can be observed in progress.

- Style shifting is patterned and adds a valuable perspective in the study of social stratification by language.

- Language is a property of a speech community and not of an individual member of that community, and a complete picture emerges only from studying the community.

Undergirding all this thinking is a commitment to the idea that variation is inherent in language and that any linguistics grounded in reality must acknowledge this fact. Labov's early work pioneered a methodology for uncovering patterns amid the apparent chaos of linguistic variation. As the field and its founder matured, so too did the understanding of the processes that shaped those patterns. In the next chapter, we examine how Labov built on his graduate work to develop a variationist theory of language.

Notes

1   This essay, "How I got into linguistics, and what I got out of it," was first published in 1987 and later revised in 1997. It is available on Labov's website: <http://www.ling.upenn.edu/~wlabov/Papers/ HowIgot.html>.

2   He began with a six-point scale but eventually refined this into a four-point scale. To add a higher degree of objectivity, Labov incorporated some acoustic analysis to verify that he was hearing the vowel differences accurately. Instrumental acoustic analysis is discussed further in Chapter Seven (see also Milroy and Gordon, 2003, or Thomas, 2011).

3   This question illustrates "the actuation problem" as formulated by Weinreich et al. (1968) (see Chapter Seven).

4   The title of his Master's thesis was "The Social History of a Sound Change on the Island of Martha's Vineyard."

5   The discrepancy in the numbers seems to stem from the fact that some of the 158 interviews were not completed.

6   A *cruller* is a type of doughnut, and *pot cheese* refers to the product known more generally as cottage cheese. Both of the local lexical items come from Dutch and thus reflect the original European settlement of New York.

7   Sociolinguists designate linguistic variables with parentheses (e.g. (r)), as opposed to the slashes (e.g. /r/) used to represent phonemes and the brackets (e.g. [r]) used to represent phonetic realizations. This notational convention was begun by Labov.

8   Voicing in phonetics refers to the action of the vocal cords. For a voiceless sound, the vocal cords are spread apart while they are pulled closer together and vibrate during the production of a voiced sound.

9   The details about this split of the short-a words are available in the *Atlas of North American English* (Labov et al., 2006).

10 Labov remarks in his 2006 commentary that labeling these "change from without" versus "change from within" might have reduced the confusion (p. 203).

11 The 2006 edition of *The Social Stratification of English* in New York City includes a new chapter that reviews 40 years of sociolinguistic studies of urban speech communities.

CHAPTER FOUR

A variationist approach to language

When the editors of the *Journal of English Linguistics* invited me to interview Labov some years ago, I jumped at the opportunity. There were, of course, a number of questions I wanted to ask, but I was especially interested in the early stages of his linguistics career. Labov introduced a new approach to the study of language and founded a field in which thousands of scholars around the globe now work. His name has been adjectivized, and Labovian sociolinguistics stands as an established part of the research landscape. How did Labov accomplish this? Was it a difficult fight to achieve recognition from the powers that be in linguistics? As Labov described the situation in our interview, "I expected that there would be a long and very romantic struggle against the established forces before the work would be recognized. That didn't happen." (Gordon, 2006, p. 336). It turns out his work was enthusiastically received from the start. Even as a graduate student he was presenting at major conferences and publishing in high-profile venues. Rather than toiling in obscurity for years to try to get his message out, Labov quickly rose to prominence.

What was it that propelled this meteoric success? What attracted a new generation of scholars as well as many established figures in the field to Labov's approach? I imagine that for many encountering Labov's work in those early days, it just made sense. Certainly the issues that he was exploring were familiar. Everyone recognized that social factors shaped speech differences, and that people varied their usage according to situation. The trouble was that existing paradigms failed to offer satisfying explorations of such matters. Many linguists were ready for a new approach. In this sense, what Labov introduced was not so much a new set of questions as a new way of answering questions that had been set aside in the past.

This chapter presents a summary of what distinguishes Labov's approach from those of others. We expand on ideas discussed in previous chapters to show how Labov built on the scholarship that preceded him and ultimately took the field in new directions. The discussion centers upon three key tenets of what has come to be known as the "Labovian paradigm":

- Variation is inherent to linguistic structure.

- A socially realistic linguistics offers valuable insights to the study of language.

- Quantitative methods can reveal patterns where casual observation sees only chaos.

We turn to each of these fundamental notions in turn.

Structured variation

Language is a highly structured system. Underpinning even the simplest utterance is a complex web of relationships that link meaningless sounds to meaningful words and that generate new meanings as those words are combined into larger strings. Linguists explore these relationships with the goal of understanding the rules governing a particular language and ultimately language in general. The structure of language derives from several components (e.g. phonology, morphology, syntax), but regularity holds throughout. I should note that linguists use "regular(ity)" to describe something governed by rules (following the Latin root *regula*, which means "rule").

Regularity is critical to language's ability to function in communication. Rules govern how units of language (words, phrases, sentences, etc.) are constructed, and having a shared set of linguistic rules is what allows two people to communicate through language. A logical extension of this observation leads us to the belief that languages should rely on a single, coherent set of rules consistently applied by all speakers. In fact, this idea, introduced in Chapter Two as the axiom of categoricity, has shaped theory and practice within linguistics throughout its history.

Saying that languages *should* behave in a certain way acknowledges that this ideal situation is not always found on the ground. Linguists, much like normal people, recognize that variation is a fact of linguistic life. We know, for example, that pronunciation, word choice, and grammar can vary among speakers of a language who represent different regional or social dialects. The traditional remedy for managing this variation advised linguists to set their analytical sights on a single dialect. Nevertheless, as Bloomfield noted (see discussion in Chapter Two), even within a single community we find that no two people speak alike in every way. This troublesome fact led many linguists to narrow their sights even further by describing the speech of the individual speaker, known as the idiolect.

The history of this thinking is outlined in the programmatic essay that Labov wrote with his mentor, Uriel Weinreich, and a fellow student, Marvin Herzog. This landmark paper, "Empirical foundations for a theory of language change" (Weinreich et al., 1968) offers a detailed statement of the principles guiding what came to be known as the variationist approach. The authors trace the traditional focus on the idiolect to the nineteenth-century linguist Hermann Paul, who held that "the language of the individual speaker-hearer encompassed the structured nature of language, the consistency of speech performance, and the regularity of change" (1968, p. 104). For Paul, language is fundamentally a psychological phenomenon, an internalized set of rules for producing utterances. To study language, therefore, you need only to access the internal grammar of the individual. In fact comparing across idiolects is the equivalent of comparing languages since every person has internalized a different linguistic system. What we think of as languages (English, French, Mandarin) do not exist except as artifacts of comparing idiolects. While such views stray far from everyday ways of thinking about language outside linguistics, Paul's influence can be seen today in the views of many prominent theorists, including Noam Chomsky.

What is especially relevant about Paul's approach for the present discussion is his motivation for isolating the idiolect as the object of study. It begins with the assumption that structure demands consistency. Thus, if one wishes to examine linguistic structure, one seeks out the most homogeneous usage, and that is found in the speech of the individual. This equation of structure with homogeneity lies at the heart of the axiom of categoricity.

In the early twentieth century, the same assumption guided the thinking of Ferdinand de Saussure, the Swiss scholar often credited with founding modern linguistics. Like Paul, Saussure maintained that language is fundamentally homogeneous. However, Saussure departs from Paul in viewing language as community property. He describes it as "the social side of speech, outside the individual who can never create nor modify it by himself; it exists only by virtue of a sort of contract signed by the members of a community" (1916/1959, p. 14). Thus, language represents a common rulebook by which speakers play. Saussure recognized, of course, that variation existed within every speech community, but he saw this as epiphenomenal. He comes to terms with the facts of linguistic heterogeneity by distinguishing *langue* (language) from *parole* (speaking). The former describes the linguistic system while the latter denotes the execution of language acts. In a telling analogy he likens *langue* to a symphony, since "what the symphony actually is stands completely apart from how it is performed; the mistakes that musicians make in playing the symphony do not compromise this fact" (1916/1959, p. 18). In this way Saussure dismisses *parole*, and with it heterogeneity, as insignificant to the primary focus of linguistic attention: *langue*. Mainstream linguistic theory continues to follow the agenda set by Saussure, and we see reflections of the *langue/parole* dichotomy in Chomsky's separation of competence from performance, as mentioned in Chapter One.

With this historical context we can better appreciate the challenge that Labov posed in the 1960s. The *langue*-centered agenda was fueled by the belief that linguistic structure requires homogeneity in order to function properly. Weinreich, Labov, and Herzog took on this received wisdom directly, exposing, for example, logical flaws with regard to language change:

> The facts of heterogeneity have not so far jibed well with the structural approach to language ... For the more linguists became impressed with the existence of structure of language, and the more they bolstered this observation with deductive

arguments about the functional advantages of structure, the more mysterious became the transition of a language from state to state. After all, if a language has to be structured in order to function efficiently, how do people continue to talk while the language changes, that is, while it passes through periods of lessened systematicity? Alternatively, if overriding pressures do force a language to change, and if communication is less efficient in the interim (as would deductively follow from the theory), why have such inefficiencies not been observed in practice? (1968, pp. 100–1)

The solution was to sever the presumed identification of structure with invariance. On this count, Labov's work provided critical evidence that linguistic structure did not presuppose homogeneity, that variation too could be regular. In his Martha's Vineyard and New York City research he offered numerous examples of sociolinguistic patterning, demonstrating that choices among competing variants were not random.

Figure 4.1 shows a simple example of such patterning. This figure comes from Labov's New York City study, and it plots the results for the (ing) variable: the alternation between alveolar and velar nasals in unstressed final syllables (e.g. *walkin'* [-ɪn] vs. *walking* [-ɪŋ]). The (ing) index shown in the Y axis marks the percentage of *–in'* use. Following the methods described in Chapter Three, Labov calculated the average (ing) indexes for four class groups (the SEC levels) across three contextual styles: casual speech (A), careful speech (B), and reading passages (C). The result is an elegant demonstration of class and stylistic stratification. The (ing) indexes for each class group perfectly parallel their distribution on the social scale not just in one speech context, but across all three, and every group decreases their use of *–in'* as they shift from casual speech to careful speech to reading. The pattern couldn't be more regular.

Findings such as these demonstrate that choices between linguistic alternatives can still be patterned even when factors governing those choices do not operate categorically. In this way they show that language relies on "orderly heterogeneity." This memorable phrase from Weinreich et al. (1968, p. 100) encapsulates a theoretical break with tradition on various levels.

The idea of orderly heterogeneity rebukes the traditional notion of "free variation" discussed in Chapter Two. In the structuralist

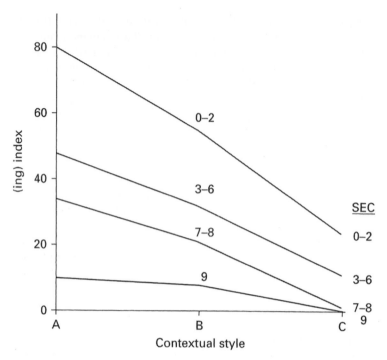

FIGURE 4.1 *Distribution of* (ing) *by social class (SEC) and contextual style in the Lower East Side study (from Labov, 2006, p. 259; reprinted by permission of Cambridge University Press).*

tradition (Saussure, Bloomfield, and their successors), free variation describes a particular kind of relationship between alternative forms, one in which the choice between the forms is not governed by rules nor does it bear any structural significance. Thus, the speaker is "free" to choose either alternative at any time. If such freedom actually reigned, we wouldn't find the clear patterning of examples like that of Figure 4.1. Instead of the random fluctuation expected of truly free variants, we see overwhelming regularity shaped by social and linguistic conditioning.

It is also significant that the orderly heterogeneity Labov and others examine is taken to be the property of a single linguistic system. The contrast here is with earlier notions of dialect mixing (see Chapter Two). The idea that variation must be the product of mixing two linguistic systems is built on the assumptions of the axiom of categoricity, and Labov reveals its shaky foundations:

> There is a kind of folk-myth deeply embedded among linguists that before they themselves arrived on the scene there existed a homogeneous, single-style group who really "spoke the language." Each investigator feels that his own community has been corrupted from this normal model in some way – by contact with other languages, by the effects of education and pressure of the standard language, or by taboos and the admixture of specialized dialects and jargons. But we have come to the realization in recent years that this is the *normal* situation – that heterogeneity is not only common, it is the natural result of basic linguistic factors. (Labov, 1972b, p. 203)

There is no need to treat variable usage as a case of switching between co-existent dialects when we accept that variability is the norm in every linguistic system.

Indeed, not only is orderly heterogeneity natural and expected, it is also highly functional. As Weinreich, Labov, and Herzog argue "nativelike command of heterogeneous structures ... is part of unilingual linguistic competence," and "in a language serving a complex (i.e. real) community, it is *absence* of structured heterogeneity that would be dysfunctional" (1968, p. 101). There are a range of technical arguments that can be made to illustrate the functional value of language variation. We saw glimpses of one such argument in Weinreich, Labov, and Herzog's comments above about the role of variation in facilitating smooth transitions during language change. Here we can consider briefly a different kind of argument, one related to issues of identity.

Language serves as a powerful tool for signaling who we are. Whenever we speak, we convey much more than the content of our words. Our pronunciation, word choices, and grammar mark our social identities. A particular usage can indicate our membership in any number of groups, some of which are defined by broad social parameters (e.g. gender, class, ethnicity) and others of which are more localized (e.g. a school clique). This ability to signal aspects of our identities stems from the existence of heterogeneous structures that link language and social categories in complex patterns. In this way an individual's usage is read in terms of a wider sociolinguistic matrix and social meaning is conveyed along with the referential meaning of the message. We saw a powerful example of this in Labov's Martha's Vineyard study where the pronunciation of the diphthongs in words such as *right* and *out* marks the speaker's orientation to traditional island life. Thus, we see one argument for the functionality of sociolinguistic variation in the way that it provides an additional channel of information.

Variables and variable rules

In the drama of orderly heterogeneity, the starring role is played by the sociolinguistic variable. A variable is essentially a set of alternative forms, the usage of which is influenced by linguistic and social factors. In the previous section, for example, we noted the (ing) variable, which comprises two variants: [ɪn] and [ɪŋ]. Sociolinguists commonly use parentheses to denote variables as separate from the slashes (e.g. /p/) and brackets (e.g. [pʰ]) used to represent phonemes and allophones respectively.

The concept of the variable is used to examine a wide range of linguistic phenomena. A sociolinguist might study phonological, grammatical, or lexical variables. Moreover, the variants of a given variable might illustrate any of several different relationships. A partial list includes:[1]

- Allophones of a single phoneme: Variants might represent phonetically different forms that alternate in the same class of words. The diphthongs (ai) and (au) from Labov's Martha's Vineyard study illustrate this type.

- Presence vs. absence of a form: The variation might stem from whether a form (e.g. a sound, a grammatical suffix, etc.) is realized or not. The case of (r) in New York City represents this type.

- Differences in the linear order of elements: Alternative word orders might be treated as a variable, as, for example, in the case of particle verbs (e.g. *I looked up the word ~ I looked the word up*). A syntactically more complicated case in this

vein is the variation between the active and passive voice
(e.g. *They allow smoking here. ~ Smoking is allowed here.*).[2]

- Lexical choices: Different words for the same meaning
  might constitute a linguistic variable. Familiar examples
  in American English include *pop ~ soda ~ coke* as terms
  for carbonated beverages and *couch ~ sofa ~ davenport ~
  Chesterfield* as alternative names for the piece of furniture.

As these examples demonstrate, the sociolinguistic variable does
not map neatly onto any traditional linguistic unit.

Whatever the nature of their relationship, the variants of a
variable do not occur randomly, but rather their usage is shaped
by linguistic and social factors. We haven't had cause to discuss
the former much since analysis of linguistic factors played a small
role in Labov's Martha's Vineyard and New York City studies.
Still, the basic idea is familiar to any student of linguistics and was
touched on in the overview of phonology in Chapter Two. It is
often the case, for example, that allophones of a given phoneme
occur only in particular phonological contexts, such as next to a
certain sound or in a certain position in a word. We mentioned the
example of aspirated stops, like the initial sound of *pipe*, which
appear in English only at the beginning of stressed syllables. We call
this a case of "linguistic conditioning," since the choice of variant is
determined by linguistic factors. It works the same way in the case
of a sociolinguistic variable except that the conditioning need not
apply categorically as it does in traditional accounts.

As an illustration of how usage of a variable reflects both
linguistic and social factors we can examine a phenomenon found
in virtually all varieties of English: *t/d* deletion in final consonant
clusters. This variable involves the dropping of a [t] or a [d] when
it appears at the end of a word after another consonant (e.g. [mɪs]
"mist"; [æn] "and"). Labov examined this variable in the study of
African American English he conducted in Harlem shortly after
completing his graduate work (Labov et al., 1968). That project
identified two key patterns of linguistic conditioning: (1) whether
the following word began with a consonant or a vowel, and (2)
whether the cluster was formed by adding the past tense suffix (*-ed*).
Labov found, and dozens of subsequent studies have confirmed,
that deletion of the final [t] or [d] occurs more frequently when

the next word begins with a consonant than when it begins with a vowel. So, for example, *last* is more likely to be pronounced as [læs] in a phrase like *last month* than in *last October*. Similarly, they found deletion happens more often when the cluster appears as part of the root of the word than when it stems from the addition of a suffix. Thus, we find higher rates of deletion for *mist* and *band* than for *missed* and *banned*. In addition to these linguistic factors, the variable deletion of [t] and [d] is also shaped by social factors such as age and social class. A sample of the results from Labov's Harlem study is shown in Table 4.1.

These data show the effects of the linguistic factors, with the highest rates of deletion occurring when the [t] or [d] appears in a simple word with a consonant at the beginning of the following word (e.g. *last month*), and the lowest rates occurring when the [t] or [d] represents the past tense suffix and is followed by a word that begins with a vowel (e.g. *missed a spot*). We also see a pattern of class stratification familiar from Labov's other New York City research. Here, lower rates of deletion are heard from the middle class than from the working class; within the latter, lower rates are heard from the upper working class, though this difference only appears in the treatment of the past tense forms.

Some early research in the variationist mode, including Labov's, tried to describe the observed patterns in detailed statements of rules. Rule-writing is common practice in linguistics as a way of denoting precisely the operations of a particular linguistic process, including the conditions under which it applies. In phonology, where this practice survives most strongly, a typical rule stipulates

Table 4.1 Deletion of t/d in consonant clusters

	Simple words		Past tense forms	
	before cons. (%)	before vowel (%)	before cons. (%)	before vowel (%)
Middle Class	60	28	19	4
Upper Working Class	90	40	19	9
Lower Working Class	89	40	47	32

(Labov et al., 1968; Labov, 1972b, p. 222)

that a particular input form is realized as some output form in a given context. This is represented with a formalism like:

$$A \to B \ / \ \_\_\_ \ C$$

The arrow represents what happens between input and output. The slash marks the conditioning environment with the underline representing the position of the affected sound. So, this rule would be read as "A becomes B when it occurs before a C"; in other words, the sequence AC is realized as BC.

To represent the process of *t/d* deletion we might begin with a rule to capture the effect of a following consonant versus a vowel.[3] This rule could simply note that [t] or [d] is dropped when it appears at the end of word after another consonant and when the following word starts with a consonant. Formally this might appear as:

$$[t]/[d] \to \text{ø} \ /C \ \_\_\_ \ \#\#C$$

The null sign indicates that the consonant is simply dropped and not changed into some other sound. A capital C is the usual abbreviation for consonant and the hashes (##) denote a break between words. Of course this rule only describes one element of the linguistic conditioning, and we'd need another to represent the deletion in simple root words rather than suffixed forms.

The problem with using traditional rules like these, however, is that they are interpreted as categorical processes. They imply that every [t] and every [d] is deleted whenever they appear in the stated environments. Traditional approaches to phonology do recognize optional rules, but these are designed to represent situations of free variation. They fail to capture many details of the pattern. For example, we know that *t/d* deletion can also happen when the following word begins a vowel. We would need a separate optional rule to represent this fact, or we could simply remove the conditioning environment to note that [t] and [d] are optionally deleted in final consonant cluster. However, neither of these choices offers a satisfactory representation of the data, specifically of the fact that all speakers apply the deletion rule more frequently when the following word begins with a consonant than when it begins with a vowel.

Labov's solution to this representational dilemma was the introduction of the variable rule. In essence, a variable rule builds into the traditional optional rule some indication of the likelihood of its application. To each rule, for example, we might assign a value "representing the proportion of cases in which the rule applies out of all those cases in which it might do so" (Labov, 1972b, p. 218). A variable rule also allows for the ranking of the relative strengths of different factors. So, for t/d deletion the rule could show that it occurs more frequently in some environments than in others. Here is one version of that rule offered by Sankoff and Labov (1978, p. 204):

$$t,d \rightarrow \langle \emptyset / \rangle C \left\langle \begin{array}{c} \emptyset \\ \# \end{array} \right\rangle \_\_\_ \# \# \left\langle \begin{array}{c} C \\ V \end{array} \right\rangle$$

Angled brackets are used to indicate variable elements. Within those brackets the conditions are ranked with the most favorable ones on top. So, this rule states that [t] and [d] are variably deleted when they appear after another consonant at the end of the word and that deletion is more common (a) when there is no morphological boundary (#) between the consonants (i.e. the [t] or [d] is not marking the past tense suffix), and (b) when the following word begins with a consonant rather than a vowel.

It is fair to say that the concept of variable rules has been controversial even within the field of sociolinguistics. The general principles that motivated them are certainly valid. All variationists acknowledge the limited perspective provided by traditional theories that held that rules were either categorical or optional. Still, questions were raised about what variable rules were intended to represent. Are they elements of the native speaker's internalized grammar? Are they descriptions of community norms? The latter would be more in keeping with Labov's general theoretical leanings (as discussed below) but might imply that all members of a speech community apply a rule in the same way; that is, at the same rate and following the same ranking of constraints. On this question Labov, with his co-author David Sankoff, note that variable rules were intended to describe "production" (Sankoff and Labov, 1978, p. 202). In this way they account for the observed patterns and do not necessarily represent the underlying network of factors that contribute to those patterns.

Variable rules are not much discussed in sociolinguistic studies today, and certainly the formalism used to write them has gone out of fashion. In fact, over 20 years ago Ralph Fasold wrote of the "quiet demise" of the variable rule. Fasold notes that variables rules were originally developed "to understand how variation works within a theory of human language" (1991, p. 9). A more cynical slant on this history might suggest that the concept represented an attempt to connect variationist research to the mainstream of linguistic theory by highlighting areas of presumed compatibility (e.g. formal representations). Whatever the motivations, the concept of variable rules remained underdeveloped. In the end, Fasold concludes we should not mourn the demise of the variable rule since "it was never any more than a display device" (1991, p. 18).[4]

Speech communities

The concept of "speech community" can be a slippery one. As noted in Chapter Two, Bloomfield cites using "the same system of speech-signals" as a defining criterion of a speech community. Clearly he was willing to overlook a good deal of variation in determining what constitutes "the same system" since he describes all speakers of English as a speech community. On the other hand, Bloomfield also defines the term in an apparently narrower sense as "people who interact by means of speech" (p. 42), which implies geographical proximity or some other means of contact among community members.

Labov's use of "speech community" is much closer to Bloomfield's narrower sense. On the question of whether members of a speech community draw on the same linguistic system, Labov offers a valuable reframing:

> The speech community is not defined by any marked agreement in the use of language elements, so much as by participation in a set of shared norms; these norms may be observed in overt types of evaluative behavior, and by the uniformity of abstract patterns of variation which are invariant in respect to particular levels of usage. (1972b, pp. 120–1)

It is this definition which licenses his calling New York City a speech community. Do all New Yorkers speak the same way? Obviously not, but they share a set of norms about linguistic behavior.

The Lower East Side study teems with evidence of these norms. For example, how often a New Yorker pronounces /r/ varies depending on social class, but all agree that /r/ should be pronounced more in certain situations (e.g. reading aloud) than in others (e.g. casual conversation). Moreover, Labov's tests show that all New Yorkers have similar subjective evaluations of r-ful versus r-less speech.

For Labov, the speech community is of paramount importance. Knowledge of language comes from studying speech communities. He shares with Saussure the view that language exists outside the individual speaker, and "The object of linguistic description is the grammar of the speech community: the system of communication used in social interaction" (1982a, p. 18). On the other hand, Labov differs greatly from Saussure and others who follow in that tradition when it comes to how to access that community grammar. As discussed above, linguists have often taken an individual's idiolect to provide an adequate reflection of the linguistic system (Saussure's *langue*), which they supposed to be homogeneous. This represents part of what Labov dubs the Saussurian Paradox: "the social aspect of language [the community's *langue*] is studied by observing any one individual, but the individual aspect only by observing language in its social context" (1972b, p. 186).

Labov strongly rejects the suggestion that an individual speaker provides an adequate window into the grammar of a speech community. Indeed, he considers the view "that the community is prior to the individual" to be "the central dogma of sociolinguistics" (2006, p. 5). As he elaborated in our 2006 interview, "We study individuals because they give us the data to describe the community, but the individual is not really a linguistic unit" (Gordon, 2006, p. 341). For a better sense of Labov's thinking we can posit, as an example, what a single New Yorker's speech might teach us about a linguistic variable like (r). Let's imagine we recorded that person in various speech contexts and measured his or her usage of (r) to find, say, that /r/ was pronounced 16 percent of the time in some context and at higher and lower rates in other contexts. What does this one person's usage tell us about how (r) functions? Not much. As Labov notes, "the language of individuals cannot be understood without knowledge of the community of which they are members" (2006, p. 5). Unless we can view our imagined speaker's usage from the broader perspective of community norms, we have no way of knowing whether 16 percent is a lot of /r/ or a little, or why that person pronounced /r/ more or less in other contexts. We certainly would have no indication that (r) was involved in change in New York City and that the change was being led by the upper end of the social scale. The study of language in its social context, therefore, is Labov's solution to both objectives in the Saussurian Paradox; it provides insights into both the individual dimension (*parole*) and the communal dimension (*langue*).

Socially realistic linguistics

Labov was certainly not the first linguist to study the social dimensions of language. The review in Chapter One highlights some examples of work in this area well before Labov's arrival in the field. Still, Labov shined new light on sociolinguistic questions and offered an innovative research paradigm around which several scholars quickly coalesced. The first step was the theoretical reorientation of letting go – or rather strongly rejecting – the axiom of categoricity and recognizing orderly heterogeneity as a normal, even necessary, characteristic of language. Once the researcher is open to the possibility of structured variation, the question becomes how to explore it. Labov's answer is a socially realistic linguistics.[5]

One dimension of this socially realistic approach is the need to recognize the social complexities of the speech communities studied. We see this in Labov's early work, especially the New York City study, through his attention to sampling. He casts a wide net in an attempt to represent the fullest range of speech possible. His objective was "a description which takes into account the distribution of language differences throughout the community, and necessarily preserves the data on the age, sex, education, occupation, and ethnic membership of the speakers studied" (2006, p. 7). To be sure, this emphasis on broad demographic parameters (e.g. sex, class, ethnicity) can be criticized as offering only a rough sketch of the social dynamics of a given speech community (see Chapters Six and Nine). Still, compared to practices elsewhere in linguistics in the 1960s, and often even today, Labov's approach comes much closer to representing a socially realistic picture.

This point reminds us that a "socially realistic linguistics" stands in contrast to some other brand of linguistics, presumably one that is socially unrealistic. As mentioned in Chapter Three, Labov entered the field with the goal of introducing a firmer empirical foundation and grounding linguistics in the study of how people actually speak. In this respect he was challenging the dominant paradigm where evidence often consisted of the native speaker's intuitions about his or her language. This paradigm is represented most prominently by Noam Chomsky, and it continues to dominate linguistic theory today. Here hypotheses about linguistic structure are tested against a speaker's (often the researcher's) sense of whether constructed examples are grammatically acceptable. Thus, the question is "Could someone say X?" and not "Does anyone actually say X?"

The view that a speaker's intuitions could provide necessary data for linguistic analysis has its roots in the Saussurian distinction of *langue* from *parole*. Since linguistics was interested in discovering the abstract structures that constituted *langue*, it made sense to avoid *parole*, which could only muddy the waters. This position hardened with Chomsky's reformulation of the distinction as competence versus performance. Competence refers to the underlying knowledge of one's native language, while performance was simply how that knowledge was implemented. Performance is seen as necessarily imperfect because it is subject to "such grammatically irrelevant conditions as memory limitations, distractions, shifts of attention and interest, and errors" (Chomsky, 1965, p. 3). The surest way to filter out such noise in pursuit of competence/*langue* is to tap the source "directly" by studying a native speaker's intuitions.

Linguists who work in linguistic theory and depend on grammatical intuitions have certainly not been oblivious to the potential flaws in their methods. In fact, there have been many studies in this area that have tested whether the grammaticality judgments proposed by linguists match those of nonspecialists. Labov reviewed some of the existing literature in 1975 when he asked "What is a linguistic fact?" What he found then, and later explorations have generally confirmed, is that many judgments made by linguists are not shared by other linguists nor by native speakers untrained in linguistics.[6]

When we survey Labov's career, we see that early on he devoted a good deal of attention to taking on the mainstream view that linguistics should pursue intuitions about language rather than actual examples of language in use. This was clearly part of his strategy for establishing a socially realistic linguistics, and he succeeded in galvanizing a movement to that end. Outside of sociolinguistics, it is fair to say that intuition-based research remains the dominant approach in many domains of linguistics (e.g. syntactic theory). Still, many trends within the field over the last few decades signal a heightened interest in empirically grounded approaches. For example, we can point to the relatively new subfield of corpus linguistics, where hypotheses about language structure and use can be tested using recently developed electronic databases of written and spoken language materials. In the realm of sounds, we see increased reliance on experimental methods in supporting theoretical claims in phonology. Whether such developments took their inspiration from Labov's critiques remains an open question. Certainly Labov and others who practice his socially realistic approach welcome this shoring up of the field's empirical foundations.

Quantitative methods

It's one thing to acknowledge variation as a crucial component of linguistic structure. It's quite another to demonstrate that the heterogeneity heard in a speech community is orderly. The study of speech differences was central to at least some branches of linguistics long before Labov set foot on Martha's Vineyard. As reviewed in Chapter Two, for example, dialect geography took exploring such differences as its *raison d'être*. Still, research in this tradition did not reveal anything like the patterned variation we see in Labov's work. Even when dialectologists adopted a socially realistic approach to representing the diversity within a community (e.g. Pederson's study of Chicago discussed in Chapter Two), their methods failed to produce a comprehensive account of sociolinguistic structures. To appreciate how Labov put the "orderly" in "orderly heterogeneity" we look to his analytical arsenal and specifically to his use of quantitative methods.[7]

We gained a sense of the value of a quantitative approach to speech data from the discussion of Labov's Martha's Vineyard and New York City studies. This research demonstrated that behind the apparent randomness of linguistic variation lies regularity. Labov showed, for example, that contrary to the characterization of an earlier researcher that New Yorkers sometimes pronounced and sometimes dropped /r/ "in a thoroughly haphazard fashion," use of this variable was highly patterned in terms of New York's stratified class system. The moral of this story is not that previous investigators were too close-minded to see the patterns; rather that their methods allowed only a limited view of the situation because they tended to focus on a relatively small sample of speakers and a restricted sample of speech data from those speakers.

Relying on a small set of speakers, especially when those speakers do not represent the diversity of the community, obviously limits the researcher's perspective. As noted earlier in this chapter, it is impossible to grasp the significance of an individual's speech behavior outside of the wider context of the speech community. This is the insight that informs Labov's pursuit of a socially realistic linguistics.

A similar logic applies in terms of the speech data observed from each individual. The interpretation of a person's usage in a given context is made easier through comparison with usage in other contexts. The cases of style shifting discussed from the New York City study, for example, guided Labov's analysis of the social meaning of the linguistic variables.

Even more fundamental than documenting stylistic variation for an individual is the need to base the assessment of the individual's usage on an appropriate dataset; that is, on a number of relevant examples. To underscore this point, we might recall that dialect geographers commonly characterized a speaker's usage of a given phoneme by the pronunciation of a handful of words. In the Linguistic Atlas of the United States and Canada, the diphthongs /ai/ and /au/, for example, were usually studied in the words *nine*, *twice*, and *wire*, and *down*, *mountain*, *house* and *out* (see Kurath and McDavid, 1961). The target words were chosen, often with historical considerations in mind, to illustrate how the sounds were pronounced in various phonological contexts. As discussed in Chapter Two, this approach assumes that an individual's pronunciation of a given word is consistent, as typically each word was elicited once by the fieldworker, and the speaker's pronunciation in that single instance was recorded.

For some variables, the dialectologist's traditional approach might make sense. I mentioned the example of "creek" versus "crick" earlier. In such a case the variation involves the choice of vowel phonemes, which is more likely to be categorical. For many other variables, however, the variation is more quantitative than qualitative. The example of (ing), mentioned above, certainly fits this characterization. We do not find that a speaker either says *walking* or *walkin'* one hundred percent of the time. Rather, everyone uses both pronunciations, and what is sociolinguistically significant is how frequently each form is used. Methodologically, we cannot understand this significance by examining a person's pronunciation in three, five, or even ten words. We need a larger sample to eliminate the statistical fluctuations and detect the overall pattern of usage.

For the reasons just reviewed, Labov's methods of analysis rely on quantification to investigate linguistic variation on several levels. His approach recognizes that an individual speaker may use different variants of a variable in the same linguistic context. For a phonological variable this might mean that a particular word is pronounced differently on different occasions. Therefore, each person's usage of the variable is examined over several tokens (examples), and some overall measure is calculated as, for example, with the centralization indexes for the diphthongs in the Martha's Vineyard study.

An individual's usage of a given variable may also be shaped by situational factors such as the physical setting, the participants in a conversation, the topic under discussion, and so on. The stylistic variation resulting from such contextual differences represents another research challenge to which quantitative methods can fruitfully be applied. Labov's usual strategy in this area is simply an extension of the basic method in the previous paragraph except that different measures are calculated for different speech contexts as we saw, for example, with the casual speech versus careful speech versus reading scores in the New York City study.

The real power of the quantitative approach comes not from describing how individuals differ in their usage of the variables, but rather from exploring correlations between linguistic variables and social parameters. These correlations are revealed when individuals are grouped into socially meaningful categories and usage means (or some other measures) are calculated so that comparisons can be made across the groups. In the Martha's Vineyard study, for example, Labov's comparison across age groups led to the conclusion that centralization of the vowels was, if the reader will forgive the pun, on the rise. The stratification of several variables in terms of social class in the New York City study was clearly shown when group means were compared.

Accountability principle

Quantitative methods are obviously about counting, but in a variationist analysis counting involves more than tallying up the occurrences of a particular linguistic form. In order to produce meaningful results, the counting must follow the "Principle of Accountability." In an early formulation of this principle, Labov defined it as the requirement:

> That any variable form (a member of a set of alternative ways of "saying the same thing") should be reported with the proportion of cases in which the form did occur in the relevant environment, compared to the total number of cases in which it might have occurred. (1969, p. 738)

Thus, researchers must remain accountable to all the data they purport to describe. They are not at liberty to pick and choose examples that support their arguments while ignoring or dismissing counter-evidence. To anyone familiar with academic argumentation in humanities fields such as literary criticism, the contrast here should be readily apparent.

Promoting this principle was very much in keeping with the goals Labov had when entering the field. He set out to strengthen the scientific basis of the field, to put linguistics on a firmer empirical footing. Acting in accordance with the accountability principle serves that purpose by making hypotheses not only testable but also falsifiable.

In practice, operationalizing the principle is not always a straightforward matter. Counting the number of occurrences of a particular form generally presents no challenge, but defining when a particular form "might have occurred" but didn't is another matter. The problem might be described as one of circumscribing the envelope of variation, and it raises fundamental questions about what it means for two forms to be "alternative ways of 'saying the same thing.'"

In the case of a phonological variable, the issue can be more easily resolved. Sounds carry no inherent meaning, no referential meaning anyway, and so we can safely interpret them as true alternatives when they appear in the same environments. New York City (r) serves as a simple example. Labov's analysis distinguishes two main variants of (r) based on whether the consonant was pronounced or dropped. The envelope of variation for (r) is defined by those words containing the /r/ phoneme since the consonant may be articulated or omitted in each of these cases. Actually, we need to fine tune this description since /r/ is subject to deletion only under some phonological circumstances. To be precise, we would define the envelope of variation as all instances of /r/ that occur before a consonant or at the end of word before a pause. For any speaker in the sample of New Yorkers, then, the total number of these instances was counted, as was the proportion of those for which the consonant was pronounced and the proportion for which the consonant was not pronounced.

With some variables, however, the envelope of potential cases is not so readily circumscribed. This is frequently the case with grammatical variables. In African American English, for example, the verb *be* sometimes appears in its uninflected form as in *He be walking*. One of the functions of this usage is to mark a regularly occurring event, and so it is known in the research literature as "habitual *be*" (see Chapter Eight). The researcher studying this construction can certainly count how often it appears, but determining when it might have appeared but didn't presents a greater challenge. What are the alternatives to habitual *be*? What is the variable of which habitual *be* represents one variant? Without answers to these questions we can't identify nonoccurrences of habitual *be*. Labov's recommendation in such cases is to trace "the relative frequency of occurrence in some globally defined section of speech, controlled for length by an independent measure like number of sentences, pages, or hours of speech" (1982a, p. 87).

This problem of circumscribing the envelope of variation hits at the core of the notion of the linguistic variable. As originally conceived, a variable represented a set of variants that were absolutely interchangeable from the perspective of linguistic structure. Theoretically a speaker could use any variant of a variable without affecting the meaning of the utterance. Here we mean the linguistic or referential meaning; variants often differ in terms of the social or stylistic meanings, which is what makes them interesting to the sociolinguist in the first place. When the concept of the variable is applied beyond the analysis of sounds, however, equivalence of meaning can be much dicier. Consider, for example, a pair such as *They broke into the liquor closet* and *The liquor closet was broken into*.

At some level these sentences represent alternative ways of saying the same thing, and they could be counted as variants of a single variable as Weiner and Labov (1983) did. Nevertheless, one might argue that they differ slightly in meaning, perhaps emphasizing different aspects of the event. Certainly the choice between active and passive voice is heavily influenced by the surrounding context, among other factors. In this way, the criterion of interchangeability for variants of a variable is stretched. Some sociolinguists resist this move. For example, in an influential essay, Beatriz Lavandera, a former student of Labov's, suggested that it was "inadequate" for investigators "to extend to other levels of analysis of variation the notion of the sociolinguistic variable originally developed on the basis of phonological data" (1978, p. 171). Labov and others, while acknowledging such criticisms, maintain that variationist analysis still offers useful insights into the choices among competing variants even when those variants involve different meanings.

Labov and statistics

The analytical path between the counting of variants and the uncovering of orderly heterogeneity is paved with statistics. Statistical reasoning has undergirded Labov's argumentation throughout his career and has become a hallmark of the variationist enterprise more generally. A full account of such reasoning and its implementation in the field lies well outside the scope of this book.[8] I highlight here a few aspects of Labov's approach to statistics.

The overarching motivation for conducting statistical analysis was laid out above. Patterns of sociolinguistic variation generally remain opaque to casual observation. Everyday experience in a speech community may lead an investigator to the recognition that members of the community vary in their use of particular forms, but an impressionistic approach cannot provide a complete picture. When the variation is a matter of the relative frequencies of the variants, quantification is needed to uncover patterns in distribution of those variants. Statistics are simply a means of managing quantitative data.

In his earliest work, Labov relied on relatively simple statistics. In the Martha's Vineyard and New York City studies, his primary statistical tool was the mean (average). All the indexes he designed for measuring phonological variation relied on averages across several token of the variable spoken by each person. Also, the comparisons across social parameters were made by examining the mean scores for members of the various groups. In the New York City study, he often presents the data in tables that simply show the distribution of speakers across several intersecting parameters (e.g. ethnicity, age, contextual style). This technique of "cross-tabulation," together with graphs like those presented in Chapter Three, was effective, though in his 2006 commentary Labov confesses, "Only the extreme regularity and independence of the social and stylistic factors made it possible to present a convincing view of the results" (p. 401).

As he came to pay closer attention to the intersection of social and linguistic factors, Labov turned to more sophisticated statistical methods. When more independent variables are involved in shaping the behavior of the dependent (linguistic) variables, the researcher must be able to sort their effects and determine which qualify as significant. As every survivor of an introductory statistics class knows, significance is a matter of how likely it is that a particular result would occur by chance. A statistically significant pattern is one that has a low probability of having surfaced randomly.

Statisticians have a number of tools for modeling the effects of multiple variables and testing the significance of observed patterns. Often these standard approaches rely on assumptions that may not hold for language data. Labov described the problem as follows:

A fundamental difficulty in applying standard multivariate techniques is that linguistic data have several unusual characteristics. First, we find that some cells, representing the intersection of various phonological and grammatical variables, are certain to be empty or very small . . . Secondly, we find most internal linguistic features are independent and do not show the typical interaction that is characteristic of social variables such as class, sex and age. Standard analyses of variance are based upon the possibility of filling all cells of a matrix evenly and the necessity of analyzing extensive interaction. (1978, p. 363)

Such concerns prompted David Sankoff and Pascale Rousseau to design a special program for the statistical analysis of variable linguistic data: Varbrul (see Cedergren and Sankoff, 1974; Rousseau and Sankoff, 1978). The name reflects the fact that this program is grounded in the concept of the variable rule. What Varbrul does, in essence, is calculate the probability of a stated variable rule applying in different environments.

Varbrul generates a statistic known as a factor value or weight. This is a number between 0 and 1 that measures each condition's effect on the rule. Generally, factor weights higher than 0.50 are interpreted as marking favoring conditions and those below 0.50 as marking disfavoring conditions. Thus, for example, in Weiner and Labov's study of the passive voice, one independent variable they examined was stylistic context. The Varbrul results for this factor showed weights of 0.54 and 0.46 for careful and casual speech respectively. Thus, careful speech is seen as slightly favoring the appearance of the passive voice while casual speech is seen as slightly disfavoring it. I add "slightly" because in Varbrul the further away from the 0.50 mark, the stronger the effects. For example, Weiner and Labov also examined the influence of a kind of syntactic parallelism – specifically, whether the would-be subject of a passive sentence had appeared as a subject in some earlier sentence in the conversation. The condition of having this parallel subject in the preceding discourse produced a Varbrul weight of 0.62 while the condition without the parallel subject had a factor weight of 0.38. These results suggest that such parallelism plays a greater role in shaping the occurrence of the passive voice.

Varbrul analysis is still used today by a number of sociolinguists. However, Labov himself tends to rely on other statistical methods, though this is largely a consequence of the kinds of data he is working with. Much of his research explores phonological variation, and he tends to rely on acoustic measurements. These data are continuous; they show a range of values. Varbrul analysis is not designed for such cases because it tests the factors influencing the application or non-application of some variable rule, which is essentially a binary choice. Other statistical techniques such as regression analysis are more appropriate in the case of continuous data.

Summary

This chapter has outlined some of the key aspects of Labov's approach to the study of language, which flourishes today under the general heading of variationist sociolinguistics. This approach is distinguished from others on theoretical as well as methodological grounds. It begins with the fundamental rethinking of how language operates encapsulated in the notion of orderly heterogeneity. Once we recognize that linguistic structure depends on variation to function, we turn to questions of how best to describe that heterogeneity. Labov's socially realistic approach attends to the diversity inherent in real speech communities and takes as its data actual speech produced in various settings. To make sense of these data Labov turns to quantitative analysis, which can reveal patterns where informal observations might see only random fluctuations.

With this overview of the distinguishing characteristics of Labovian thought and practice we can better appreciate his contributions to linguistic study. The following chapters explore Labov's insights across various areas of the field. We turn first to his work on stylistic variation and his contributions to the study of discourse analysis.

Notes

1 This list comes from Walt Wolfram (1991), who provides a fuller typology and discussion of the concept of the linguistic variable.

2 Labov has done much more research on phonological variables than grammatical ones, but he did examine the use of the passive voice in a co-authored paper. See Weiner and Labov (1983).

3 This discussion paraphrases the argument in Labov (1972b, pp. 216–23).

4 Fasold's article offers a thorough critique of the variable rule concept. Interested readers may also consult Walt Wolfram's essay from the same volume, which discusses how the introduction of variable rules altered previous notions of the sociolinguistic variable (see Wolfram, 1991).

5 "Socially realistic linguistics" was used by Labov (2006, p. 11) in reviewing previous studies of language in its social context, specifically in reference to Antoine Meillet's writing. Hymes (1974, p. 196) later applied the term to describe how Labov's approach differs in orientation from other areas of sociolinguistics.

6 More recent reviews of these issues are provided by Schütze (1996), Kepser and Reis (2005), and Wasow and Arnold (2005).

7 My goal in this discussion is to highlight the central issues related to
   the use of quantitative methods. Readers interested in practical advice
   for implementing such methods in their own research may wish to
   consult Milroy and Gordon (2003) or Tagliamonte (2006).

8 More details about the use of statistics in sociolinguistics can be
   found in Fasold (1984), Guy (1993), Milroy and Gordon (2003), and
   Tagliamonte (2006).

CHAPTER FIVE

Speech styles and discourse

Consider the following description of a crime:

> The suspect, a male caucasian of medium build and aged approximately 25 years, gained access to the premises and proceeded to bust up the joint before departing the area in a late-model black sedan that was tricked out with some sick rims.

No doubt you're struck by the oddity of certain phrases in this passage. While it mostly employs the peculiar language of police reporting, it also contains phrases like "bust up the joint," "tricked out" and "sick rims" that seem decidedly out of place here. The strangeness of these phrases is not a matter of grammar or content – they violate no grammatical rules and they add relevant information – but rather a matter of form. Every time we speak or write we face a vast array of choices in how we construct our message. Among the factors that guide our decisions about linguistic forms is the communication context. In the context of a police report it is appropriate to use vocabulary like "gained access to the premises" and "late-model black sedan," but not to use phrases like "bust up the joint" and "tricked out." By the same token, the latter phrases might be perfectly appropriate in the context of a conversation among friends while the others (e.g. "gained access to the premises") would sound strange.

These differences illustrate the dimension of language commonly referred to as "register." Registers are varieties of a language associated with particular contexts of use. The term often appears in discussions of relatively distinctive varieties such as "legalese" or "baby talk." Still, there is more to register variation than the handful of such readily identifiable varieties might suggest at first. We vary our usage according to situation in myriad, often subtle, ways affecting vocabulary, pronunciation, and grammar. Indeed the ability to make these adjustments is a crucial element of our communicative competence (see Chapter One and Hymes, 1972).

Registers constitute one element of intra-individual (or intra-speaker) variation, or variation within an individual's usage. This term signals a contrast with "inter-individual variation," which describes differences across speakers including those constituting regional and social dialects. In the Labovian tradition, intra-individual variation is generally treated under the heading "style."

As we saw in Chapter Three, Labov has been interested in stylistic variation since his graduate studies. In fact, his approach to style in the New York City study stands as one of the most innovative aspects of that project. Recall the frustration of previous researchers who found New Yorkers varying their pronunciation in an apparently haphazard manner; for example, dropping [r] one minute and pronouncing it in the next. Labov showed that this variation was far from random. By systematically investigating how New Yorkers spoke in a range of contexts, he revealed patterns of stylistic stratification just as regular as those of class stratification. Significantly, Labov showed that the same linguistic variables participated in both dimensions. Some scholars (e.g. Kenyon, 1948) operated under the assumption that linguistic differences in the stylistic dimension (i.e. those related to context or function) were distinct from those in the social dimension (i.e. those between groups of speakers). Labov found, however, that both kinds of variation may draw on the same pool of linguistic forms. Thus, for example, rates of pronouncing [r] are lower among working class speakers than among middle class speakers, but they're also lower in conversational speech than when reading aloud.

Many key concepts in variationist sociolinguistics stem from Labov's work on style. These include theories about which forms of language are the most systematic and how social awareness of usages affects language change. But Labov's approach to style has been even more influential in the realm of methodology. We see this most clearly in his approach to data collection through the sociolinguistic interview, a technique that has dominated the field since its introduction in Labov's New York City study. This chapter considers the significance of Labov's research on style for both methodology and theory in sociolinguistics. We look first at the techniques he developed to investigate stylistic variation and turn later to some of the lessons learned from this investigation.

The sociolinguistic interview

Sociolinguists, by definition, engage in the study of language in its social context. If we consider the ubiquity of language across the vast array of human activities, we see that the possibilities for sociolinguistic research are truly endless. Nevertheless, in the variationist arena one approach to mining the raw material for sociolinguistic analysis has prevailed over others: the interview. Interviewing is an established technique across the social sciences, and within linguistics it has served as the primary tool in many fieldworkers' arsenals. Nevertheless, the way that sociolinguists structure their interviews differs significantly from common practice elsewhere, within linguistics and beyond. Before detailing Labov's approach to interviews, it's helpful to consider the context in which it was developed.

As we saw in Chapter Four, the central premise of Labov's work is the notion of orderly heterogeneity which maintains that variation is inherent in linguistic structure (that's the heterogeneity bit) and that it is patterned (that's the orderly bit). This conception of how language works was first fully developed by Weinreich et al. (1968), and it represented a clear break from the thinking that had dominated linguistics since the early part of the century. Still, there was at least one branch of the field for which the gospel of orderly heterogeneity represented less of a heretical challenge: dialect geography. The existence of linguistic variation is, of course, a guiding premise of dialectology, but even in this field we find that traditional theory and methods offered a rather limited perspective on that variation (see the discussion in Chapter Two for further details and examples). Most relevant here is the way that intra-speaker variation was investigated or rather how it was largely ignored.

The methods of dialectology were designed to explore categorical usages. They tested whether a person said A or B, and they generally did so by asking directly "What do you call X?" If a person alternated between forms, sometimes saying A and sometimes B, then this approach had no systematic way of capturing that variation. Remember that dialect geographers carried out their research through fairly structured interviews, posing a series of questions to elicit each person's usage with regard to hundreds of linguistic variables, most of which were related to word choice and pronunciation. Two aspects of this approach are especially significant here: (1) that an individual speaker's usage of a given variable was typically recorded as a response to a single elicitation, and (2) that the entire interview consisted of questions and answers about language.

This brief review of dialectologists' methods helps us appreciate the innovation that Labov's approach represents. As he has often acknowledged (e.g. 2006, p. 22), his methods of data collection grew out of the dialect geography tradition. Nevertheless, Labov's commitment to pursuing orderly heterogeneity led him to explore new methods, which expanded the range of speech studied and, in so doing, the range of linguistic variables examined. Central to this revolutionary approach was the development of the methodology that's come to be known as the sociolinguistic interview.

We can better understand how (and why) Labov parts company with dialect geography by recalling parallel developments in other branches of sociolinguistics. Of particular relevance is the work of Dell Hymes and John Gumperz, who pioneered approaches to language grounded in research methods from anthropology, particularly from ethnography. In that tradition, the researcher often adopts a role of participant-observer, immersing him- or herself in local cultural practices. The goal is to paint a rich picture of the broader social context of those practices and, in a sense, to understand them on their own terms. We find this objective reflected in, for example, Hymes's emphasis on exploring a broad range of elements comprising a "communicative event" – the participants, the setting, the nonverbal communication, and so forth – rather than just the language produced (see Chapter One).

In developing the sociolinguistic interview, Labov sought to blend the dialectological and ethnographic traditions, adopting the advantages and avoiding the disadvantages of each approach. Thus, the interview format favored in dialectology offers a relatively efficient means of surveying large numbers of people, and the fact that the same basic protocol is used in each interview makes it easier to compare the results across the sample of people. Still, the traditional interview conducted by dialectologists relied on direct questions about linguistic usages and collected generally brief and self-conscious responses. On the other hand, a researcher engaged in long-term participant-observation likely has access to a wide range of speech events and hears (and possibly records) a fuller repertoire of speech from each member of a community. The ethnographer also gains insight into the social dynamics of the community by being immersed in it. But, this approach demands a tremendous time commitment as researchers often spend months or even years in the communities they study. It may also be difficult to compare the findings from one community with those from others when the data are gathered in very different ways.

After weighing the pros and cons of these techniques, Labov arrived at the peculiar hybrid we know as the sociolinguistic interview. It has the basic structure of an interview – a one-to-one interaction between a questioner and a respondent – but it seeks a level of access more on par with that afforded the ethnographer. Thus the interviewer poses questions designed to elicit speech that, in form, accurately represents the interviewee's repertoire and that, in content, shines light on the social dynamics of the speech community. The ideal interview is one in which the interviewee speaks freely and at length, sharing an insider's perspective that paints a picture of local social practices.

The subject of how much and what kinds of speech are sampled in a sociolinguistic interview highlights fundamental issues in varia-tionist theory and method. For example, one of the most significant distinctions between Labov's approach and that followed by dialectologists relates to the quality and quantity of data collected. The sociolinguistic interview seeks to record extended samples of free-flowing conversational speech as the primary source of data. This pool of speech material opens up possibilities that aren't available with the more limited data gathered by traditional dialectology. Most importantly, it allows for the investigation of non-categorical usages. When you have recorded an hour or so of a person's unscripted speech, you can explore the relative frequencies of competing forms in that person's usage. To return to an example discussed earlier (Chapters Two and Four), all speakers of English vary in their pronunciation of the suffix *–ing* (e.g. *walking*, *fishing*), sometimes pronouncing it with a velar nasal [ŋ] and sometimes with an alveolar [n]. In the course of an hour's conversation we're likely to utter hundreds of words with *-ing*, and so counting how often this suffix is pronounced with the velar nasal (e.g. *walking*) and how often with the alveolar nasal (e.g. *walkin'*) across a long conversation provides a good measure of a person's usage of this kind of variable. Crucially, this method offers insights into usages for which a single response (or even two or three responses) during direct elicitation would be meaningless.

The sociolinguistic interview also differs from the dialectological approach in seeking to observe less self-conscious usage. The linguistic-atlas-style interview consisted of hours of questions about language. No attempt was made to disguise the purpose of the exchange which was to document how the interviewee spoke. In this way, much of the data collected represented the interviewee's reporting of his or her usage rather than an observation of actual usage.[1] When we consider how ideas about correctness (see Chapter Two) might lead someone to misrepresent their own speech, it's easy to imagine potential problems with such a direct approach. Such concerns certainly guided Labov in developing his interview techniques. The goal of recording extended samples of unscripted speech stems not just from a need for a certain amount of data. The quality of the data also matters, and on this count, the best speech occurs when the interviewee monitors his or her usage the least.

For Labov, then, the "best speech" corresponds in most cases to just the opposite of what that term describes in popular discussions. Evaluations of the "best" and "worst" English are ordinarily based on how closely one follows prescriptive rules. The sociolinguist, however, typically wants to capture samples of speech that is as far removed from the normative influence of prestige dialects (e.g. Standard English) as possible. Labov terms this style of speech "the vernacular," and he makes clear why researchers should fix their eyes on this prize:

> Not every style or point on the stylistic continuum is of equal interest to linguists. Some styles show irregular phonological and grammatical patterns, with a great deal of "hypercorrection." In other styles, we find more systematic speech, where the fundamental relations which determine the course of linguistic evolution can be seen most clearly. This is the "vernacular" – the style in which the minimum attention is given to the monitoring

of speech. Observation of the vernacular gives us the most systematic data for our analysis of linguistic structure. (1972b, p. 208)[2]

The kind of "hypercorrection" Labov has in mind here certainly includes cases of statistical overshooting where a person or group uses some variant with higher frequency than expected, given their social position.[3] No doubt Labov also has in mind hypercorrection of a more usual sort which typically involves the overextension of a linguistic rule (e.g. *foots* for *feet*). At a phonological level this includes cases of adding sounds that didn't apply historically, such as a normally *h*-dropping Briton saying "high hate" for *I ate*.

The vernacular, as Labov defines it, is the form of language we use in our most spontaneous moments, when we give little or no thought to how we might sound. It is how we talk in relaxed conversations with trusted friends. Adopting the vernacular as the target of analysis puts the sociolinguist in a challenging position. How can the speech used in a research interview approximate the spontaneity of a conversation between close friends? This question is part of a broader dilemma that Labov terms the "Observer's Paradox": "the aim of linguistic research in the community must be to find out how people talk when they are not being systematically observed; yet we can only obtain these data by systematic observation" (1972b, p. 209).

The hybrid approach of the sociolinguistic interview stems from Labov's wrestling with the Observer's Paradox. Interviewing is a form of systematic observation, but the format of the interview is designed to prompt the vernacular speech that the interviewee would use when not under observation. Labov has developed a range of strategies to elicit "casual" speech. The most famous of these is the "danger-of-death" question mentioned in Chapter Three. This and other techniques for mitigating the effects of observation are discussed further below.

While recording vernacular usage stands as a key objective, the sociolinguistic interview has other bases to cover as well. Remember the ultimate goal is to record a wide sampling of the interviewee's speech repertoire – casual as well as more careful speech – and to gain insight into the social world of the community and the interviewee's position in it. Thus, for the interviews conducted in his extensive study of the Philadelphia speech community, Labov designed questions to explore "contrasting attitudes and experiences among various sub-cultures" and to gather information that would allow researchers "to trace the patterns of communication among members of the neighborhood, and establish the position of the speaker in the communication network" (1984, pp. 32–3).

At the same time, Labov builds a high degree of flexibility into the sociolinguistic interview and actually encourages the fieldworker "to isolate from a range of topics those of greatest interest to the speaker, and allow him or her to lead in defining the topic of conversation" (1984, p. 32). Here we get a sense of what makes the sociolinguistic interview decidedly odd as a speech event. While operating within the basic format of an interview, the researcher makes conversational moves that push against the boundaries of that genre. Recognized rules of interaction govern the interview as an event; it is framed as an opportunity for information sharing where one party (the interviewer) asks questions and the other party (the interviewee) provides answers. In this format, the control over the conversation rests with the interviewer, who chooses the topics discussed by asking all the questions. The sociolinguist attempts to reverse the usual dynamic by letting the interviewee direct the discussion.

Issues such as these have spurred criticism of Labov's approach to interviewing for decades. An influential early challenge came from Nessa Wolfson (1976), who argued that sociolinguistic interviews can not produce "natural" speech because they are "unnatural" events. Labov's technique begins as a recognized event, the interview, but turns into something closer to an informal conversation with, Wolfson argues, problematic results:

> From the point of view of the subject, this is not only an unexpected turn of events, but a truly unnatural speech situation. The subject is frequently quite mystified about why a total stranger, armed with a tape recorder, should want to engage him in conversation. He feels that something is very wrong, and he is correct; the rules have been broken and he has no idea what his role should be. (Wolfson, 1976, p. 196)

Wolfson's observations on the strangeness of the sociolinguistic interview are well taken. Still, we must ask whether "unnatural speech situations" can produce linguistic data that are of value to the researcher. For Wolfson, the answer was clearly "no," but her pessimism partly stems from the fact that she was studying personal narratives. She found that the kinds of stories people tell in response to interview questions differ significantly from those that arise spontaneously in everyday conversations. By contrast, Labov and other sociolinguists have typically relied on interviews to study phonological and grammatical variables. The patterns of variation associated with these features arguably depend less on the larger speech setting than do questions of which discourse genre (e.g. story, lecture, etc.) to use.

While not immune to problems, the sociolinguistic interview has proven to be a useful tool for gathering speech data. Like all research methodologies, it serves well in some investigations but is not intended to fit every bill. Labov has recognized this from the start and developed alternative approaches like the rapid and anonymous survey that was used in New York department stores (see Chapter Three). More recently, the field's methodological horizons have expanded greatly with sociolinguists pursuing a wide range of techniques. Still, the interview remains a core strategy in the researcher's toolbox.

Isolating contextual styles

In discussions of sociolinguistic methods, the spotlight often falls on casual speech and how best to capture the elusive vernacular. Nevertheless, a full account of variation in a given speech community needs to cast a wider net, one that catches various samples of each speaker's stylistic repertoire. As noted above, the sociolinguistic interview is designed to act as such a net. It elicits speech produced during a range of tasks or, in Labov terms, a variety of contextual styles.

Before exploring the details of those contextual styles, it is useful to recall the guiding principles behind Labov's design of the interview. As mentioned in Chapter Three, Labov conceives of stylistic variation as related to how much attention the speaker pays to his or her speech. The vernacular, by definition, stands at one end of the stylistic continuum where the lowest degree of attention is given to the form of speech used. At the other end we find the speech produced during tasks like reading words aloud, where speakers more closely monitor the form of their speech (their pronunciation).

Various parts of the sociolinguistic interview seek to explore different points along that continuum and thus to produce a rich profile of each interviewee's repertoire.

In his studies in New York City and Philadelphia, Labov explored the more careful end of the stylistic continuum through reading tasks. These include story passages, lists of words, and series of minimal pairs – words like *guard* and *god* or *ferry* and *furry* that differ (for some speakers) by a single sound. The attention-to-speech model informs these choices, predicting that speakers will concentrate most on their pronunciation when reading minimal pairs. If they can produce the relevant sounds differently, then this is the context where they're most likely to do so since the minimal pair draws their attention to those sounds. Reading a list of words in isolation also encourages focus on pronunciation since there is no message to convey. Still, compared to the minimal pair reading, interviewees are less aware of which sounds in those words might be under scrutiny. With the story passages the interviewee has to think about meaning and how the words go together into sentences. This presumably takes some of the focus away from the task of pronouncing. To encourage less formal performances, the instructions ask the interviewee to read "as naturally as possible," just as you might "if you were telling the story yourself" (Labov, 2006, p. 62). Moreover, the content of the passages is informal, as are the vocabulary and grammar. They are personal narratives – in the New York City interviews, one recounts a childhood story – and not news reports or other genres associated with more "proper" language.

The reading tasks actually account for a small portion of the interview, and they are typically done at the end of the process. Most of the hour or more of recorded speech comes from answering questions. In a successful interview, these responses will veer away from the usual back-and-forth exchange into the territory of free-flowing conversation. To explore such stylistic differences Labov distinguishes "careful" from "casual" speech.

Careful speech constitutes most of the talk produced during a sociolinguistic interview. Indeed, Labov defines it as "the type of speech which normally occurs when the subject is answering questions which are formally recognized as 'part of the interview'" (2006, p. 59). This speech is "careful" in the sense that interviewees choose their words deliberatively as they construct answers to particular questions – at least more deliberatively than during an emotional exchange or other casual speech context. We should not assume, however, that interviewees focus primarily on how they express themselves in answering interview questions. The care is given more to what they say than to how they say it. Labov provides points of reference, noting that "[i]t is certainly not as formal a situation as a public address, and less formal than the speech which would be used in a first interview for a job, but it is certainly more formal than casual conversation among friends or family members" (2006, p. 60).

For the researcher hoping to explore the full stylistic continuum, the stiffest challenge comes in capturing casual speech. After all, this is the everyday language that people use when "they argue with their nearest and dearest, scold their children, or pass the time of day with their friends" (Labov, 2006, p. 64). As the Observer's Paradox reminds us, a researcher would not normally have access to this style. The challenge of gaining such access is especially formidable in the context of an interview. Nonetheless, Labov developed techniques that work to meet the challenge. I noted previously his danger-of-death question which is designed to elicit an emotionally charged narrative. Labov also includes questions about childhood topics that typically produce a turn toward the casual. In the New York City study, for example, he asked about children's games and the songs that often go with them. Many of these rely on rhymes that only work with a vernacular pronunciation, such as the r-lessness required by:

Glory, glory Hallelujah,
The teacher hit me with a ruler. (Labov, 2006, p. 69)

In addition to steering the conversation toward certain topics in pursuit of a casual style, Labov also took advantage of opportunities to capture speech outside the normal one-on-one interview. In one example mentioned in Chapter Three, an interview was interrupted by a phone call, and Labov recorded the interviewee speaking casually with her cousin. A more common occurrence involves children or other family members appearing during the interview. Often the interviewee breaks away from speaking with the researcher to address those third parties, and in so doing switches to a more casual style.[4]

Similar effects can be achieved through a more intentional break from the usual interview format. In their research in Harlem, for example, Labov and his colleagues found that some of the African American children and teenagers seemed very reluctant to talk at all in one-on-one interviews even though the interviewer was also African American and someone they knew from the neighborhood (see Labov, 1972a, p. 207ff). To counteract this apparent verbal inhibition, the researchers turned the recording sessions into more of a party, by playing games, providing snacks, and most importantly by having two or more children in the conversation. These group sessions proved to be a rich vein of spontaneous speech as the children spoke to each other as much if not more than to the "interviewer." Since Labov and his colleagues were interested in linguistic features associated with African American vernacular such as copula deletion (e.g. *You the best*), this approach proved critical. The quantitative analysis of this speech revealed that the young people used vernacular features at much higher rates in the group sessions than in the individual interviews.

The Harlem study introduced an element of participant observation to the process of collecting speech data. Labov's Philadelphia project did the same through different means. Some of the fieldworkers for the Project on Language Variation and Change built a strong rapport with community members. This was a long-term project, and the interviewers, who were graduate students in Labov's program at Penn, spent a good deal of time in the communities and interviewed many of the same individuals on several occasions. As a result, their recording sessions came to resemble conversations between friends more than questions and answers between strangers. We see evidence of this in the content of these exchanges, in which "interviewees" share personal information, gossip freely about neighbors, and generally speak their minds (e.g. Labov, 2001b, pp. 334–5).

When it comes to speech produced within the context of the usual sociolinguistic interview, the stylistic divisions are not always so easy to determine. How can the researcher draw a line between casual and careful speech? Labov's approach relies on identifying situations within the interview that are likely to promote casual speech. These include the danger-of-death stories and discussions of childhood mentioned earlier. In his New York City study, he sought verification of a style shift in these situations by examining how the interviewee's voice changed. He listened for "channel cues" of a switch to casual speech in the form of changes in tempo, pitch, volume, breathing rate, and laughter (see Labov, 2006, p. 72). Clearly the goal in considering these cues was to offer greater objectivity to the determination of what's labeled casual speech and to avoid assuming that all speakers adopt this style when telling a story about how they almost died or about their childhoods. Nevertheless, later researchers, and even Labov himself, have largely abandoned this approach. A common complaint stems from the fact that despite their apparent objectivity, these channel cues are, in fact, interpretable in various ways. How can we tell whether a faster tempo signals that a speaker is anxious or enthusiastic? How can we distinguish nervous laughter from that which occurs in relaxed contexts?

In more recent work, Labov (2001a) has laid out a revised process for distinguishing casual and careful speech within the sociolinguistic interview. He presents a decision tree that guides the researcher through a series of steps to separate elements of the interview. While most of the spontaneous (unscripted) talk that occurs during the interview is treated as careful speech, the model identifies four categories of casual speech. Included here are the familiar cases of speech directed toward family members or anyone else other than the interviewer, and talk about childhood memories. Personal narratives in response to the danger-of-death question or others also count as casual speech. The final category comprises tangents, which Labov defines as "an extended body of speech that deviates plainly from the last topic introduced by the interviewer, and represents the strong interest of the speaker" (2001a, p. 92). As noted above, Labov's protocols for interviewing prize such tangents because they signal a breakdown of the typical question-answer format and movement toward spontaneous conversation.

While his approach to stylistic variation has changed in some details over the years, Labov continues to be guided by the same principles. It is important to recognize that the techniques described here were developed with particular research goals in mind. The unusual structure of the sociolinguistic interview allows Labov to systematically probe how speakers shift their usage across various contexts. The different contextual styles that Labov compares are understood as points on a continuum, marking how much attention one pays to speech. This and other aspects of Labov's model have met with some criticism, as discussed below, but it's hard to deny the fruitfulness of the approach. In case after case we see that speakers vary their usage of linguistic features across the contextual styles. More importantly, for Labov's assumptions, this variation patterns as expected with pronunciations associated with formality or the standard dialect appearing least often in casual speech and gradually increasing in frequency as one moves to careful speech and then to reading passages, to word lists, and to minimal pairs. The graphs from Labov's New York City study presented in Chapter Three illustrate this common finding.

Insights from the study of style

Until recently, stylistic variation has played second fiddle to inter-speaker ("dialect") variation within sociolinguistics. While acknowledging the ubiquity of style shifting, researchers have generally concentrated their attention on linguistic patterns related to social factors such as class, gender, ethnicity, and so on. Style certainly has not been ignored, but sociolinguists' investigations in this area have typically served as means to an end rather than an end in themselves. Labov observes that "the direct study of style-shifting in social groups has been an auxiliary undertaking designed to throw light on the main findings of the community pattern" (2001a, p. 86). He is speaking here in general about the field he pioneered, but this certainly describes his own treatment of style as a research topic.

From the beginning of his career, Labov has investigated style in conjunction with other types of sociolinguistic variation. In his New York City study, for example, he examined style shifting in relation to social stratification by class, and the figures presented in Chapter Three illustrate how these two types of variation often run in parallel. In Figures 5.1 and 5.2 we see a similar parallel patterning of social and stylistic variation. These data come from Labov's Philadelphia project and show the distribution of the variable (dh). This variable, which Labov also examined in New York City, describes the alternation in the first consonant in words like *these* and *those* which is sometimes pronounced as a [d] and sometimes as the standard fricative [ð].[5] Labov calculates an index which represents a kind of average usage of (dh) on a scale of 0–200, where zero would indicate consistent use of the fricative variant (e.g. *these* and *those*) and 200 would indicate consistent use of the stop variant (e.g. *dese* and *dose*).[6]

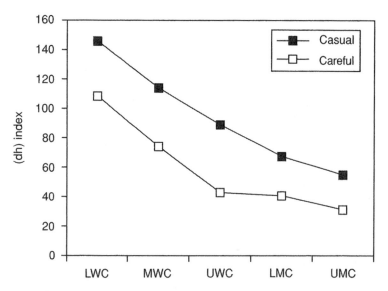

FIGURE 5.1 *Variation in the pronunciation of* (dh) *by social class and style in Philadelphia (from Labov, 2001b, p. 96; reprinted by permission of Wiley-Blackwell).*

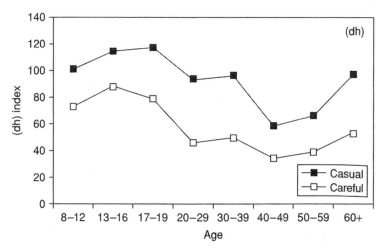

FIGURE 5.2 *Variation in the pronunciation of* (dh) *by age and style in Philadelphia (from Labov, 2001b, p. 102; reprinted by permission of Wiley-Blackwell).*

The picture in Figure 5.1 reveals class stratification much like that seen in the New York City examples. The (dh) indexes decrease as we move up the socioeconomic ladder from the lower working class (LWC) to the middle working class (MWC), the upper working class (UWC), the lower middle class (LMC), and to the upper middle class (UMC). Stylistic variation is explored here through the simple comparison of casual and careful speech. We see that all social groups agree in the direction of style shifting, using the stop form (e.g. *dese* and *dose*) more in casual speech.

This same stylistic consistency is found in Figure 5.2 where the speakers are grouped by age rather than social class. In Philadelphia, as elsewhere in the English-speaking world, the variation in (dh) suggests a stable pattern. This phonological feature is not undergoing change, and the picture in Figure 5.2 supports this interpretation. Rather than a clear trajectory of either rising or falling indexes across the generations, we find a series of ups and downs. These findings illustrate a common pattern in which features of non-standard dialects tend to be used less by middle-aged adults than by both younger and older generations. What's significant for the present discussion is the fact that the index scores for casual and careful speech undulate in tandem. Just like the social classes in Figure 5.1, each age group uses more of the stop form (e.g. *dese* and *dose*) in casual speech.

The symmetry between social and stylistic variation is by no means a coincidence. These do not represent independent dimensions of our sociolinguistic reality. Rather distinctions of style are modeled on those related to social stratification. It seems that a linguistic feature must first vary in usage across groups of people before speakers will draw on it to mark shifts of style. As Labov explains, "speakers derive their stylistic parameters from observations of social differences in the use of language" (2001a, p. 87).

Investigating the correlations between social and stylistic variation led Labov to propose a typology of linguistic variables based on which dimensions they vary in (see, e.g. 1972b, p. 314). Most of the usages that sociolinguists investigate show distinctions in both the social and the stylistic dimensions. For some of these cases, we find that people are well aware of a particular pronunciation or grammatical form and associate it with some social group. In Labov's terms, variables that bear this kind of overt social awareness are labeled "stereotypes." A case like (dh) illustrates this type, since pronunciations like "dese" and "dose" are associated with working class speech in Philadelphia and other urban communities. Stereotypes are often represented in particular words or phrases and may carry a popular label. Thus, we hear one of the stereotypes of "Brooklynese," or working-class New York in general, in the phrase "toity-toid" for *thirty-third*. Similarly, the variation in (ing) is popularly described as "dropping the g," a stereotype reinforced orthographically by *–in'* (e.g. *fishin'*).

It is possible for a variable to show social stratification and style shifting but not bear overt social awareness. In fact, such variables, which Labov labels "markers," may be the most common type. The case of (æh) in New York City operates as a marker. As noted in Chapter Three, New Yorkers sometimes pronounce this vowel with the tongue low in the mouth (i.e. [æ], which most dialects have in *trap* and *cat*) and sometimes with a much higher tongue position (i.e. close to the [ɪ] of *bit* and *lid*). Labov found a clear pattern of class stratification for this variable with raised variants of the vowel more common among the working class than the middle class. He also recorded the usual pattern of stylistic variation with all groups using lower (more like [æ]) variants in careful speech than casual and even more so when reading. Still New Yorkers show little conscious awareness of this variable, and so it does not function as a stereotype.

The final category in Labov's typology is an "indicator," which denotes usages that serve to differentiate social groups yet show no stylistic variation. Thus, indicators signal membership in some group, but members of that group do not adjust their usage across speaking contexts. We see an example of this type in the phenomenon known as the "*cot/caught* vowel merger." With this change, which is active in many regions in the US, the distinction between the vowels of words like *lot* and *thought* is lost so that pairs like *cot ~ caught, Don ~ dawn, knotty ~ naughty* come to be pronounced as homophones. In many communities, this merger can be heard with some groups and not with others – most often we find a generational separation – but it is rare for speakers to vary their usage in different stylistic contexts.

The typology of stereotype, marker, and indicator serves as a useful model for describing differences in the treatment of stable variables, but Labov has also incorporated it into his theories of language change. A fuller discussion of this work will be given in

Chapter Seven, but for now we might note that the different types of variables correlate with different stages in the development of a linguistic innovation. Thus, an indicator is characteristic of an early stage while stereotypes relate to changes that have been active for much longer.

The way that Labov draws on evidence of style shifting to develop broader theories about community-wide variation and change underscores my earlier suggestion that the study of style serves mostly as a means to an end for Labov. He investigates stylistic variation because it provides insights into the sociolinguistic status of particular variables, which in turn may shine light on larger forces shaping variation in a speech community. This approach is very much in keeping with his general perspective on the proper object of sociolinguistic analysis. As described in Chapter Four, Labov's focus always remains on the community and not the individual speaker. This may help us appreciate Labov's interest in style. He finds it valuable in so far as it helps paint a picture of the community, but he has little interest in more micro-level explorations that seek to understand why individuals make particular linguistic choices.

Critiques and new directions

Labov's work on stylistic variation has been enormously influential, particularly with regard to setting a methodological agenda. The sociolinguistic interview with its peculiar goal of capturing the speech of a friendly conversation within the format of a question-and-answer exchange has served as the workhorse of the field. Nevertheless, the thinking that informed the design of the interview has met with stronger objections. Many scholars have questioned Labov's conception of what causes people to shift their styles across various contexts.

An easy criticism to level against Labov's attention-to-speech model relates to its apparent limitations. Can we explain all shifts of style in terms of how much attention a person pays to his or her speech? Consider how you vary your speech over the course of a day. In my case, for example, on a given day I might speak with many different people from my family, to my colleagues, to students, and (ignoring my mother's advice) to various strangers. Certainly my speech varies greatly across these situations in vocabulary, grammar, and pronunciation. But is this due to differing levels of attention? Do I pay more or less attention to my language when I'm talking with a co-worker at the copy machine than when I'm chatting with a fellow dog-owner in the park?

Clearly Labov's model cannot account for all style shifting, but we must remember that it was never meant to do so. This point may not have been readily appreciated on the basis of his early work such as the New York City study. More recently, however, Labov has been explicit in acknowledging the limited scope of the attention-to-speech account, noting that it "was not intended as a general description of how style-shifting is produced and organized in every-day speech, but rather as a way of organizing and using intra-speaker variation that occurs in the interview" (2001a, p. 87). In other words, attention paid to speech does not govern all our stylistic choices, but it can help us make sense of the shifts made during a sociolinguistic interview, which of course is structured so as to induce the speaker to vary the degree of attention paid to his or her speech across different tasks.

As for more general accounts of style shifting, a number of scholars have offered alternatives to Labov's model. One of the most influential proposals comes from Allan Bell, who conceives of style as governed principally by concerns about audience. The essence of his account, known as "Audience Design," holds that we adjust our usage according to the people we are talking with and whoever else might be listening.[7] This approach obviously takes the exploration of style well beyond the interview context. Many other researchers have followed Bell into this territory, and the study of style from such broader perspectives remains a very active area of scholarship.[8] Labov, however, has not pursued this general theorizing about the nature of stylistic variation much in his own work.

Even if we accept Labov's model for what it is – an account of style shifting within the sociolinguistic interview – we might question its assumptions. Of particular interest here is whether the contextual styles that Labov isolates are properly treated as points on a continuum. Can attention to speech or, indeed, any single factor account for the typical style shifting observed in an interview? The assumption that the contextual styles constitute a continuum is reinforced by Labov's analysis, especially by his representation of style as a single dimension, as in the various graphs from Chapter Three. Arranging the styles in this way implies that the difference between

casual and careful speech is somehow equivalent to that between
careful and reading style, which is equivalent to that between reading
a story passage and reading a list of unconnected words.

Especially problematic is the assumption that speech produced
for the various reading tasks (stories, word lists, minimal pairs)
occupies a single continuum with spontaneous conversation.
This view has been challenged by several scholars. In her study
of phonological variation in Belfast English, for example, Lesley
Milroy (1987)[9] found that some vernacular pronunciations that
were very frequent even in the relatively careful speech of the
interview were virtually nonexistent in reading contexts. Milroy's
speakers seemed to draw on a distinct phonological repertoire
for reading, rather than from the same continuum employed
for spontaneous speech. Such findings underscore the fact that
reading and writing involve different cognitive processes than does
speaking. Moreover, literacy practices commonly carry ideological
baggage related to the standard language. Asking an interviewee to
read something aloud may trigger a kind of dialect switch akin to
a bilingual's alternation between languages and not just a stylistic
adjustment within one variety.

Criticisms related to the treatment of reading tasks highlight
a larger limitation of Labov's model. The stylistic continuum
Labov posits derives ultimately from an opposition of vernacular
and standard dialects.[10] His definition of "vernacular" explicitly
associates this style with a lack of attention paid to speech. At the
other end, it makes sense to equate increased attention with the
use of more standard speech. Many of the linguistic variables map
neatly onto this opposition. With (dh), for example, the standard
form (e.g. *these* and *those*) alternates with the nonstandard form
(e.g. *dese* and *dose*), and style shifting is measured in terms of
relative use of these variants. In some speech communities, like New
York City and Philadelphia, the variation between the vernacular
and the standard poles seems to be appropriately represented on
a single continuum. Nevertheless, in other communities a much
greater separation exists between the local vernacular and the
standard. Belfast stands as one example of what have been dubbed
"divergent-dialect communities" (see, e.g. J. Milroy, 1992). In
these linguistic ecosystems, we find less complementarity between
vernacular and standard; a stylistic shift away from the vernacular
is not necessarily toward the standard and vice versa.

Even for the communities that Labov has studied we might question the appropriateness of the implied vernacular-standard continuum. As Penelope Eckert notes (2001), the linguistic variables that Labov investigates often have quite different sociolinguistic profiles and thus bear distinct social meanings. For example, it makes some sense to consider a variable like (dh) as an alternation between a standard and a vernacular form (e.g. *these* vs. *dese*), but a variable like (ing) operates differently. The "vernacular" form of (ing) (e.g. *walkin'*) often signals casualness and informality rather than nonstandardness (see Chapter Nine). The broader lesson of such examples is that these kinds of differences in social meaning tend to get lost with an approach like Labov's, which puts more emphasis on demonstrating style shifting rather than explaining its motivations.

Criticism of Labov's approach to stylistic variation has revealed many of its limitations. Alternatives to the attention-to-speech model, such as Bell's Audience Design Theory, have spurred a wider discussion about the nature of style that goes well beyond talk in sociolinguistic interviews. Indeed, understanding how speakers adjust their usage to convey particular social meanings has blossomed into one of the most active areas of research today. Much of this work adopts a very different approach to the problem from Labov's; for example, treating styles as actively constructed from an array of linguistic features that work together to make social meaning. This research is at the heart of what Eckert calls the "third wave" of variationist sociolinguistics discussed in Chapter Nine.

Labov's discourse analysis

Throughout this chapter we have explored Labov's thinking about the ways that people adjust their speech according to situation and how and why linguists might study such stylistic variation. In addressing these questions Labov has commonly concentrated on specific speech features such as the phonological variable (dh). Indeed, it is fair to say that most of Labov's work over the course of his career – research in stylistic variation as well as social and historical variation – has dealt with relatively small and readily segmentable units of language like the pronunciation of particular vowels or consonants or the use of particular grammatical features.

Such features have served as the bread and butter of variationist sociolinguistics more generally, owing to their suitability for quantitative analysis. Nevertheless, Labov has turned his analytical eye to bigger chunks of language from time to time. In fact he has maintained an interest in discourse analysis for several decades, and while his publications in this area have been relatively few, his work has proven to be quite influential.

The label "discourse analysis" covers a wide range of practices across several scholarly fields. Some discourse analysts examine spoken language and some examine written language. Some concern themselves with relatively broad questions of the rhetorical effects of prepared texts and some attend to more localized social actions performed by people engaged in everyday conversation. Within linguistics, work in discourse analysis is generally distinguished from other approaches by (a) its consideration of rules and patterns that operate on larger stretches of language beyond the boundaries of the sentence, and (b) a commitment to examining "real-life" samples of language in use rather than examples invented on the basis of intuitions. The latter orientation is, of course, shared across sociolinguistics.

Labov's earliest interest in discourse analysis developed organically from his general research paradigm. As discussed earlier in this chapter, the methodology of the sociolinguistic interview elicited particular kinds of speech, and one of the most valuable was the personal narrative. Through the danger-of-death question and other prompts, Labov sought to record people telling stories from their pasts. Labov became interested in the function and structure of these narratives, and published a landmark study with Joshua Waletzky in 1967 titled "Narrative analysis: Oral versions of personal experience."

Scholarly explorations of narrative were certainly nothing new even in 1967, but much of the research had examined carefully constructed narratives of the kind told by professional storytellers or found in literature. Though not the first to do so, Labov and Waletzky turned their attention to the more spontaneous narratives that we tell in everyday interactions. Some of the narratives they analyzed took five to ten minutes to tell while others consisted of just a few clauses recited in less than a minute. By examining these relatively pared-down narratives, they hoped to isolate the basic elements, to clarify what makes a narrative a narrative.

Much of Labov and Waletzky's discussion considers the formal dimension of this question of how narrative differs from other types of discourse. They define the basic units of narrative by distinguishing different kinds of clauses. They note, for example, that narratives do not consist of a simple series of sentences recounting events in the same order they occurred in; instead, the relationship between the clauses of a narrative and the events or situations they describe is more variable. Some clauses convey information that can be mentioned at virtually any point in the story while others are more restricted in terms of the temporal sequence. The latter type is critical to Labov and Waletzky's definition of narrative. When two clauses must appear in a certain order for the coherence of the narrative, they are said to be separated by a "temporal juncture" (p. 20).[11] A narrative is defined as "any sequence of clauses that contains at least one temporal juncture" (p. 21). Thus, using their example, something as brief as "I shot and killed him" constitutes a narrative. This represents, of course, a bare minimum, and most narratives are far more elaborate.

Labov and Waletzky also set forth a general model for the structure of narratives, one that relates the component clauses to broader functions. Figure 5.3 illustrates a modified version of that model which helps visualize the narrative process and the relations between the elements.

Narratives are often prefaced with a brief summary statement, which is meant to "encapsulate the point of the story" and which Labov labels "the abstract." The narrative proper typically begins with "orientation," designed to identify the timeframe as well as the people, place, and situation relevant to the events. The recounting of events follows in the "complication" or "complicating action" section. Describing what happened is one function of a narrative, but it is not the only purpose. Labov and Waletzky stress the evaluative function of narrative as well. People use stories to make a point. A narrative that leaves the listener asking "so what?" fails on this score. Narrators address this concern in the "evaluation" component, which is defined "as that part of the narrative that reveals the attitude of the narrator towards the narrative by emphasizing the relative importance of some narrative units as compared to others" (Labov and Waletzky, 1967, p. 32). In essence, this is when the narrator steps back from the action to offer some kind of comment on its significance.[12] This evaluation may then be

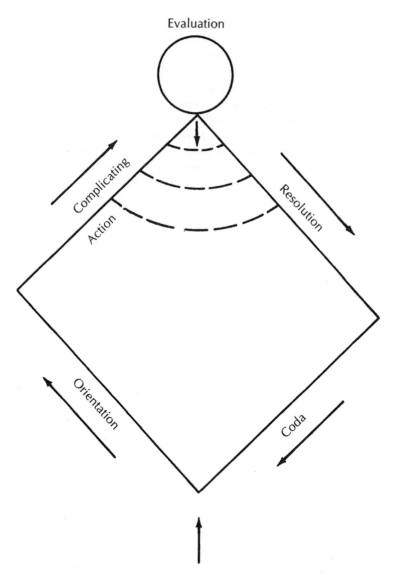

FIGURE 5.3 *The structure of personal narratives (from Labov, 1972a, p. 369; Copyright © 1972 University of Pennsylvania Press. Reprinted with the permission of the University of Pennsylvania Press).*

followed by a result or "resolution" section, which describes further happenings; that is, things that occurred after the most noteworthy event (see Labov, 1997b, p. 414). A final element in the narrative structure is the "coda," which serves the purpose of "returning the verbal perspective to the present moment" (Labov and Waletzky, 1967, p. 35). Codas may explicitly signal the end of the story (e.g. "that was it") or might connect some aspect of the story to the present (e.g. "and I still see him every now and again").

After laying out a model for the structural analysis of narratives in the 1967 paper, Labov's follow-up discussions have explored broader issues related to why we tell stories and how they function as social action. For example, he has reflected on the tension between a narrative's reportability – how noteworthy are its events – and its credibility – how believable are the events (see 1982c and 1997b). Reportable events are by definition less common, which may lead to their being harder to accept as true. Thus, he notes that narrators recounting highly reportable events tend to devote more effort to establishing their credibility (1997b, p. 407). Labov has also explored age-related differences in narrative technique, noting, for example, that young narrators (children and adolescents) tend to have less evaluation in their narratives than do adults (see 1972a, pp. 393–6).

To be sure, Labov's work on narrative analysis has not been immune to criticism. One familiar challenge stems from the material he analyzes. Most of the narratives Labov examines were elicited in the context of the sociolinguistic interview, and therefore might be considered less natural than the kinds of stories that people tell in informal conversations between friends. Emanuel Schegloff, for example, has noted that narratives told in conversational contexts are often more interactional and even co-constructed by the participants (see Schegloff, 1997). Some scholars have reported difficulties in applying Labov's models to material they collected as the pieces of the narrative are not as readily isolatable as Figure 5.3 suggests (see for example Mishler, 1997).

Despite such critiques, it is clear that Labov's contributions to the study of narrative have been enormously influential. Among other achievements, this work has drawn attention to the value of studying nonliterary narratives and has demonstrated that people with fairly low levels of education can produce sophisticated and effective narratives.

In addition to his work on narrative, Labov has sketched broader theories of how and why speakers carry out social actions through talk. He offered some thoughts on the subject in the landmark "The study of language in its social context" (see 1972b, pp. 252–8), but a much fuller presentation appeared in *Therapeutic Discourse* (1977), which he co-authored with David Fanshel, a professor of social work.

Labov has framed the fundamental question driving sociolinguistics as understanding "why anyone says anything" (e.g. 1972b, p. 207), and in *Therapeutic Discourse* he explores that question more elaborately than in any of his other works. The study presents a fine-grained analysis of speech that tries to look beyond what is said in order to uncover what is meant. The fact that there's more to our messages than what's literally expressed in our words is certainly well known. Intonation, hesitations, and other accompaniments to the words convey meaning as well. What Labov and Fanshel examine, however, is "an even larger body of implicit activity" that is nonverbal and not easily translated into simple propositions. They note that:

> [M]ost utterances can be seen as performing several speech acts simultaneously. The parties to a conversation appear to be understanding and reacting to these speech acts at many levels of abstraction. As we see it now, conversation is not a chain of utterances, but rather a matrix of utterances and actions bound together by a web of understandings and reactions. (1977, pp. 29–30)

In referring to speech acts, Labov and Fanshel draw on work by philosophers of language such as J. L. Austin and John Searle. Their speech act theory offers a way of examining how people do things with language. It helps us understand, for example, how something phrased as a question can really serve as a request (e.g. "Can you pass the salt?").

Labov and Fanshel also take inspiration from sociologists like Harvey Sacks and Emanuel Schegloff who developed the field of conversation analysis. Research in this area typically involves detailed analysis of naturally occurring speech with an overarching goal of understanding how what makes conversational interactions coherent. The basic questions are often along the lines of *Why did person A say that and why did person B respond in that way?*

Labov and Fanshel weave strands from both the speech act theorists and the conversation analysts into their approach. They introduce a multilayered method of navigating the "matrix of utterances and actions" that is conversation. The book examines speech from a therapy session between an experienced psychotherapist and her patient, Rhoda P., a 19-year-old woman suffering from anorexia nervosa. The level of detail and the thoroughness of the analysis may shock readers unfamiliar with this style of research. The study covers nearly 400 pages and treats just 15 minutes' worth of speech.

The framework introduced by Labov and Fanshel examines the language of the therapy session on several levels. They present a "cross-sectional analysis" that breaks down each utterance to explore what is said (the actual words), how it is said (the paralinguistic or "channel" cues like intonation and tempo), and why it is said (the speaker's intent and what is accomplished). At one point in the session, for example, Rhoda reports on a conversation with her mother, who Rhoda feels is spending too much time away from home helping Rhoda's sister with a new baby. Rhoda describes asking her mother "Well, when do you plan to come home?" Labov and Fanshel (1977, p. 160) note the tone of exasperation in Rhoda's voice. This cue supports the interpretation that even though it is phrased as a request for information, Rhoda's question really operates as a request for action and more indirectly as a challenge to the mother, implying that she is neglecting her responsibilities. In the context of the therapy session this reported interaction between Rhoda and her mother operates at another level, serving as evidence that Rhoda has carried out a suggestion from the therapist to express her needs and emotions.

The connections between the level of the utterance (what is said) and the speech act (what is done) rely on various "rules of discourse," which Labov and Fanshel detail. These are the unspoken codes of verbal conduct that explain "how the speaker knows what to do, and how the listener knows what has been done" (p. 74). For example, the interpretation of Rhoda's question to her mother rests on a "rule for indirect requests," which specifies the conditions under which something phrased as an informational question is taken as a request for action (p. 82).

As was the case with Labov's work on narrative, some aspects of the analysis in *Therapeutic Discourse* have been challenged by critics, but the work certainly introduced a valuable new way of exploring interactive talk. As one reviewer of the book put it,

Labov and Fanshel "have focused on some of the most empirically intractable features of verbal behavior no less than on the more abstract features of speech acts" and "have systematically related these seemingly disparate aspects of communication ... within a comprehensive, internally consistent, and reasonable model" (Russell, 1979, p. 178).

Such comments remind us that Labov's work in discourse analysis is not as far removed from his other pursuits as it may at first appear. Even though the kinds of linguistic material he's examining here differ significantly from the features he examines, for example, in the New York City study, his general approach to the data is consistent. Thus, we see in his discourse research, as we have seen elsewhere, a drive to introduce more empirical methods and to bring a higher level of accountability to the language material examined. The results are also similar as Labov looks into an apparently chaotic arena of free-flowing speech and manages to uncover general patterns.

Notes

1 At least this is true of responses to direct questions of the type "What do you call X?" Dialect geographers also employed less direct techniques (e.g. "Tell me about the buildings on your farm."), but the context was always a metalinguistic one.

2 For slightly different formulations of this "Vernacular Principle" see Labov (1972c, p. 112, and 1984, p. 29).

3 See the discussion of (r) in Chapter Three.

4 Labov (2006, p. 67) describes such a case of style shifting from an African American woman he interviewed in New York City.

5 The variation for (dh) involves an intermediate form, which is phonetically an affricate (see Labov, 2001b, p. 78).

6 More information about how such indexes are calculated is provided in Chapter Three.

7 Bell first elaborated his theory in the seminal paper "Language style as audience design" (1984).

8 The volume by Eckert and Rickford (2001) collects a representative sample of approaches to style in the last couple of decades. An overview of this work can be found in Schilling (2013) or Coupland (2007).

9   A summary is available in Milroy and Gordon (2003, Chapter Eight).

10 By "standard" I mean the prestige dialect, what we generally think of as "proper" or "correct" and commonly associate with formal education (see Chapter Two).

11 I reference the pages from the 1997 reprinting of the article in the *Journal of Narrative and Life History*. This special issue of the journal includes 47 contributions reflecting on the 30-year legacy of Labov and Waletzky's study.

12 Narrators vary in the degree to which their evaluations are embedded within the narrative framework. Sometimes an explicit statement of the morale of the story is offered, and sometimes the message is conveyed more subtly (see Labov and Waletzky, 1967, pp. 34–5, for examples).

CHAPTER SIX

The "socio" of sociolinguistics

When the field is called "sociolinguistics," it comes as little surprise that questions at the intersection of language and society permeate the scholarly conversation. If, as Labov maintains, the fundamental question posed to the field lies in understanding "why anyone says anything" (1972b, p. 207), then it makes sense to look to a range of potential explanations. Certainly we must pursue answers in language structure; our linguistic choices are always governed by the grammar, phonology, and other components of the language system; but purely linguistic explanations can take us only so far in understanding any given utterance. Why does, for example, someone say *walkin'* as opposed to *walking* ([-ɪn] versus [-ɪŋ]) in a particular situation? Or why does one person use one pronunciation 57 percent of the time and the other 43 percent of the time, while another person uses them at different rates? From the perspective of language structure (the morpho-phonology of English), these pronunciations function simply as alternative ways of saying the same thing. We know, however, that they do not say the same thing from a social perspective. They convey different messages about the speaker, the setting, and other dimensions of the speech context. Thus, in order to fully appreciate these and all linguistic choices, we need to consider social forces as well.

Variationists traditionally explore the role of social factors in terms of the broad demographic criteria on which people might be categorized. These include social class, gender, ethnicity, and age, and the chapter is organized around these social parameters.[1] As a preface to this discussion, it's helpful to sketch a general model for how these elements contribute to sociolinguistic variation. Differences that pattern according to demographic criteria (class, ethnicity, etc.) are commonly framed as social dialects. This term implies a linkage to geographical or regional speech differences. As a way of understanding why social distinctions produce (or at least correlate with) linguistic differences, we might draw a parallel to regional dialects. How do speech differences between regions arise? Part of the answer lies in the fact that languages change over time as new words are coined, pronunciations are modified, grammatical structures evolve, and so on. Changes produce dialect differences when they affect the speech of one group but not the speech of others, as happens when an innovation takes root in one location but fails to spread to others. What might cause an innovation not to spread? One approach to this question focuses on patterns of communication. Our ways of speaking are shaped by the people we speak with. People or groups who are in regular communication will likely influence one another linguistically. This explains how a change that arises in a community might be generalized to that population, and it also predicts the limits of the change's diffusion. Those limits will tend to correspond to boundaries of the communication network. Where discontinuities appear in that network dialect differences will mount. The basic model was framed by Bloomfield in his principle of density of communication (1933/1984, pp. 46, 326–8; see also Labov, 2001b, pp. 19–20).

In the case of regional dialects, the discontinuities of communication often result from natural barriers. Thus, in the US the Appalachian Mountains correspond to a major dialect boundary between the South and the Midland regions. In England a number of dialect isoglosses (boundary lines) run through The Fens, an eastern region that was historically marshland. When it comes to barriers to communication, however, we find that social divisions can operate as effectively as geographical ones. In many societies, being a member of a particular class, ethnicity, or some other category determines, to a large extent, the people we talk with. The kinds of meaningful interactions that shape our speech habits generally take place within and not across social categories. In these interactional patterns the seeds of social dialect divisions germinate.

As we'll see below, this model of dialect differentiation offers a useful framework, but it does not suffice as a means of explaining why social factors shape linguistic variation. For one thing this traditional view underplays the ways that speech differences might be actively constructed. As we consider situations where the social differences correlate less clearly with points of communication breakdown, as, for example, with gender, we sense the limitations of the dialect model. Here the notion that speakers serve as agents in the creation of sociolinguistic variation has strong appeal if we want to explain how speech differences could arise between groups in regular communication (see Chapter Nine).

This chapter surveys Labov's research on the role of several social factors in the construction of language variation and change. Labov commonly frames the issues around a set of broadly defined social variables. Thus we find throughout his writings discussions of the effects of social class, sex, ethnicity, and age on patterns of linguistic variation. It would be a mistake, however, to assume from this that Labov ignores how patterns of variation are shaped by more localized social factors or by individual speakers. Both his New York City (2006) and Philadelphia (2001b) studies demonstrate his willingness to look beyond simple demographics. Still, wrestling with the effects of those broader factors certainly stands as a central occupation in his work. On this score his contributions have been many. The variationist approach provides an ideal toolkit for unmasking the complex correlations between speech and the social identities of the speakers.

Social class

When we ponder the kinds of social factors that are likely to correlate with linguistic differences, socioeconomic status or class comes quickly to mind. Still, the way we perceive class and how it operates may vary widely, as I frequently discover when I raise the issue with students. For some, class seems synonymous with wealth; they see a person's class as simply a function of that person's bank balance. Others view class in more abstract terms as a matter of status so that higher class people (and things) carry more prestige than lower class ones. The issue becomes even more vexed when people are asked about their own class. There is still a good deal of truth to the traditional quip that most Americans think they're middle class.[2]

The difficulty that my students and others have in coming to grips with class reflects J. K. Chambers's observation that class is an "inherently fuzzy" concept, especially in comparison to other variables that sociolinguists examine such as age and sex (2008, p. 40). In industrialized societies we recognize a basic division between the working and middle classes, often coded in the metonyms "blue collar" and "white collar" from the attire suited to work in a factory versus an office. These labels reflect the salience of occupation as an element of social class. To be sure, job categories offer a more productive way of approaching class than wealth or income. After all, many college professors earn less than many plumbers, but a professor represents the middle class and a plumber the working class. Still, social class is about more than one's profession. It typically functions as a pervasive cultural divide that shapes our lives in various tangible and intangible ways.

Of concern here are the ways that class shapes our language. Sociolinguistic research has revealed that class-based variation is widespread and manifest in a range of linguistic dimensions. Variationist studies have commonly focused on phonological and grammatical variables in exploring the influence of class, but other research has examined class in terms of broader discourse patterns.[3] Social stratification by class has been central to Labov's research agenda since his New York City study. This work has not only led to a greater appreciation for the complex role of class in linguistic variation, but it has also informed crucial aspects of Labov's broader thinking about language, including his conception of speech community and his understanding of the forces driving linguistic change.

We begin our survey of Labov's research on class-based variation with a question that he had to face before embarking on that research: How is social class best measured? We can acknowledge that class is multidimensional cultural construct, but in order to explore it as a social variable in a variationist (statistical) analysis, the researcher must have a method of categorizing people by their socioeconomic status. This raises the question of which criteria best serve as indicators of class status.

In his New York City project, Labov had the advantage of piggy-backing onto an existing sociological study, the Mobilization for Youth Program. As noted in Chapter Three, that program constructed a ten-point scale based on occupation, education, and income. Labov collapsed some of these categories in his analysis. He frequently broke the scale up into five class groups: lower, lower working, upper working, lower middle, and upper middle. But sometimes he presents the results with fewer categories and occasionally with more categories.[4] As he notes, "there is no reason to assume that each [variable] is affected by the class structure to the same extent" (2006, p. 155).

For his Philadelphia research,[5] Labov developed a socioeconomic index similar to the one used in New York. Again, people are distinguished by their education and occupation, but here a scale of "residence value" (i.e. market price of the home) replaces the income factor used earlier. These three factors were combined in the calculation of a composite index for each Philadelphian surveyed. Values on the scale ranged from 0 to 16, but in his analysis Labov typically groups the sample into six categories: lower working, upper working, lower middle, middle middle, upper middle, and upper class (2001b, p. 63). He also considers two other measures: "house upkeep," which relates to whether homeowners maintain their houses in good condition or let them deteriorate, and "social mobility," which codes whether a person's socioeconomic status is higher or lower than that of his or her parents (2001b, pp. 63–6).[6] These factors allow Labov to make finer-grain distinctions within certain class groups, but they are not formally incorporated into the composite index.

The statistical methods that Labov relies on (mostly multivariate analysis) allow him to explore class-related effects in various ways. In fact, he is able to examine the relative importance of each component of his composite socioeconomic index to the overall variation. These tests reveal that occupation functions as the most significant factor followed by education and finally by residence value (2001b, p. 118). Nevertheless, Labov argues that the composite index offers the most reliable measure overall, even though breaking out the individual components can offer insights into the social meaning of particular variables. For example, occupation seems to correlate strongly in the case of variables established early in one's life, a finding that Labov suggests may reflect the link between occupation and family history. For variables acquired later in life and subject to more conscious manipulation, education seems to play a greater role. The case of (r) in New York City illustrates the latter scenario, while (dh) illustrates the former (Labov, 2001b, p. 114).

While Labov's methods for measuring social class have varied somewhat, his research has repeatedly demonstrated the significance of this factor across different communities and different linguistic features within the same community. Indeed it's clear that investigations of class-based variation were crucial to the establishing the very field of variationist sociolinguistics. As argued in Chapter Four, patterns of class stratification emerging from Labov's New York City study provided overwhelming evidence of the "orderly heterogeneity" on which the whole endeavor was premised.

Moreover, those patterns usually hold across a range of speech styles even when rates of usage vary dramatically from one stylistic context to another. We saw this common pattern earlier (e.g. Figures 3.1 and 5.1) where each group remains in the same position in the class hierarchy despite altering their usage from casual to careful speech and to reading style. As it happens, Labov sees this stylistic pattern as an expected by-product of class-based variation. He proposes a general axiom that "the correlate of regular stratification of a sociolinguistic variable in behavior is uniform agreement in subjective reactions towards that variable" (1972b, p. 249). As discussed in Chapter Four, the shared sociolinguistic norms that are evident in such patterning form the bedrock of Labov's concept of the speech community.

Exploring the motivations that produce the correlation described by this axiom draws our attention to other fruitful questions about how social class shapes sociolinguistic variation. When we consider why speakers shift their usage of a variable like (th) or (dh), we might look to the fact that variation involves an alternation between a standard form ([θ] or [ð]) and a nonstandard form ([t] or [d]). It's easy to appreciate why someone's usage might reflect a higher rate of standard forms in the relatively formal tasks of reading aloud and answering questions in an interview. Labov's attention to speech model of style shifting is, in fact, premised on the idea that the more formal tasks will produce speech that is more standard as one shifts away from the vernacular (see Chapter Five).

But this evidence that speakers of all classes recognize one form as more standard, which is to say more correct and more proper, raises an interesting question: Why do they not use that form in their casual speech as well? Cases like (th) and (dh) represent stable sociolinguistic variables; they are not involved in sound change. Given the apparent advantages of using the standard pronunciations, we might expect that they would come to supplant the nonstandard forms. As Labov observes:

> Why don't all people speak the way that they obviously believe they should? The usual response is to cite laziness, lack of concern, or isolation from the prestige norm. But there is no foundation for the notion that stigmatized vernacular forms are easier to pronounce; and there is strong evidence of concern with speech in large cities. Careful consideration of this difficult problem has led us to posit the existence of an opposing set of covert norms, which attribute positive values to the vernacular. (1972b, p. 249)

This notion of opposing norms is captured in the distinction between "overt prestige" and "covert prestige."[7] Standard forms (e.g. *think, these, walking, I don't have any*) carry overt prestige associated with education, mainstream success, and so on. The value of the non-standard forms (e.g. *tink, dese, walkin', I don't have none*) stems from their covert prestige associated with toughness, localness, and so on. Thus, patterns of sociolinguistic stratification are maintained because social classes differ in their orientations to these different types of prestige.

The examples discussed so far illustrate stable patterns of variation, but social class serves as a powerful factor in situation of language change as well. Popular views on this subject often suppose that change is a top-down process. Innovations arise among the upper classes who strive to distinguish their speech from that spoken lower down the social ladder. Of course those lower groups, driven by the allure of overt prestige, eventually close the linguistic gap by adopting the upper-class innovation, and the process must begin anew. Or so the story goes. In actuality, Labov and others who have explored the sociolinguistics of language change offer a very different portrait of the process.

The variationist methodology opened new windows onto the process of language change by refining the study of active changes (see Chapter Seven). Investigating changes while they are in progress offers a richly detailed view of how innovations spread through the language system and through and across communities of speakers. With regard to social class, these investigations have shown a common pattern of changes beginning neither at the top nor the bottom of the scale, but rather in the middle. From this evidence, Labov formulates his "Curvilinear Principle":

> Linguistic change from below originates in a central social group, located in the interior of the socioeconomic hierarchy. (2001b, p. 188)

The label "curvilinear" refers to the pattern revealed when usage is compared across social classes as shown in Figure 6.1.

This diagram illustrates the general curvilinear pattern rather than plotting results for a particular sociolinguistic variable. Labov has found ample evidence of this pattern in his studies of New York City and Philadelphia, as have researchers examining other speech communities (see, e.g. Labov, 2001b, chapter 5). The curve bends from the high levels at which the interior groups use the innovative forms. Sometimes the lead appears in the upper working class and sometimes in the lower middle class. Crucially the more peripheral groups, those on the high and low ends of the hierarchy, trail in their adoption of change.

Labov specifies that this curvilinear pattern typifies the progress of changes from below. He is drawing on his distinction of the social meaning of changes. Changes operate either above or below the

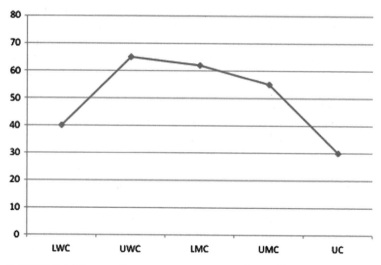

FIGURE 6.1 *The curvilinear pattern represented visually.*

level of social awareness. Most of the changes that Labov and other sociolinguists have explored fall into the latter category; they do not rise to the level of conscious awareness as they spread through the speech community.

By contrast, we expect a different class profile to emerge in the case of a change from above. These changes carry significant social salience, and often involve the introduction of a prestige form from outside the local community. One of the classic cases of a change from above is New York City (r). This change involves increased pronunciation of /r/ in words like *fourth* and *floor*. Labov's findings on (r), which we examined in Chapter Three, are reproduced here as Figure 6.2. The data for casual and interview speech (styles A and B) clearly show that the upper middle class (group 9) take the lead in this change, pronouncing /r/ at higher rates than the groups below them. Thus we see the pattern represented in the popular view described above: an innovation introduced into the community from the top of the social scale. We should keep in mind, however, that such cases of change from above are far outnumbered by the more common change from below.

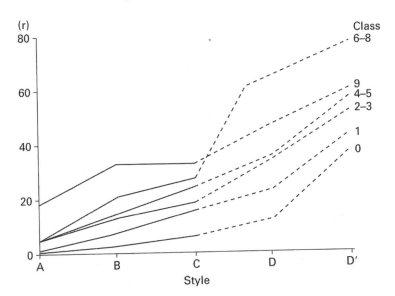

FIGURE 6.2 *Distribution of* (r) *by social class and contextual style in the Lower East Side study (from Labov, 2006, p. 152. Copyright © 2006 William Labov. Reprinted with the permission of Cambridge University Press).*

The findings on (r) also highlight another intriguing class-based pattern as noted in Chapter Three. The consistent class stratification of the left-hand side of Figure 6.2 is disrupted on the right-hand side by the high (r) values of the lower middle class (group 6–8) in reading the word list (style D) and the minimal pairs (style D'). Labov describes this as hypercorrection since these speakers "go beyond the highest-status group in their tendency to use the forms considered correct and appropriate for formal styles" (1972b, p. 126). This statistical trend seems to reflect broader sociolinguistic attitudes. Members of the lower middle class show a "hypersensitivity" to stigmatized speech forms, a tendency that applies even to those forms they regularly use in their own casual speech (1972b, p. 130). The subjective reaction tests that Labov carried out in New York City offer empirical support for a general picture of linguistic insecurity among this group.

Labov suggests that this linguistic insecurity and the hyper-correction it produces serve as powerful forces propelling language change. Drawing on the New York City (r) data, he argues that adults in the lower middle class, and perhaps especially women, play a key role in spreading the incoming prestige norm beyond the highest social groups (see 1972b, chapter 5). The model that Labov has in mind is clearly that of a change from above. Still, it is interesting to note that the lower middle class is often at, or near, the forefront of changes from below as well according to the curvilinear principle. Perhaps the insecurity that seems to come as part of their interior position in the social hierarchy may also spur their adoption of innovations more generally, even those that carry no overt prestige.

This review has highlighted some of the insights that Labov has drawn from his study of class-based variation. This research benefits from the kinds of large-scale surveys he conducted in New York City and Philadelphia. Such projects were fairly common in the early decades of variationist research. For example, Roger Shuy directed a major study of Detroit speech in the late 1960s (see Shuy et al., 1967), and Peter Trudgill carried out a project very similar to Labov's in the English city of Norwich (1974).[8] More recently, not only have large urban projects become less common, but the study of class as a social variable seems also to have dropped off. Some of the reasons for this turn in the field are discussed in Chapter Nine.

By way of concluding this discussion of Labov's work on social class, I should note that his general approach, while frequently adopted in the field, has attracted criticism. Indeed some sociolinguists have challenged the general model Labov assumes.[9] The method that Labov follows, where class is measured on some multi-point scale based on factors like education and occupation, reflects a particular view of social class. In this "functional" paradigm, society operates "as an integrated system, its various parts (classes) performing different functions and receiving different rewards according to the importance of their functions to the system" (Rickford, 1986, p. 216). This model assumes that society operates by a kind of consensus. Labov's emphasis on shared norms as defining the speech community serves as a clear reflection of this orientation. Some social theorists criticize this approach and argue that the primary social dynamic governing the relations between the classes is one of conflict, not consensus. According to this Marxist model, conflict stems from the fact that people differ in terms of their relationship to the economic market and thus have differing opportunities and access to power, material goods, and so forth. In notions like covert and overt prestige we seen hints of how this model might play out in Labov's theories of sociolinguistic variation. Still, he has not implemented such a conflict model of class into his research.

Social networks

Decades of research by Labov and others make it clear that linguistic variables often pattern neatly with social class. Correlations between language use and class abound in the literature. However, identifying that working class people use more of form A and middle class people use more of form B is just a first step. Class categories (e.g. working, middle, upper) may help organize sociolinguistic results, but they do not explain them. Even the criteria that such categorizations are based on have limited explanatory value. To make sense of the patterns we must dig deeper and try to understand the mechanisms that produce class-related (and other) sociolinguistic correlations.

The study of social networks offers a productive approach in this regard. The basic concept is quite simple: your social network comprises the people you interact with. Straightaway we sense the explanatory advantage this offers over more abstract notions like class. As sketched in the introduction to this chapter, patterns of communication underpin the basic model of sociolinguistic differentiation. The study of social networks pursues the fundamental truth that our speech is shaped by those we talk with.

Sociolinguists engaged in this pursuit draw on the insights of social network theory as developed in other fields. This work highlights how social networks differ structurally. Some networks involve a group of people who interact frequently and in a variety of contexts. Consider, for example, a neighborhood where many of the people are close friends, some work together at the same company, and some are members of the same extended family. Such a tight-knit network contrasts with one characterized by less-frequent, more-unidimensional contacts. Someone who lives some distance from family and who does not work at the same place as his or her neighbors has a more diffuse social network. As it happens, these different types of network structures often correspond to class divisions. The kind of close-knit network where everyone knows everyone else through a variety of connections typifies traditional working class communities while more loose-knit and diffuse networks characterize middle class communities.[10]

Labov has explored the sociolinguistic dimensions of such differences of network structure. This work often focuses on how individuals differ in terms of their positioning within a given network. In his early work in South Harlem, for example, he investigated the social networks of African American adolescents by mapping friendship relations (see Labov et al., 1968; Labov, 1972a, chapter 7). Figure 6.3 represents one social network studied in this way. During the fieldwork, each boy was asked "Who are all the cats you hang out with?" and Figure 6.3 plots their responses. The solid lines connect boys who named one another, while the dashed lines represent nonreciprocal responses with the arrow pointing from the namer to the person named.

From this style of "sociometric" diagram we see that some members of this network of boys hold more central roles than others. Roger, for example, with his reciprocal hang-out connections to six others clearly occupies a more core position than Gary, who was named by just three others and identified just one connection (Billy) on his own. Even more peripheral are people like Lesley and Curtis whom nobody named but who claim to hang out with one of the more of the central members of the group. These boys represent a common social type known in African American culture as

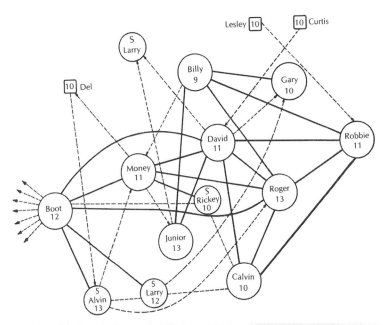

FIGURE 6.3 *The "hang-out pattern" of a group of Harlem adolescents (from Labov, 1972a, p. 262; Copyright © 1972 University of Pennsylvania Press. Reprinted with the permission of the University of Pennsylvania Press). Numbers indicate the boys' ages.*

the "lame." Despite growing up in the neighborhood, lames remain largely isolated from vernacular culture.

We see evidence of this isolation in Labov's examination of how usage of features of African American vernacular varies across a social network like that in Figure 6.3 (see 1972a, chapter 7). He reports, for example, that lames typically use the stop pronunciations of (dh) (e.g. *dese* and *dose*) at lower rates than the central members of the group. Similar discrepancies appear in the results for grammatical features as well. Thus, the pattern of "copula deletion," in which the verb *be* is omitted (e.g. *He nice.*), is rarely used by lames but appears quite commonly in the speech of the core group. Such findings have important implications for the study of African American English, discussed more fully in Chapter Eight. They serve here as an illustration of the kinds of insights a social network analysis provides sociolinguists.

Labov's Harlem research demonstrates how linguistic variation correlates with integration in a social network. He took up this issue again in his Philadelphia project, where he developed a much more elaborate means of measuring network integration. The Philadelphia fieldwork often involved multiple interviews with the same speakers over a period of months or even years. This extended contact meant that Labov and his fellow researchers gathered useful ethnographic detail about the social networks in the neighborhoods they studied in depth. Their interview protocols also included a series of questions exploring interactions within the neighborhood. From this material they constructed a series of "communication indices" (see Labov, 2001b, chapter 10). For example, to examine how many neighbors each interviewee had contact with, the researchers asked for a count of the number of "people on the block the person would *say hello to, have coffee with, visit with, invite to a party, go out with,* or *confide in*" (2001b, p. 336). This index offered a measure of how plugged into the social network of the block a person was. For a somewhat different approach, Labov's team also explored how localized each person's friendship patterns were by simply asking how many of their friends lived on the block. As we might expect, Labov found a strong statistical correlation between these measures. It makes sense that someone who has a high level of contact with many neighbors would also have a higher proportion of his or her friends among those neighbors.

The sociolinguistic patterns arising from this network analysis came as a greater surprise. Labov concentrates on how adoption of several sound changes correlates with his "communication indices." One of these changes involves the fronting of the nucleus (the first vowel) of the diphthong /au/ of *house* and *loud* so that it comes to sound more like the [æ] of *bat*. This is one of the "new and vigorous" changes gaining ground in Philadelphia speech. In terms of its social class distribution, it illustrates the curvilinear pattern typical of changes from below. The network analysis finds a strong correlation between progress in the change and integration in the neighborhood as measured by how many people on the block one has regular interaction with. However, the correlation works the opposite way with regard to the index of how localized one's friendship network is. Labov found that the people with a higher percentage of friends from outside their local block tend to take the lead in this and other sound changes (see 2001b, p. 338).

As it happens, this finding fits with other research on how network structures shape the diffusion of innovations. In sociology, economics, and other fields researchers have explored how new technologies and ideas spread. What this work has often shown is that innovations rely on different kinds of relationships to spread. Diffusion from one community to another depends on people with diffuse social networks to carry the innovation across groups. But in order for the innovation to penetrate into a new community it needs to be adopted by influential locals who serve as a model for others to follow. Among the first sociolinguists to explore these mechanisms in the spread of language change were James and Lesley Milroy (see, e.g. Milroy and Milroy, 1985). Labov draws on their work and others' in his portrayal of the leaders of language change, one of the central themes of his 2001 book. A key characteristic of these leaders is their somewhat unusual positioning in their social networks: their friendship ties link them to people beyond their immediate neighborhoods, but they nevertheless function as core members of their local networks (see Chapter Seven).

While social network has played a supporting role in Labov's research when compared to other variables such as class and gender, it has turned in some memorable performances. Some researchers seem to view social network as an alternative to class as a variable in sociolinguistic analysis. For Labov, however, the two clearly offer complementary perspectives on the issues. Thus, we have seen examples of how exploring relationships within social networks can help account for linguistic patterns that differ among people who would be categorized as members of the same social class (e.g. the lames have the same socioeconomic status as the core members of the Harlem hang-out networks). By the same token, Labov argues that we need the perspective of the class distribution within the broader speech community to appreciate the linguistic patterns observed at a more local level.

Gender

One of the most consistent findings across 50 years of sociolinguistic research has been the observation of variation along gender lines. Almost every study that has investigated this issue has discovered linguistic differences between men and women or boys and girls.

This vast literature includes countless studies of the US, the UK, and other English-speaking societies, but patterns of gender-based language differences are by no means confined to English or even to other European languages and cultures. Gender has been shown to play key sociolinguistic roles in speech communities around the world.

On the one hand, the fact that linguistic differences frequently pattern in terms of gender may come as little surprise. After all, gender operates as a powerful force shaping behaviors of various kinds in most (perhaps all) societies. Many cultures expect males and females to dress differently, pursue different occupations and interests, and generally act differently in many social settings. Thus, we might expect speech behavior to fall subject to such cultural prescriptions as well.

On the other hand, the prevalence of gendered language differences can seem perplexing in comparison to other sociolinguistic factors. Recall the premise of the basic model of dialect differentiation mentioned earlier: speech distinctions arise when barriers of some sort separate groups of people and inhibit communication. Obviously geographical separation acts to limit communication between groups, and many social divisions, such as class, religion, ethnicity, and so on operate with similar effects. But herein lies the logical problem posed by a notion of "genderlects": segregation by sex is much less prevalent in many parts of the world. Certainly in western cultures, males and females do not generally live apart from one another, but rather are raised in the same households, often educated in the same schools, and, most importantly, interact on a regular basis almost every day of their lives. Thus, it is hard to see how a model of linguistic differentiation prefaced on barriers to communication might account for gender patterns.

For this reason many sociolinguistic discussions of gender stress the active role that speakers adopt in constructing their linguistic selves. The basic idea is that in a given community men and women speak differently not because they lack exposure to the other sex's pattern, but rather as a means (one of many) of constructing gender identities. This approach is in keeping with a view of gender as a social force, rather than a static property. As Eckert and McConnell-Ginet framed it:

> "Gender" becomes a dynamic verb. We speak of practices (and traits and activities and values) as "gendered" where they enter in some important way into "gendering" people and their

relations. That is, gendered practices construct members of a community "as" women or "as" men (or members of other gender categories), and this construction crucially also involves constructing relations between and within each sex. (1992, pp. 462–3)

It's no doubt clear from this discussion that "gender" is far from a synonym for "sex." The latter describes biological distinctions such as male and female, while the former denotes the broader cultural dimensions of that divide. Linguistic variation, at least the kind that sociolinguists explore, is a matter of gender. We are not usually interested in how anatomical differences between males and females contribute to speech differences, but rather in how language serves as one of the "gendered practices" that Eckert and McConnell-Ginet see as constructing membership in gender categories. Nevertheless, incorporating such a nuanced view of gender into the typical variationist analysis presents definite challenges. How many gender categories should be recognized? How can the fluidity of membership in the categories be coded?

Labov and other sociolinguists usually sidestep such issues or rather postpone their consideration. The usual methodology treats gender as a simple binary that divides the sample population into males and females. Statistical analysis may reveal correlations between linguistic forms and either males or females, but the researcher seeks explanations for these patterns in cultural dimensions of the male/female divide. In this way, findings derived from an analysis of sex-based differences are interpreted through the frame of gender.

Labov has been interested in the sociolinguistics of gender throughout his career. In his New York City research, for example, he uncovered significant differences between men and women in the use of several linguistic features. He reports that men use the stop variants of the (dh) variable more than do women; that is, men are more likely to say *dese* and *dose* for *these* and *those*. Still, in Labov's report (2006) such findings took a back seat to his discussion of class-based variation. Gender features more prominently in Labov's work on Philadelphia speech. There he found significant gender differences with each of the dozen or so linguistic variables he investigated. For example, he reports that women are more likely than men to pronounce the (au) diphthong of *how* and *cow* with more of fronted starting point (i.e. [æʊ] instead of [aʊ]).

As it happens, the patterns that Labov uncovered in his research have proven to be extremely common in the sociolinguistic literature on gender. Recognizing these similarities across numerous studies, Labov formulated a set of general principles. Thus, the New York City pattern with (dh) represents a trend seen with linguistic features that distinguish standard from nonstandard speech. Labov captures this trend with the following principle:

> For stable sociolinguistic variables, women show a lower rate of stigmatized variants and a higher rate of prestige variants than men. (2001b, p. 266)

As we saw in his treatment of class-based variation, Labov draws a distinction between stable variables and those involved in language change. In New York City, as in Philadelphia, (dh) functions as a stable variable. The same stability characterizes a variable like (ing), the alternation between [ɪŋ] and [ɪn] in the –*ing* suffix (e.g. *fishing* vs. *fishin'*), and, in accordance with the above principle, Labov finds that women use the stigmatized [ɪn] variant at lower rates than men in Philadelphia (2001b, p. 265). Both (dh) and (ing) function as sociolinguistic variables in many English-speaking communities around the world, and these same gender patterns have been reported by several other researchers. Indeed, the generalization that women use stigmatized forms less and prestige forms more applies to many other linguistic variables in many other languages (see citations by Labov, 2001b, p. 266).

Labov also postulates general principles covering situations of language change. Closely related to the above principle is his formulation that:

> In linguistic change from above, women adopt prestige forms at a higher rate than men. (2001b, p. 274)

Recall that a change from above carries significant social salience, usually because it involves the introduction of a prestige form from outside the local community. New York City (r) stands as one of the best-known examples of this type of change, and in his dissertation research Labov found that the adoption of the incoming rhotic (r-ful) pronunciation was more advanced among women than among men. As with his previous principle, Labov cites several other studies reporting the same gender pattern (2001b, p. 274).

The principles are phrased here as descriptions of what women do more or less than do men, but they could also be phrased in the reverse. In fact, Labov originally cited the first principle as "men use a higher frequency of nonstandard forms than women" (1990, p. 205). Either formulation serves as a description of the facts, but if we want to explore explanations for how the gender patterns arose, we might ask which group is more responsible for the observed differences. Do the tendencies described here stem from men's embracing of stigmatized forms and rejection of prestige forms or from women's embracing of prestige forms and rejection of stigmatized forms? Labov definitely sides with the latter interpretation, noting that "women are as a rule the active agents of sexual differentiation" (1990, p. 239). He unites the two principles above as reflecting women's "linguistic conformity" to mainstream values. Evidence that such conformity is a greater concern for women than for men can be found in patterns of style shifting, where women often show more extreme shifting toward prestige usage in more careful speech contexts (e.g. reading). The results from the social evaluation tasks that Labov carried out in his New York City study are also relevant here (see Chapter Three). In that work he found that women generally scored higher on his test of linguistic insecurity and also commonly over-reported their use of prestige forms on his self-evaluation test. Both of these findings are consistent with the suggestion that women are more attuned than men to the social evaluation of particular linguistic usages.

The portrait of women's linguistic inclinations is complicated by Labov's final principle:

In linguistic change from below, women use higher frequencies of innovative forms than men do. (2001b, p. 292)

We find overwhelming support for this principle in the sociolinguistic literature (see Labov, 2001b, pp. 279–90). The case mentioned above of the fronting of the (au) diphthong of *how* and *cow* in Philadelphia illustrates this tendency. Similarly, Labov notes that women lead in the New York City raising of (æh), as in *bad*, and (oh), as in *bought*. There are reported cases where men seem to lead changes, such as the centralization of the (ai) and (au) diphthongs on Martha's Vineyard. Still, these counterexamples are relatively rare in comparison to the main trend.

At first blush, this principle might appear to serve as a complement to the previous principle on women's role in language change.
It might seem reasonable to combine these statements into a
generalization that women lead linguistic changes whether they
operate above or below the level of social awareness. The problems
with such a generalization become apparent when we try to posit
some kind of unifying motivation.

As we've seen, women's adoption of changes from above
makes sense as an offshoot of their greater use of prestige forms
and avoidance of stigmatized forms in the case of stable variables.
Changes from below, however, bear very different social profiles.
By definition, they do not carry the overt prestige of changes from
above and of the forms associated with the standard side of the
standard/nonstandard divide. In fact, changes from below may hold
some degree of stigma, though speakers are generally not conscious
of such connections. For example, using his subjective reaction test,
Labov showed that many New Yorkers rate speakers with innovative
(i.e. raised) pronunciations of the (æh) and (oh) vowels as suited
only for occupations at the bottom of the socioeconomic scale.[11]
This last principle, therefore, seems difficult to reconcile with the
previous two. If women are concerned with linguistic prestige, why
should they participate in changes that don't bring greater prestige
and may actually bring stigma? Labov frames the situation as "The
Gender Paradox," which he summarizes as follows:

> Women conform more closely than men to sociolinguistic norms
> that are overtly prescribed, but conform less than men when they
> are not. (2001b, p. 293)

To put it another way, women are conservative when standard or
prestige forms are at issue and innovative when they're not.

It is easy enough to understand the possible motivations driving
women's conservative behavior given the social benefits of using forms
associated with "proper" speech as opposed to those associated with
the vernacular. Explaining women's inclination toward innovation
presents a stiffer challenge, and, in fact, this remains an open question
in the field.[12] Labov has explored these issues by examining how
gender interacts with other social variables, especially class.

When differences between men and women are examined in
conjunction with class stratification, we see that the gender effects

vary tremendously across the socioeconomic ladder. In many cases Labov finds the strongest differentiation between the sexes in the second-highest status group (typically the lower middle class) (1990). This result is especially interesting when we remember that this group also plays a crucial role in language change leading to the curvilinear pattern that typifies most changes from below. Labov suggests that the position of this group in the social hierarchy produces a sense of class insecurity, including about their linguistic behavior. As we've seen, a similar argument has been offered to explain women's speech. Labov offers a more positive spin on this issue by framing the feelings of social insecurity as concerns with social mobility (2001b, p. 277). Thus, women act not out of anxiety over losing status, but rather with the goal of improving their status. Labov furthermore suggests that women's traditional leading role in child-rearing may be a factor. He raises the possibility of interpreting "the linguistic conformity of women as a reflection of their greater assumption of responsibility for the upward mobility of their children" (2001b, p. 278).

Labov weaves these suggestions into a general proposal about the life course of language change (see Chapter Seven). Through his Philadelphia research he has identified several sound changes of varying time depth. Some are very recent, while others are nearly complete. Exploring this material, he finds that gender differences tend to be rather slight in the early stages of change. This fits with a more general tendency for incipient changes to lack any strong social associations.

As the change advances it develops an association with one or the other gender, most commonly with women. Interestingly, in this still early stage we often see a strong split between women and men in the lower end of the social scale. Labov interprets this as men "retreating or resisting a female-dominated change" (2001b, p. 308).[13]

The next generation typically shows a sharp acceleration of the change that, because of the low levels of the innovation heard among the older men, is especially marked in the men's usage. In Labov's research and in many other studies, we often find that men's participation in changes lags behind about one generation. In Philadelphia, for example, Labov reports that the degree of fronting of the diphthong (au) found with men in their 30s and 40s is comparable with the degree of fronting found with women in their 50s and 60s (see 2001b, p. 304). Again, Labov looks to women's traditional responsibilities in child-rearing as a way of understanding such findings, and he suggests that "men are at the level of linguistic change characteristic of their mothers because they acquired their first use of these variables from their mothers" (2001b, pp. 306–7). Labov is quick to point out that this is far from the complete story and that men's and women's usage is shaped by a range of factors over the course of their lives. Still, it is an intriguing observation, and one that might offer a new perspective on the proposed innovativeness of women. Maybe it's not the case that women are characteristically more inclined to innovation than men. Maybe both sexes are equally so inclined, but because of their role as primary caregivers, women have more of an opportunity to transmit the changes they've adopted to the next generation.

In subsequent generations, the basic gender division is repeated as the change spreads further through the speech community. As it reaches completion, the gender divide lessens as men eventually catch up to women of their age cohort. At this final stage the change may simply become a general characteristic of local speech in which case it is adopted by the entire community. Alternatively, the innovative usage may develop into a stable sociolinguistic variable in which case the first principle would come to apply.

Labov's work on gender has been highly influential. As is often true, Labov succeeded in framing a productive conversation with his general principles. Researchers have looked to their own work to see whether it supports or refutes Labov's generalizations. They also have continued his efforts to look beyond the descriptive statements for explanations. In recent years, much of this latter work has followed a different path. As discussed further in Chapter Nine, many scholars have taken to heart the idea that gender is performative and dynamic and have looked beyond the statistical correlations that form the basis of much of Labov's argumentation, preferring instead to explore the construction of gender in a range of everyday activities.

Ethnicity

In pluralistic societies like those studied by Labov, distinctions of ethnicity often have a role to play in sociolinguistic variation. This makes sense given how ethnic divisions have, historically at least, shaped settlement patterns in broad regional terms as well as on a more local level (e.g. ethnic neighborhoods). In this way, ethnicity affects communication networks in much the same way as social class does. But, we might expect especially clear ethnic patterns with regard to speech when we consider the kinds of differences at issue. To be sure, ethnicity is a slippery term that is applied to a wide range of situations. In the context of American cities like New York and Philadelphia, ethnicity most commonly describes one's family descent, often specifically the place one's ancestors immigrated from. Thus, prominent ethnic identities include Italian, Irish, and Puerto Rican. This section highlights Labov's work related to ethnicities of this type, but we should bear in mind that for Labov, and for sociolinguistics more generally, the study of variation related to ethnicity has been dominated by interest in African American English, the topic of Chapter Eight.

With ethnic groups defined by historical immigration, as they typically are in the US, one reason to expect sociolinguistic differences along these lines stems from the connection between immigration and "foreign" languages and dialects. The process of shifting from the heritage language of the first-generation immigrants to English may influence the development of ethnic dialects as elements of that language's lexicon, grammar or phonology are carried over to shape the variety of English spoken in later generations. Several examples of these "transfer" effects appear in the literature. The most obvious cases involve borrowed vocabulary from the heritage language such as the Yiddish words *chutzpah* and *schlep*, which characterize Jewish speech.[14] We see a somewhat trickier case in the Chicano English use of *barely* as in "I barely broke my leg." As Carmen Fought, who studied with Labov at Penn, notes, this use of *barely* to describe a recent event ("I have just broken my leg") seems to stem from a translation of Spanish *apenas*, which is used with this meaning as well as with others that *barely* serves in most varieties of English (see Fought, 2006).

Labov has found evidence of such transfer effects much harder to come by. In fact, he observes with great surprise that ethnicity in general functions as a minor factor in shaping the sociolinguistic variation he examines (2001b, p. 247). He did identify some ethnic patterns in his New York City research. The clearest examples involve the lead by Italians in the raising of (æh) (the vowel of *bad*) and the lead by Jews in the raising of (oh) (the vowel of *bought*). These results suggest an interesting twist on the usual account of transfer effects from heritage languages. When learning English, native speakers of Italian often substitute a low vowel [a] for the English [æ], and native Yiddish speakers typically use a low [ɒ][15] for English [ɔ]. If these heritage phonological effects were to carry over, then we might expect to find in later generations correlations between Italian ethnicity and lowering of [æ] and between Jewish ethnicity and lowering of [ɔ]; but, of course, we find just the opposite phonetic trend. This leads Labov to speculate that the ethnic patterns arose from second- and third-generation Italians and Jews seeking to avoid the stigma of their parents' and grandparents' accented English. But in eschewing the low vowels of their ancestors, they overshot the phonetic mark and produced raised pronunciations as a kind of hypercorrection (Labov, 2001b, p. 247).

Labov also examined the potential influence of ethnicity in Philadelphia, where the prominent groups include Italians, Irish, and Germans. With a few minor exceptions, he finds little evidence of the kinds of sociolinguistic divisions based on ethnic differences reported in other speech communities. Perhaps most surprising is the fact that ethnicity plays no significant role in the variation related to many sound changes active in Philadelphia speech. As he notes, ethnicity "has proved to be weaker and less general in its effects than gender, age, and social class" (2001b, p. 259).

While Labov's assessment accurately describes the role of ethnicity relative to many other social variables, we should not misconstrue it as a claim that ethnic differences have become irrelevant in American English. Research on Cajun English in Louisiana, Lumbee English in North Carolina, and Chicano English in the Southwest and elsewhere belies such a claim (for an accessible review of this literature, see Wolfram and Schilling-Estes, 2006). Moreover, Labov has in mind ethnic differences related to the voluntary immigration of mostly European people. As discussed in Chapter Eight, African American English stands as a special case, and Labov has argued that the difference between black and white ethnic identities plays a central role in linguistic variation and change across the US.

Conclusion

True to the scholarly banner they work under, sociolinguists approach the study of language with an eye on the fact that it is fundamentally a social phenomenon. For Labov, this project has generally taken the form of an exploration of how major social factors operate in the construction of linguistic variation. Those factors include social class, gender, and ethnicity among others, and in this chapter we have highlighted the fruit borne of Labov's efforts. Certainly we must count among his significant contributions the many general patterns he has uncovered such as his principles describing gender differences and the curvilinear class distribution. Such findings have provided a framework that has guided decades of productive research.

To be sure, Labov's approach has not escaped criticism. In addition to questioning particulars like his model of social class mentioned earlier, some scholars have challenged the general methodology and the broad-strokes approach it takes to the consideration of social dynamics. Labov's analysis mainly relies on a common set of social variables defined by demographic criteria. This raises the criticism that the researcher presumes to know what factors shape the sociolinguistic variation before the analysis proceeds. An alternative might explore social divisions defined by more localized criteria reflecting the dynamics of a particular speech community.

Another frustration with Labov's research stems from his emphasis on establishing correlations between social factors and linguistic variation. In his fullest treatment of these issues (in his massive 2001 book), Labov devotes much of the discussion to gathering rather complicated statistical proofs in support of general principles like those reviewed here. The argumentation at times becomes impenetrable to readers untrained in this style of quantitative reasoning. Even specialist readers may lose sight of the forest for the trees. The impressive detail with which Labov surveys the territory of sociolinguistic variation, documenting the interaction of social and linguistic variables from multiple directions with multiple statistical models, can overshadow his considerations of what it all means.

The phenomenon is certainly not unique to Labov's research. Walt Wolfram described the challenge facing variationists some 20 years ago:

[E]xamining the interactional effect of social variables has become increasingly sophisticated, typically involving multivariate statistical analyses of data ...With all the advances, there remain underlying theoretical and methodological issues related to the examination of co-varying social and linguistic variables. The search for underlying social explanation has now replaced the more superficial examination of background demographic variables, but this search can sometimes be elusive. (1993, pp. 201–2)

As the scientist's mantra states, correlation does not imply causation. Establishing a statistical connection between variables does not constitute an explanation. Labov regularly acknowledges this distinction, and, as we've seen throughout the chapter, he has advanced ideas about the underlying social and psychological dynamics that shape the patterns he documents.

The kinds of explanations that Labov has suggested often paint the social world with broad strokes. People are described by the generalized social categories of his analysis. Thus, to explain an observed pattern, the question takes the form "Why do upper-working-class people (or women or Italians) do this?" Any answers to such questions necessarily rely on generalizations about the groups. Dissatisfaction with this approach has fueled a move by some sociolinguists away from dependence on predetermined social categories. Some researchers have challenged Labov's approach at a more fundamental level, and a radical reframing of variationist methodology has emerged, as we'll see in Chapter Nine.

Notes

1 Age, as a social variable, is most relevant in the study of language change, and so I will save a discussion of age-related variation for Chapter Seven.

2 A 2008 national poll found that 53 percent of Americans considered themselves "middle class," including some 40 percent of people earning less than $20,000 a year and one-third of people earning over $150,000 (see Pew Research Center, 2008).

3 British sociologist Basil Bernstein is one of the best-known scholars in this area. He explored differences in middle class and working class styles of communication. Central to his theorizing were the concepts of "elaborated" versus "restricted" codes, said to characterize the middle and working classes respectively. His early work came under

criticism from Labov and others who saw it as fostering a deficit view of nonstandard dialects (see Chapter Eight). Ivinson (2011) offers a convenient overview of Bernstein's work with relevant citations.

4 See, for example, his analyses of (th) and (dh) where the class continuum is broken up differently (2006, p. 156).

5 Labov has reported on the Philadelphia research, formally known as the Project on Linguistic Variation and Change, in various venues. The fullest presentation of this material appears in his 2001 book, the second volume in his *Principles of Linguistic Change* series.

6 Labov also explored effects related to social mobility in his New York City project. Among his findings, he reports that speakers who have moved up the socioeconomic ladder from their parents often use linguistic variables at levels associated with the class above even their newly achieved one (see Labov, 1966b).

7 These terms themselves were popularized by Trudgill (1972) based on the cited passage from Labov. Labov himself spoke of "covert prestige" in answering questions about his paper at the 1964 Lake Arrowhead conference (see Labov, 1966a).

8 Labov gives a full list of such projects in chapter 15 of the second edition of his New York City book (2006).

9 See, for example, Milroy and Milroy (1992), Rickford (1986), and Woolard (1985).

10 James and Lesley Milroy have explored the intersections between class and social network and its sociolinguistic effects in their work (see, e.g. Milroy, 1987, Milroy and Milroy, 1985, Milroy and Gordon, 2003).

11 Actually, Labov found that some respondents were unreasonably harsh in their evaluations and rated the most innovative speakers as not qualified even for working class positions such as factory work (see 2006, chapter 11).

12 Wolfram and Schilling-Estes (2006) offer a useful overview of approaches to these issues.

13 Labov acknowledges his colleague Anthony Kroch as first proposing this interpretation (see Kroch, 1978).

14 Actually it's clear that both *chutzpah* and *schlep* have spread beyond Jewish speakers today.

15 The [ɒ] designates a low back rounded vowel. It's not common in American English but is used by many British speakers in words like *lot* and *sock*.

CHAPTER SEVEN

Labov as historical linguist

In the most general sense, historical linguistics describes that branch of the field dedicated to the study of language change. Questions of how and why languages evolve over time have been central to linguistics from the start. Throughout the nineteenth and twentieth centuries some of the most significant achievements in the field came from the study of historical connections within the Indo-European family of languages. Scholars traced the history of English, Latin, Greek, Sanskrit, and the roughly 200 other languages that make up this family. By systematically comparing the daughter languages, they succeeded in reconstructing a detailed picture of the structure of the common ancestor, Proto-Indo-European, a language thought to have been spoken some 6,000–9,000 years ago.

Interest in language change has dominated Labov's research agenda, though he has set his sights on more recent developments. Still, he has wrestled with many of the same issues as traditional historical linguistics throughout his career from the landmark studies he carried out in graduate school to his *opus magnum* on the subject, the three-volume *Principles of Linguistic Change* (1994, 2001b, 2010). This diachronic emphasis comes as little surprise. After all, language variation and language change go hand-in-hand. Change is essentially variation projected in the temporal dimension. Just as synchronic variation involves one group preferring usage A to usage B while a different group prefers B to A, language change appears as people at one time preferring A to B, and people at some later time preferring B to A. Moreover, the same methodology developed for studying sociolinguistic variation at one point in time shines new light on the study of language change.

This chapter sketches Labov's methodological innovations in the exploration of linguistic change and highlights key insights resulting from this work. We will see some of the many ways in which Labov has broken new ground, but we will also note that he has taken up many traditional topics and long-standing debates in the field of historical linguistics. His research in this arena is guided by a principle of "using the present to explain the past" (see, e.g. 1994, chapter 1). He argues that exploring how language works today can enhance our understanding of historical developments, and nowhere is this clearer than in the case of uncovering the forces that drive linguistic change.

The study of change in progress

Traditionally in historical linguistics the study of language change meant the study of the past. Scholars explored changes that had taken place centuries or even millennia ago. This approach focused on the endpoints of the change process: the original form and the new form. What happened in between these stages received less attention. With regard to sound change – the type of most interest to Labov – the consensus among historical linguists envisioned a gradual process. Obviously people do not go to sleep at night pronouncing things one way and wake up pronouncing them differently. Rather, phonetic change begins with the introduction of an innovative pronunciation that is used by a minority of the population at first. This new form competes with the original over time and slowly gains ground with each generation until it completely supplants the original.

From this description of the process we can sense why historical linguists traditionally felt they had to confine their explorations to the study of completed changes. Language change seemed too messy to be investigated as an active process. Thus, we cannot observe changes directly but only detect them after the fact. We have to know how the story ends – which form wins out – to make any sense out of the apparent chaos of the transition from one usage to another. As Bloomfield (1933/1984) framed the problem, variability in pronunciation abounds at all times due to a wide range of factors from situational differences (e.g. how fast or slow we're talking) to physiological differences (e.g. vocal tract sizes of men vs. women). Thus, "[e]ven the most accurate phonetic record of a language at any one time could not tell us which phonemes were changing" (1933/1984, p. 365).

The variationist paradigm rises to this methodological challenge. Labov argues that systematic observation of variation within a speech community can detect active changes.[1] His initial demonstration of this came in his study of Martha's Vineyard, and he refined the techniques in his explorations of New York City and Philadelphia. Today, this approach, which has come to be known as the study of language change in progress, has developed into a mainstay of sociolinguistic research.

The advances in the study of language change that Labov initiated stem from the notion of orderly heterogeneity that lies at the heart of the variationist program (see Chapter Four). Labov recognizes that variation is not random, but rather patterned. In the exploration of language change, patterns correlating with age offer crucial insight. Comparing the usage of speakers of different generations presents a kind of window into the past. We refer to such a view as "apparent-time" in contrast to the "real-time" perspective gained by comparing usage at two distinct points in time. The basic idea holds that examining the speech of a 70-year-old provides a picture of the language as it was spoken six decades ago when that person first acquired it. Comparing that picture with one based on the speech of young people today allows the researcher to track changes over time.

The reliability of apparent-time evidence depends on the assumption that our speech does not change significantly over the course of our lives. At first blush, this might seem a flawed assumption. After all, how many of us would agree that we talk the same way today as we did in our teenage years? When we think about vocabulary, for example, we might suppose that there are many words we use today that our 16-year-old selves would never use and vice versa. But this is not the dimension of language that Labov has in mind. The features of interest here are less subject to change over the course of one's life because they operate as part of one's core grammar or phonology. These aspects of our linguistic knowledge tend to be set during childhood as we acquire our native language and tend to remain stable over time. Anyone who has tried to learn a second language as an adult or even a teen can appreciate this point. Our native linguistic tendencies represent a significant hurdle to achieving fluency in another language, and in a similar fashion they also serve as a brake on our ability to modify our basic phonology and grammar over our lifetimes.

Since Labov first drew on it, the apparent-time hypothesis has been tested in several studies (see Labov, 1994, chapter 4). The strongest test involves a real-time check on the results. For example, a researcher might return years later to a speech community where earlier the generational pattern had suggested a change was in progress. Several researchers have followed up on Labov's study of New York City, including recreating his department store survey. These projects have generally confirmed the inferences of change Labov drew and they mark how far the innovations have spread since the mid-1960s (see Labov, 1994, pp. 86–94).

In a more direct test of the assumptions behind apparent-time reasoning, researchers might examine not just the same community, but actually the same people at different points in time to see whether a person's usage remains stable across the lifespan. For practical reasons, this approach is less common though Sankoff and Blondeau (2007) report on one such study of sound change in Montreal French. Their results demonstrate that most people do not alter their basic phonology over time, but, interestingly, those who do change tend to follow the direction of the overall community. Thus, adults may adopt an innovation that they did not favor in their youth. Even with such cases, however, the generational comparison will suggest a change in progress. Thus the basic picture emerging from apparent-time evidence remains valid, though the Montreal findings advise researchers to tread cautiously when interpreting the time-depth of inferred changes.

When we observe generational differences in the usage of some linguistic variable, the interpretation that a change is active may quickly leap to mind. As Labov cautions, however, not all differences in apparent time stem from changes in progress. Sometimes such differences represent stable "age-grading," where every generation recreates a consistent pattern of variation. We saw an example of this in the case of (dh) discussed in Chapters Five and Six. Labov's representation of the age distribution of this feature in Philadelphia is reproduced in Figure 7.1.

We examined these findings on (dh) in Chapter five as an illustration of the consistent stylistic difference found with every age group

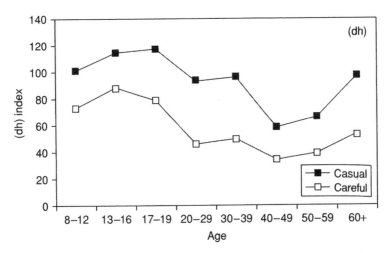

FIGURE 7.1 *Variation in the pronunciation of* (dh) *by age and style in Philadelphia (from Labov, 2001b, p. 102; reprinted by permission of Wiley-Blackwell).*

between casual and careful speech. Here we focus on the age pattern. If this were a change in progress, we'd expect a steady rise as we move from the older to the younger ends of the graph. Instead we see undulations with relatively high scores among teenagers and the oldest adults and lower scores among middle-aged adults and children. As it happens, this distribution represents a common finding with stable vernacular variables. The higher index scores indicate greater usage of the nonstandard pronunciations (e.g. *dese* and *dose*). We often find that adolescents and older adults use vernacular forms at higher rates than do others. Labov reports that certain grammatical features of African American vernacular show a similar distribution (see 1972a, pp. 284–5). To explain the pattern we might look to the behavior of middle-aged adults, whose reduced usage of nonstandard forms may reflect their position in the mainstream workplace.[2] The relevant point here is that the social forces undergirding patterns such as that in Figure 7.1, whatever their nature, endure over time and function to reproduce the same age-grading in each generation.

Such stable patterns complicate the interpretation of apparent-time evidence, and researchers must proceed cautiously to distinguish cases of regular age-grading from situations of change in progress.

The surest means of establishing that some change is underway lies in gathering supporting evidence from real time. Assuming the researcher doesn't wish to wait for several years to track usage over time, the best strategy is to look to the past. We see examples of this approach in Labov's use of linguistic atlas data collected in the 1930s and 1940s in his studies of Martha's Vineyard and New York City (see Chapter Three). Even though that dialectological research employed very different methods from Labov's, the material served to anchor his observations in real time and supported his interpretations of how the dialects were changing.

Labov's work and countless other sociolinguistic studies have made the case that language change can be observed while in progress, but we might ask, given the methodological challenges, why anyone would bother with this approach. What benefits does studying changes from this perspective carry? Specific answers to this question abound in this chapter and throughout the book, but I would characterize the general value of the sociolinguistic exploration of change in progress as a matter of scale. Traditional historical linguists often operate on a deep timescale and explore long-range trends that take place over centuries or longer. Sociolinguists, by contrast, typically deal with smaller slices of time. These varying approaches examine language change through very different frames of reference.

Imagine, for example, that we wanted to examine a historical change like the Great Vowel Shift, which altered the pronunciation of many English vowels beginning some 500 years ago. How would we trace the development of such a change? What evidence would we have about how the vowels sounded before and after the Shift and about how they changed in between? Obviously we have access only to written records from the period, but we might find indications of how the relevant sounds were pronounced in variant spellings since orthographic standards were not fixed then. Useful as this evidence is, it has clear limitations with regard to the phonetic details it can reveal. Moreover, written evidence paints an incomplete picture of the social variation related to the shifting vowels. For one thing, we don't always have details of the social backgrounds of the authors, and, more significantly, a large percentage of the population remains completely unrepresented given that over two-thirds of the people of England could not read and write at that time.

The lack of detail available when exploring changes from the past is certainly not an issue in the study of active changes.[3] If anything, the latter produces too much detail, and the challenge lies in sorting through the evidence to reveal significant patterns. We explored many of the sociolinguistic dimensions of this challenge in Chapter Six, where, for example, we considered the role that social class plays in shaping a change's progress. Of course the ability to draw on recordings of actual speech as opposed to written records opens the study of sound change progress to valuable phonetic details.

In general, therefore, the study of active changes offers a portrait of much higher resolution than that available from examining historical changes. The variationist approach serves to bring the process into tighter focus, and ideally shines fresh light on the mechanisms that drive language change. In this way the perspective shifts from the endpoints of a change – what the original form was and what it became – to the inner workings of the process – how and why one form came to replace another.

A variationist theory of language change

For a broader perspective on how the study of active changes might illuminate the change process, we turn to the seminal statement of the issues made by Weinreich et al. (1968). The authors trace the thinking that has dominated historical linguistics for over a century and highlight the limitations of this pursuit. As advertised, they present an alternative approach meant to lay the "empirical foundations for a theory of language change." This alternative is drawn from what we call today the "variationist paradigm," and at the heart of this programmatic essay lies a powerful defense of the central tenet of this paradigm: orderly heterogeneity is inherent in language structure. Without variation there would be no change, and embracing that variation brings new dimensions to the study of change. Weinreich, Labov, and Herzog frame the dimensions of the scholarly engagement with language change around five key problems:

1 Constraints Problem: What is a possible change? The historical record documents a wide range of changes in all areas of language, but the possibilities are not endless. What constraints exist "on the form, direction, or structural character of linguistic changes" (Labov, 1994, p. 115).

2 Transition Problem: How does a language pass from one state into another? What processes shape the intervening stages in a change situation?

3 Embedding Problem: How are innovations embedded in the linguistic matrix? How do they fit in the phonological or grammatical structure and interact with other elements of that system? By the same token, how are innovations embedded in the social matrix? What social factors shape the diffusion of a change through and across speech communities?

4 Evaluation Problem: How are changes evaluated by the speech community? Do they carry prestige or stigma or do they operate below the level of social awareness? How is the course of change affected by social perceptions?

5 Actuation Problem: How and why is a change activated? "Why do changes in a structural feature take place in a particular language at a given time, but not in other languages with the same feature, or in the same language at other times?" (Weinreich et al., 1968, p. 102).

Traditional historical linguistics has dealt with many of these problems, but the nature of the available evidence limits such investigations. The lack of phonetic detail in written records, for example, means that researchers must rely on speculation in positing the intervening stages of a historical sound change. Also, the social dimensions of language change were given little attention in traditional approaches as in the field more generally. Thus, any consideration of the embedding problem would deal only with linguistic structure, and issues related to the evaluation problem might go completely unaddressed.

Labov's approach to the study of change in progress brings a fruitful perspective to all of the above problems. As noted earlier, observing the change process as it happens opens a window on the mechanisms propelling it. The ability to flesh out a detailed portrait of an active change has particular relevance to the transition and embedding problems. Insight into the evaluation problem may come directly from the kinds of subjective reaction tests Labov employed in his New York City study or indirectly from consideration of stylistic variation.

The actuation problem has proven a tougher nut to crack. Certainly traditional approaches as well as variationist research have brought greater understanding to the linguistic and social factors that spur change. In the case of sound change, for example, the research literature teems with demonstrations of how the pronunciation of one sound can be altered in a particular direction under the influence of a neighboring sound. Labov discusses several examples of such "triggering events" related to vowel changes (2010, chapter 5). Nevertheless, the reason why these kinds of interactions between sounds lead to a change at a particular time and in a particular speech community usually remains a mystery. Given the multitude of social and linguistic factors acting on a language at any time, it's hard to predict what changes will take place. In fact, even accounting for the actuation of a documented change from the past presents a substantial challenge.

The life cycle of change

While we must acknowledge the difficulty of pinpointing the catalyst of a change, variationist research has succeeded in tracking how innovations progress. Labov has formulated a general model to describe the life course of linguistic change (1972b, pp. 178–80). In keeping with his usual focus, Labov frames the model as an account of sound changes, but many aspects can certainly be applied more generally to innovations in other areas of language.

Change begins with the usage of some form of a linguistic variable becoming generalized to members of a certain subgroup of the speech community. In the earliest stages the innovative form bears no social awareness; speakers do not adjust their usage by style. Labov refers to variables of this type as "indicators." They mark group membership but function below the level of consciousness.

Younger generations of the original subgroup acquire the innovative usage and advance it beyond the levels of their parents. Labov labels this process "hypercorrection from below" and sees it as a response to the same social pressures that inspired the original adoption of the new form to mark group membership. As we've seen elsewhere, Labov uses "hypercorrection" to describe a statistical pattern of overshooting an expected numerical target. This process differs from cases involving overextending standard or "correct" forms by using them in the wrong grammatical contexts (e.g. *She is a person whom reads a lot.*) which is also called hypercorrection. At this stage the change still operates from below and speakers do not make conscious adjustments in their usage of it.

Eventually the change spreads beyond the original group, first to neighboring groups within the social spectrum and later to the speech community as a whole. This does not imply that all social groups employ the innovative forms with the same frequency. The subgroup in which the change originated will continue to lead the process as shown, for example, in the common curvilinear class distribution discussed in the previous chapter. At this stage speakers may remain unaware of the variation at a conscious level, but they do adjust their usage by contextual style. In Labov's terms, such a variable operates as a "marker," and the consistent pattern of style shifting across all groups demonstrates that the variable has developed into a community norm.

Complications arise as an innovative usage becomes more firmly established in a speech community. The scenario described thus far is one of "change from below," in which the innovation spreads in the absence of conscious awareness. In some cases, speakers come to take more notice of the variation related to such changes. This may lead to a stigmatization of the innovative usage led by the highest status group, those at the upper end of the socioeconomic ladder. Here we might find speakers across the social spectrum making "a sporadic and irregular correction of the changed forms towards the model of the highest status group – that is, the prestige model" (1972b, p. 179). The evidence of this phenomenon can be found in patterns of stylistic variation where use of innovative forms drops off in careful speech. Labov calls such behavior "hypercorrection from above." It serves as a driving force in "change from above" and seems to be especially characteristic of the lower middle class as noted in Chapter Six (see also Labov, 1972b, chapter 5). In the case of change from below, such hypercorrection serves as a kind of backlash that may stall the progress of the change. If the stigma associated with a change becomes extreme, the variable may develop into a "stereotype," a usage that is the subject of overt comment, and may eventually disappear from the community.

Of course not every change meets with such resistance. Many innovations that begin as changes from below proceed through a speech community and eventually come to represent the new stable norm. In the later stages of a change, social differences begin to even out as those groups who lagged behind catch up and the innovative forms achieve near categorical usage by all members of the speech community.

The overall course of language change often follows the pattern depicted in Figure 7.2. This is the well-known S-shaped curve that models a wide variety of changes, linguistic and otherwise. This model depicts the progress of change over time in a way that is consistent with Labov's description.[4] In the early stages, use of innovative forms catches on slowly and remains limited to certain segments of a population. At some point, however, the change experiences a rapid increase in its adoption and usage levels rise quickly. In the later stages the rate of adoption again slows, but eventually the change reaches completion.

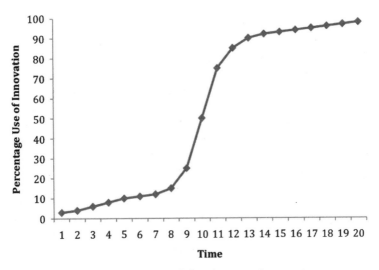

FIGURE 7.2 *The S-shaped curve of the adoption of innovations.*

How do changes spread? Social factors

The life cycle of change that Labov describes provides a road map for researchers exploring ongoing changes. It offers helpful diagnostics for determining the status of potential changes such as the presence or absence of stylistic variation. Still, it leaves open many central questions about the process. We may wonder, for example, how an innovative form comes to be an indicator of some subgroup in the early stages of change and why that usage spreads beyond the membership of that subgroup. Answers to the former question probably depend greatly on circumstances particular to each change. For example, the centralization of diphthongs on Martha's Vineyard involves a pronunciation variable that had been a minority feature of local speech for several generations before its usage accelerated in the twentieth century.

With regard to the second question, however, we might expect some generalizable description of the factors driving a change's spread through the community. Labov's treatment here remains rather vague. Thus, in describing the expansion of change, he notes "To the extent that the values of the original subgroup were adopted by other groups in the speech community, the sound change with its associated value of group membership spread to these adopting groups" (1972b, p. 178). Labov may have in mind cultural values similar to those implicated in his conception of "covert prestige" – notions like toughness and belonging to the local community (see Chapter Six) – but this connection is not made explicit.

Labov does have much more to say with regard to social profile of those people who drive the progress of language change. Much of the discussion of social factors in the previous chapter bears on this issue. Thus, we have noted that changes in progress tend to be dominated by women more than men. We also observed in the common curvilinear class pattern that speakers from the interior of the social scale, typically the upper working class, tend to lead language changes. Looking beyond such demographic characterizations, Labov has argued that leaders of change often occupy an unusual position in terms of their social networks. They function as central players in their local (neighborhood) groups – the kinds of people that everyone on the block knows and respects – but their friendship ties connect them to other networks as well.

To explore the mechanism behind such findings, Labov looks to the research literature from sociology and communication studies on how changes in opinions and cultural practices spread (see 2001b, pp. 356–63). He finds an especially strong parallel to linguistic change in fashion choices. Studies in this area have identified a two-step process of influence. Mass-media campaigns do not affect the majority of people directly. Rather, innovations (e.g. new fashions) must first be adopted by local opinion leaders, and it is these influential people who inspire others to join in. Interestingly, the social profile of the fashion leaders bears a number of similarities to that of the leaders of language change. Both types of leaders tend to be women who represent the middle ranks of the class scale and who have strong ties within their local communities as well as beyond.

Labov fills out his profile of the leaders of change by considering personality traits. The communication indexes he developed for the Philadelphia project (see Chapter Six) offer some insight when interpreted from this perspective. For example, we might read the question about how many people on the block one might say hello to, have coffee with, and so on, as a measure of gregariousness. Labov pursues this issue further by exploring the personal histories and attitudes of several individuals found to be in the avant-garde of sound change in Philadelphia.

One of the most memorable of these individuals is a woman named Celeste, who was interviewed several times over a period of 17 years.[5] Many of the stories Celeste recounted in her interviews contribute to a picture of her as an outgoing, strong-willed person who is not afraid to speak her mind. For example, she grew up in a traditional Italian family headed by a controlling father, but she notes that, as a teenager, she regularly defied her father by sneaking out for dates. In adulthood she clearly has assumed a leadership role in the neighborhood, and she offers many stories of how she organizes community efforts, such as taking up collections for flowers when someone passes away. On the basis of Celeste's case and others, Labov summarizes the characteristic leaders of change:

[T]hey are women who have achieved a respected social and economic position in the local networks. As adolescents, they aligned themselves with the social groups and symbols that resisted adult authority, particularly when it was perceived as unfairly or unjustly administered, without deviating from their upwardly mobile path within the local social structure. (2001b, p. 409)

This social profile sketches common personality and other traits of the leaders, but we should be careful in considering the connection of such traits to linguistic behavior. Speech does not operate at the same level of conscious control as does fashion or many other cultural practices. We wouldn't want to say that participating in a sound change directly represents the kind of resistance to authority that we find in Celeste's personal history. Rather, Labov suggests that the profile of the leaders of change typifies someone with a particular kind of "social trajectory," one that brings them in contact with a wide range of people who might shape their speech habits in their formative years and one that drives them to positions of influence within their local networks as adults (2001b, pp. 409–10). In this way they come to serve as the crucial intermediaries in the two-step flow of communication by which innovations diffuse.

How do changes spread? Linguistic mechanisms

Labov's variationist methodology, with its sampling from a wide spectrum of a speech community, opens windows on the social forces that shape the course of language change, but it also allows a fresh perspective on the linguistic dimensions of the process. One of the most significant demonstrations of the value of Labov's approach in this regard comes in his investigation of how sound change advances through the structure of a language. This issue lies at the heart of the transition and embedding problems described above. At one time a sound is pronounced in a certain manner in all the words that contain it, and later that sound has a different pronunciation in all (or some) of those words. What happens in between these stages? How is the new pronunciation carried through the language?

This question has fueled a long-standing debate within historical linguistics about the basic unit of sound change. Does change operate on words or on phonemes?[6] In other words, when an innovation occurs, does it spread from word to word or does it affect all instances of the phoneme equally, without regard for the words containing them?

The traditional view holds that sound change works at the level of the phoneme. Bloomfield summarizes this position by noting that "sound-change is merely a change in the speaker's manner of producing phonemes and accordingly affects a phoneme at every occurrence, regardless of the nature of any particular linguistic form in which the phoneme happens to occur" (1933/1984, p. 353). The development of this claim is commonly attributed to the Neogrammarians, a group of nineteenth-century scholars who devoted much of their efforts to exploring historical relations within the Indo-European language family. For the Neogrammarians and others tracing genetic connections among languages, evidence of the regularity of sound change abounded. When we compare related languages, we find consistent patterns of correspondence between sounds. For example, a /t/ in English commonly corresponds to a /d/ in Latin (e.g. *tooth*/*dens*; *two*/*duo*; *eat*/*edere*). We interpret such evidence as stemming from the fact that words like English *tooth* and Latin *dens* come from the same source in their shared parent language (Proto-Indo-European). Whatever sound the words originally had later developed into a /t/ in English and a /d/ in Latin. If sound change didn't operate across the board, modifying each instance of a phoneme, but rather every word developed on its own, these kinds of correspondences wouldn't appear. The outcome of sound change would be more a matter of random chance. Thus, we might find that the original sound appears as a /t/ in some words but a /d/ in others and maybe a /p/ or a /k/ in still others, all within a single descendant language.

As it happens, exceptions to sound change do occur, but they tend to be shaped by phonological effects. Thus, a phoneme might develop one way when it appears at the beginning of a word but another way when it appears at the end or in the interior. Indeed, these hardly count as exceptions to the regularity of sound change; they're really just a fine-tuning of the description of when a change applied. However, it is crucial to note that rules describing a sound change traditionally take into account only phonological factors such as position in a word, which other sounds occur next to the changing sound, and so on. Other factors such as the meaning or grammatical function of the words containing the changing phoneme do not factor into the equation.

This Neogrammarian view of sound change envisioned the process as phonetically gradual but lexically[7] abrupt. Changes operate over fairly long terms and develop in small steps. But each step affects all instances of a phoneme at the same time, and thus applies to the entire word stock containing that phoneme. Incidentally, this presumed phonetic gradualness also factors into the traditional dismissal of the possibility of studying changes in progress. Change was felt to proceed slowly and by imperceptible degrees, making the process unobservable until it had gone to completion.

During the 1970s, challenges to Neogrammarian conceptions of sound change began to coalesce around a radically different view. One of the leading scholars in the development of this alternative view was William Wang. Based initially on material from the history of Chinese, Wang demonstrated that sound changes do not always carry through the entire word stock of a language. Instead he cites examples suggesting that a particular change may be interrupted and may affect some of the words containing the original sound, but not all of those words. Importantly, there was no phonological distinction between the changed words and the unchanged words. In other words, whether the change applied or not seemed to have no basis in the surrounding phonological context of the original sound. As we just noted, the Neogrammarian view of change has difficulty accounting for such phonologically random outcomes.

Wang interpreted such cases as evidence that sound change did not apply simultaneously across the board, but rather spread from word to word. This view came to be known as "lexical diffusion." As the converse of the Neogrammarian position, it posited that the process of sound change was phonetically abrupt but lexically gradual. Thus, when a change is underway, it involves the substitution of one pronunciation for another, with a perceptible phonetic difference between those pronunciations. But the new pronunciation appears at first in a subset of words and expands its range over time. Often the change proceeds through all the words of the language containing the relevant sound and no lexical exceptions appear. In such cases, the outcome of lexical diffusion would be identical to that of Neogrammarian change.

As you can imagine, this debate is one that can benefit greatly from methods designed to investigate the change process while it is active. Labov first took up the issues in a 1981 paper in *Language*, the premier journal for American linguistics, and expanded his discussion in the first volume of his *Principles of Linguistic Change* (1994). Looking to examples of ongoing sound changes from his Philadelphia study and others, Labov finds evidence consistent with both proposed processes. Some changes appear to proceed as predicted by the Neogrammarian model while others seem to be driven by lexical diffusion.

One of the examples Labov explores involves the vowels /u/ and /o/. Traditionally, these vowels are articulated with a retracted tongue position; that is, with the back of the tongue raised slightly toward the back of the roof of the mouth. In Philadelphia (and in many other dialects of English) these vowels participate in changes that produce a more fronted articulation (i.e. the tongue moves forward in the mouth). Labov tracked the progress of these changes in minute phonetic detail using acoustic measurements. I have more to say about this methodology below, but here we might simply note that acoustic analysis allows the researcher to measure precisely various aspects of the speech signal. In the cases of /u/ and /o/, this analysis revealed that Philadelphians pronounce the vowels with varying degrees of fronting. When the acoustic measurements are plotted graphically, they show a continuous distribution from front to back. This picture is consistent with the kind of phonetic gradualness inherent in the Neogrammarian model of sound change. The changes to these vowels do not involve an alternation between two or more discrete pronunciations.

Furthermore, the fronting of /u/ and /o/ seems to proceed with no regard for the meaning or grammatical category of the words containing the vowels. Labov does find clear differences in the degree of fronting between certain sets of words – for example, *too* tends to be fronted more extremely than *tool* – but these differences reflect distinct phonological contexts. Some environments favor the change and others disfavor it, but these conditioning patterns are definable in phonological, not lexical, terms. This issue lies at the heart of the debate between Neogrammarian change and lexical diffusion. Does the progress of a change depend on its phonological environment or on the words containing the sound? To test this question directly, Labov examines pairs of homonyms in the speech of an active participant in the changes. He compared the degrees of fronting of dozens of examples of the pairs *too* and *two* and *know* and *no*, and his statistical analysis revealed no significant difference between the homonyms. It appears, therefore, that these changes apply equally across a phonological context regardless of the particular lexical item containing that context, just as the Neogrammarian view predicts.

Labov finds a very different pattern of change in the case of "short *a*" in Philadelphia. This label describes the vowel of *bat* and *bad* that is traditionally pronounced as the low front [æ]. In many parts of the US, however, we hear alternative pronunciations of this vowel involving raised forms such that *bad* might sound something like *bed* or even *bid*. This raising operates as an active sound change in Philadelphia (as in New York City), but it takes a course very different from the one seen with /u/ and /o/. For one thing, raising of /æ/ seems to result in phonetically discrete pronunciations. Labov demonstrates this pattern with acoustic data which show that raised examples are clearly separated from unraised examples in vowel space.

The question of which factors govern the change also distinguishes the short *a* case from that of /u/ and /o/. We need not bother here with the details, which are quite complex, as we note simply that the raising of /æ/ seems to reflect both phonological and non-phonological conditioning. Labov shows that Philadelphians never produce the raised variants in certain phonological contexts. For example, /æ/ remains low when followed by a voiceless stop consonant, as in *bat* and *tap*. On the other hand, the raised forms are used almost universally when the vowel appears before a nasal consonant as in *ham* or *ban*. Of particular relevance to the issue at hand is the evidence that phonological conditions cannot completely account for the observed patterns. For example, raising does not generally apply when a voiced /d/ follows the vowel, as in *sad* or *fad*, but three /d/-words stand as exceptions: *mad*, *bad*, and *glad* do undergo raising. Similarly, we find exceptions to the use of raised pronunciations next to nasal consonants in the case of past-tense forms of strong verbs like *ran*, *began*, and *swam*, in which only the low vowel occurs. We even have indications of a homonymic pair being distinguished since the /æ/ in the noun *can* (e.g. *tin can*) illustrates raising while the vowel in the auxiliary verb *can* (e.g. *we can*) remains low. Labov concludes that the observed patterns result from lexical diffusion.

Drawing on these and other examples of sound changes in many languages, Labov puts forward a general account of the difference between Neogrammarian change and lexical diffusion. He suggests that certain kinds of sound changes travel through a language via the former process and other kinds via the latter. His proposal relies on the fact that phonemes operate as members of classes and subclasses, which reflect elements of the pronunciation as well as their distribution in the language (e.g. which positions in a word a sound can occupy). Thus all languages make a primary distinction between vowels and consonants, and languages like English divide vowels into subclasses of tense (or "long") and lax (or "short"). The English tense vowels include those in *boot* and *boat*, while the lax vowels include those in *book* and *bit*. These subclasses differ in various ways that need not concern us at the moment. What's important for Labov's proposal is that a change like the raising of short *a* in Philadelphia represents a change from one subclass (lax vowels) to another (tense vowels). By contrast, with a change like the fronting of /u/ and /o/, the classification does not change – these remain tense vowels – and only their phonetic ranges shift.

Labov predicts that the changes across subsystems, such as substituting one class of vowel for another, will rely on lexical diffusion while changes within a subsystem, such as gradually altering the articulation of a phoneme, will proceed according to regular, Neogrammarian change. Underlying this contrast, Labov suggests, are distinct kinds of phonological rules: "We have located Neogrammarian regularity in low-level output rules, [which specify the articulation of sounds,] and lexical diffusion in the redistribution of an abstract word class into other abstract word classes" (1994, pp. 541–2). In this way he provides support for both views of the mechanism driving sound change and, more importantly, posits an account of why some changes will proceed via one and some changes via the other.

General patterns of sound change

One of Labov's strengths as a scholar lies in his ability to see beyond the particulars of the situations he studies and to formulate generalizations from his observations. We've seen illustrations of this tendency in his consideration of social influences as, for example, in his statements about differences between men and women in situations of language change (see Chapter Six), and his work on Neogrammarian change versus lexical diffusion illustrates the same basic approach applied to broader characterizations of linguistic patterns. In line with the latter focus on language-internal dynamics of sound change, Labov has dedicated a good deal of his research attention to two common types of change: mergers and chain shifts.

A merger occurs when the distinction between two phonemes is lost, when two formerly separate sounds become one. Mergers take place quite commonly, and historical linguists have documented them in the history of languages all over the world. Labov has explored the phenomenon of merger in active changes. One of the most significant of these mergers in progress for North American dialects of English involves the loss of the distinction between the /ɑ/ of *cot, tock*, and *Don* and the /ɔ/ of *caught, talk*, and *dawn*, known as the "*cot/caught* merger." This change has been well established in some regions (e.g. eastern New England, Canada) for at least half a century, but it appears to be spreading rapidly in other areas (e.g. the western US).

Returning to a theme introduced earlier in this chapter, Labov's work on mergers illustrates the ways that variationist methods can bring a new perspective to the study of traditional topics. Exploring mergers in progress allows for a more detailed view of the mechanisms at work. In light of the previous discussion, for example, we might wonder whether mergers operate by lexical diffusion or regular Neogrammarian change. As it happens, examples of both types appear in the sociolinguistic literature. Some mergers rely on a word-by-word recategorization from one phoneme class to another, a process known as "merger by transfer." Other mergers involve the kind of phonetically gradual shifts associated with Neogrammarian-style change, illustrating "merger by approximation" (see Labov, 1994, p. 321). The *cot/caught* merger generally operates in this latter fashion. A change of this type raises further questions about how the phonemes actually come together. Does the *cot/caught* merger, for example, result from a movement of the *cot* vowel up into the space of the *caught* vowel, or from the movement of the *caught* vowel down into the *cot* vowel's territory? Alternatively, both vowels might shift toward each other and meet somewhere in between.[8] Studying active changes through recordings of actual speech makes possible fine-grained phonetic analysis, which allows the researcher to test which of the various scenarios applies. Work by Labov and others finds evidence in support of all these possibilities. In fact,

FIGURE 7.3 *Chain shifting illustrated.*

the *cot/caught* merger seems to be carried out in different ways in different regions. Sometimes the resulting merged pronunciation resembles the original *cot* and sometimes *caught*, and still other times it sounds like something intermediate between the two.

Labov's methods have also proven fruitful in the examination of chain shifts. The term "chain shift" describes a coordinated series of changes in which a shift in the pronunciation of the first sound spurs a phonetic adjustment by the second. Thus the changes represent a kind of chain reaction. Figure 7.3 represents the process abstractly. In this simple scenario, sound A enters the phonetic space occupied by B, and B leaves that space. Linguists normally differentiate between two types of chain shifts depending on the timing of the changes. If the chain begins with A moving into B's space causing B to abandon its home territory, then it illustrates a "push chain." If, however, the process begins with B vacating the space which spurs A to shift, then we have a "drag (or pull) chain." The distinction between these types is not original to Labov. Much like mergers, chain shifts have long been known to historical linguists. For example, scholars of the history of English commonly cite the Great Vowel Shift as an example of chain shifting.

Labov and others engaged in the study of sound change in progress have identified many examples of chain shifts. For example, in the Great Lakes region of the US a pattern known as the Northern Cities Shift is heard. This shift affects the pronunciation of six vowels, as shown in Figure 7.4. The vowel symbols in this diagram are placed according to their positions in vowel space, which represents the position of the tongue, and the arrows denote the directions each vowel shifts toward. The coordination implied by the chain-shift model seems clear when the changes of the Northern Cities Shift are plotted in this way. Labov suggests that the Shift began with the movement of /æ/ (as in *bat*), which prompted a drag chain from /ɑ/ (as in *box*), which in turn dragged /ɔ/ (as in *bought*) down. Later shifting of /ɛ/ (as in *bet*) put pressure on /ʌ/ (as in *but*), resulting in a push chain. The backing of /ɪ/ (as in *bit*) seems to come last and may represent a direct parallel to the shifting of /ɛ/ (see Labov, 2010, p. 112).

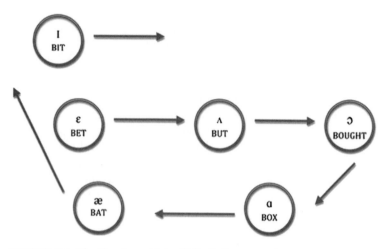

FIGURE 7.4 *The Northern Cities Shift (following Labov, 2010, p. 15).*

Labov has drawn on examples of active changes like the Northern Cities Shift, together with examples from the historical record like the Great Vowel Shift, in order to formulate general principles describing how vowels change during a chain shift. He notes, for example, that some types of vowels tend to rise and other tend to fall in vowel space during chain shifts (see 1994, p. 116). From the perspective of the general issues outlined by Weinreich et al. (1968), this work relates to the constraints problem as Labov wrestles with notions of what is and isn't possible in a vowel shift.

   Chain shifts and mergers have relevance to a number of central issues in the study of sound change, none more fundamental than the question of why language changes; and Labov has brought his insights to bear on this question. His discussion focuses on the causes and consequences of these changes from a functional perspective. In essence, he pursues the question of whether the communicative function of language plays a role in the course of sound change. We can appreciate why chain shifts and mergers might figure in this discussion if we consider the repercussions of such changes. A merger results in the loss of a phonemic distinction, which means that some words that previously had different sounds will now have the same sound. On the other hand, a chain shift preserves the contrasts between the shifting sounds, and indeed the basic model (as well as representations of shifts like those presented above) can make it tempting to interpret the process as fundamentally driven by concerns about maintaining distinctions. In fact, one of the pioneers in the exploration of chain shifting, André Martinet (1952), offered an account of the process that explicitly appealed to such motivations. Labov, by contrast, proposes an alternative account that is very much in keeping with his general skepticism about functionalist explanations.[9] To his mind, sound change operates by mechanical principles and not by concerns about preserving or maximizing the capacity of a language to convey information (see 1994, chapter 19, for a summary of his argument). In support of this view he notes that mergers – despite their destruction of phonological contrast – occur with great frequency, probably even more commonly that chain shifts. Moreover, he presents anecdotal and experimental evidence that both of these kinds of sound change result in misunderstandings within and across dialect regions (see 2010, chapters 2 and 3).

It appears, therefore, that many sound changes not only do not enhance the communicative function of language, but may actually threaten this function. Lest we conclude from such evidence that change represents a purely destructive force, Labov reminds us that communication is but one function of language (2010, p. 371). Sociolinguistic research provides ample evidence of the fact that we do much more with language than simply transmit information to others. Thus, while an innovative pronunciation might increase the potential for certain kinds of miscommunication, it clearly serves social and other functions that adopters of the change find valuable.

The Atlas of North American English

Beginning in the 1990s, Labov took his work on sound changes in a new direction by exploring the phonological landscape of the entire English-speaking continent. He directed a survey of sound patterns across the US and Canada that resulted in *The Atlas of North American English* (ANAE), a large-format volume bursting with over 120 maps charting the results (Labov et al., 2006). At first glance it might seem ironic to describe this style of work as a "new" direction given its obvious similarities to the dialect geography tradition (see Chapter Two). After all, dialectologists have engaged in the same tracking of the distribution of usages across large regions for well over a century, and they even publish their work in linguistic atlases.

Closer examination reveals, however, that Labov's approach to regional dialectology very much reflects the priorities of sociolinguistics. We see this most clearly in the kinds of linguistic phenomena Labov and his team explore in the ANAE project. Whereas traditional dialectologists generally tracked the retention of older forms – for example, the survival of Dutch words like *cruller* and *stoop* in areas of Dutch settlement like the Hudson Valley – ANAE concentrates on recent and ongoing sound changes including the *cot/caught* merger and the Northern Cities Shift mentioned earlier. This emphasis on change in progress led Labov to a methodology that further distinguishes this work from the older dialect geography approach. Rather than NORMs (non-mobile, older, rural males), Labov sought to survey a more diverse sample of people. The team interviewed a total of 762 speakers ranging in age from 12 to 89. They focused almost exclusively on urban areas, recording at least two people from every city with a population over 50,000 and more people from large metropolitan centers like Chicago and Atlanta. The ANAE sample was skewed in favor of women (480 female participants to 282 males) and relatively younger speakers (462 of the 762 were aged 20–40 years). This bias was introduced intentionally to provide the most detailed picture of those people expected to represent the vanguard of sound change.

ANAE's separation from its dialect-geographical roots appears even stronger in their techniques for data collection and analysis. First, Labov and his team relied on modified versions of the sociolinguistic interview to gather the speech samples. Interviews were carried out over the telephone, which saved much time and expense over traditional fieldwork. For some of the linguistic features the analysis relied on auditory coding. Thus, to determine whether a person has the *cot/caught* merger, the researcher listens carefully to the pronunciation of relevant words and transcribes what he or she hears. Most of the findings, however, derive from acoustic analysis.

Acoustic phonetics examines speech as sound waves using a variety of tools. Spectrographic analysis has proven especially valuable in this regard as it provides a visual representation of the speech signal. The researcher can then measure with great precision various dimensions of the signal. A full treatment of this topic lies outside the scope of the present discussion.[10] I focus here on how Labov and others apply acoustic analysis to the study of vowels.

We produce vowels by shaping our mouths in various ways so that the sound created by forcing air from the lungs and through the larynx (voice-box) resonates. The frequencies at which the sound waves resonate relate to the size of the cavities we create in the vocal tract by opening our mouths, rounding our lips, moving the tongue back and forth, and so on. Spectrographically, the resonances associated with vowels appear as horizontal bands of energy called "formants." The first two formants, abbreviated F1 and F2, have proven especially useful because they correlate closely with the traditional articulatory dimensions used to differentiate vowels. The first formant, F1, corresponds to vowel height and the second formant, F2, corresponds to frontness. Thus, by measuring F1 and F2, researchers can plot the positions of vowels in phonetic space. This technique offers a precise way of comparing the effects of sound changes across individual speakers, as illustrated in Figure 7.5. These diagrams offer a view of the vowel spaces of two ANAE subjects: James W., a 78-year-old from Chicago, Illinois and Martha F., a 28-year-old from Kenosha, Wisconsin. Several examples of words containing each of the six vowels shown in the diagrams were analyzed and their F1 and F2 frequencies were measured. What's plotted here are the average F1 and F2 values calculated by the ANAE researchers.

The vowels shown are those involved in the Northern Cities Shift, and we can see evidence of the Shift in both of these speakers' vowel spaces. James W. appears to represent an early stage in the Shift. He has raised /æ/ but the other vowels appear in roughly their standard positions. Martha F., however, seems more advanced in the Shift. Her /æ/ appears quite raised, she has fronted /ɑ/, and her /ɔ/ seems to have lowered. Also her /ɛ/, /ɪ/, and /ʌ/ appear to have shifted toward the back of vowel space. With a difference of 50 years between these speakers, we have an apparent-time illustration of this change in progress.

Labov pioneered the use of acoustic analysis in the study of sociolinguistic variation several decades ago. He incorporated spectrographic measurements in his Martha's Vineyard study (1963),

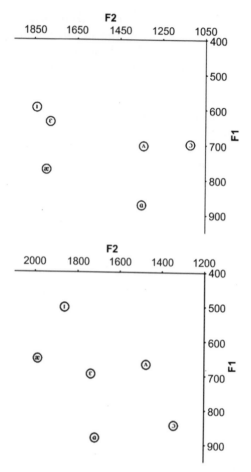

FIGURE 7.5 *Average F1 and F2 values for the vowels of the Northern Cities Shift in the speech of* (a) *James W., age 78, and* (b) *Martha F., age 28 (based on Labov et al., 2006, pp. 198–9).*

but the landmark report *A Quantitative Study of Sound Change in Progress* (Labov et al., 1972) offered a fuller demonstration of the fruitfulness of these techniques. In those early days, the analysis relied on specialized machinery and the measuring had to be done by hand. In the last 20 years or so, software has been developed, making spectrographic analysis possible on personal computers and incorporating instrumental means of measurements.

Labov and his collaborators on the ANAE used formant frequency data and other kinds of acoustic analysis to explore phonetic variation in broad regional terms. They tracked the geographical ranges of several widespread features, and also identified a number of more localized patterns. As an illustration of the former, they showed the reach of the Northern Cities Shift to stretch from western New England across the Great Lakes region and westward into states like Minnesota. The *cot/caught* merger is found to have an even wider influence. From earlier research by dialect geographers (e.g. Kurath and McDavid, 1961) we knew that the merger had taken root in eastern New England (e.g. Boston) and western Pennsylvania (e.g. Pittsburgh). ANAE revealed, however, the spread of the merger across a large span of the West and also showed that it is gaining ground in parts of the South.

From findings like these, the ANAE produced a new – or perhaps it's more accurate to say updated – picture of the regional dialects of North American English. In terms of its broader impact, the ANAE's findings serve as a clear counterweight to the popular belief in the homogenization of American English. Many people assume that regional speech differences are dying out, having been leveled due to improved mobility, the standardizing influence of the broadcast media, or other developments of the last half century. ANAE shows that not only are regional dialects not melting away, but that their differences are actually being reinforced by recent innovations.

One of the more intriguing dimensions of the ANAE results is how closely they parallel earlier research by dialect geographers. The boundaries between dialects drawn by ANAE (see Labov et al., 2006, p. 148) bear a striking resemblance to those established in the mid-twentieth century by Hans Kurath and other dialectologists (see Figure 2.3). This is surprising when we recall that those boundaries were determined on the basis of very different types of people and linguistic features. Labov and his colleagues read these similarities as reflecting "the enduring influence of the original regional patterns of the settlement of English-speaking North America" (Labov et al., 2006, p. 303). In this way, we might take the linguistic patterns as indicative of broader cultural differences that were shaped by the earliest settlers and continue to manifest in patterns of communication, constructions of regional identities, and so forth.[11]

Conclusion

The fundamental fact that languages change presents something of a challenge to traditional conceptions of linguistic structure as dependent on absolute regularity and homogeneity. As we saw in Chapter Four, Weinreich et al. (1968) identified this conflict in the dominant paradigm of the day:

> After all, if a language has to be structured in order to function efficiently, how do people continue to talk while the language changes, that is, while it passes through periods of lessened systematicity? Alternatively, if overriding pressures do force a language to change, and if communication is less efficient in the interim (as would deductively follow from the theory), why have such inefficiencies not been observed in practice? (pp. 100–1)

When we accept the idea that variation is a normal, even necessary, characteristic of language, the ubiquity of linguistic change becomes less perplexing and we can focus on understanding the relationship between the variation observed at a single point in time and the longer-term diachronic trends. Labov's research record teems with evidence of the fruitfulness of this approach. He has blazed new trails by exploring the social embedding of linguistic changes and painting a picture of the pivotal players in their advancement through and across speech communities. He has also made major contributions to our understanding of the linguistic dimensions of the change process, offering, for example, empirical confirmation that sound change can spread either by lexical diffusion or in a regular, Neogrammarian fashion.

Labov's many and varied contributions here all flow from his refinement of the theory and methods for studying language change in progress. This approach has provided a new perspective on the change process and has also led to a much richer description of the inner workings of that process. Many historical linguists have recognized the value of the sociolinguistic exploration of change in progress, and a fruitful scholarly dialogue has developed between these subfields.

Notes

1   Labov commonly credits Louis Gauchat as a pioneer in the study of
    sound change in progress though Gauchat's work drew on qualitative
    descriptions of usage. Gauchat compared generations of French
    speakers in the Swiss Village of Charmey around the turn of the
    twentieth century and described several ongoing innovations. His
    inferences were confirmed by follow-up research carried out 25 years
    later (see Labov, 1994, pp. 85–6, 2006, p. 12).

2   Eckert (1997) offers more discussion of the linguistic consequences of
    different stages in life (see also Milroy and Gordon, 2003, pp. 35–9).

3   In recent decades many scholars have collected enormous databases
    of written texts from the history of English and other languages.
    These databases have been digitized and allow researchers to trace
    linguistic developments in much greater detail than was possible with
    traditional methods (see Chapter Nine).

4   Labov frames the basic mechanisms underlying the S-shaped curve
    in terms of communication networks and rates of contact among
    innovative and conservative speakers (see 1994, pp. 65–7).

5   Labov notes that the fieldworker Anne Bower developed a deep rapport
    with Celeste over the years, and the recordings resemble a conversation
    between friends much more than an interview (2001b, p. 386).

6   In Chapter Two, I discuss the basic concept of the phoneme. Briefly,
    linguists define "phoneme" as a distinctive category of sound in a
    language. A phoneme serves as an abstract type of sound that may
    vary in its actual articulation. For example, native speakers of English
    consider *fan* and *fad* to have the same vowel sound, but actually the
    /æ/ of *fan* is pronounced with nasalization as some air flows through
    the nasal cavity during its articulation while the air flows only
    through the mouth for the vowel of *fad*.

7   Linguists refer to the word stock of a language as its "lexicon" and
    things related to this aspect of language as "lexical."

8   As another possibility, the distinction could be lost by both vowels
    expanding their traditional ranges in vowel space to produce a
    complete overlap. This relatively rare situation is known as "merger
    by expansion" (see Labov, 1994, pp. 321–3).

9   Labov's account of chain shifting relies on the notion of "probability
    matching," a phenomenon by which humans and other animals
    adjust their behavior unconsciously to match the frequencies of
    events in their environments (see Labov, 1994, pp. 580–3).

10 For an introduction to this area of study see Thomas (2011).

11 Labov explores the cultural history related to many of the major dialect divisions in his 2010 book. He has also developed theories of how linguistic features like the Northern Cities Shift spread geographically. In this work he has drawn special attention to the differences between transmission of changes across generations of inhabitants of a single community and diffusion of changes from one community to another by means of contact between adult speakers (see 2007 and 2010).

CHAPTER EIGHT

African American English: Lessons learned, lessons taught

In popular conception, language works as a vehicle for transmitting information from one mind to another. In this way language serves a practical function; it is a tool for communication. Therefore, we shouldn't expect people to care much about any particular linguistic tool as long as the one chosen can get the job done. But here we start to see the limitations of such a narrow conception of what language does. Language provides a system for making meaning (of various kinds), but it also means something to its users. The author Toni Morrison described what language means to her and many other African Americans in a 1981 interview:

> [Language] is the thing that black people love so much – the saying of words, holding them on the tongue, experimenting with them, playing with them. It's a love, a passion. Its function is like a preacher's: to make you stand up out of your seat, make you lose yourself and hear yourself. The worst of all possible things that could happen would be to lose that language. There are certain things I cannot say without recourse to my language. It's terrible to think that a child with five different present tenses comes to

school . . . to be told things about his language, which is him, that are sometimes permanently damaging. (quoted in Rickford and Rickford, 2000, pp. 4–5)

Morrison is speaking not about language in general, but about the patterns of speech associated with African Americans. As we'll see, her eloquent expression of the value of African American language marks a sharp contrast with the harsh treatment it receives in mainstream culture and some academic circles.

Labov's scholarly engagement with African American English began with his dissertation project – several African Americans were included in the survey of the Lower East Side – but took the main stage when he turned his attention uptown. The study of south Harlem (Labov et al., 1968) explored a wide range of phonological and grammatical features of African American speech, but it also sought a better sense of the social context in which those speech forms thrived. Looking back on this work, Labov described it as "one of the most fascinating intellectual and social adventures of my life" (1997a).

This research shaped Labov's thinking on a number of critical issues. The methodological challenges and rewards of working with the Harlem adolescents led him to refine his concept of the vernacular as an element of stylistic variation (see Chapter Five). The theoretical puzzles posed by the complex grammatical patterns observed with "copula deletion" – where the linking verb *be* is omitted (e.g. *He __ happy.*) – inspired Labov's development of variable rules (Labov, 1969; see also Chapter Four). His experience is not unique. In the decades since the pioneering work in Harlem, the dialect spoken by many African Americans has inspired countless studies and today represents one of the most productive areas of research within the variationist paradigm.

Without a doubt this research has generated insights of tremendous value within linguistics, but it has also proceeded with higher purposes in mind. Misperceptions about nonstandard speech patterns including those associated with African Americans abound and often have real consequences for users of these speech varieties. Fighting such ignorance has motivated many linguists, and certainly Labov has stood in the vanguard of such efforts.

This chapter reviews Labov's engagement with linguistic and social issues related to the language of the African American speech community. His work in this area highlights a side of his career that we have only glimpsed previously in this book. He entered linguistics with a goal of changing how scholars think about language, hoping to demonstrate the value of studying the everyday speech of ordinary people. In Labov's work on African American speech, we find this goal expanded as he has endeavored to shape perceptions well beyond the community of scholars.

What is African American (Vernacular) English?

Before delving into Labov's work related to the speech of African Americans, some preliminary remarks will provide a useful orientation for readers with only a general sense of the dialect. The distinctiveness of various aspects of African American language has long been noted. It has been represented, and often parodied, in literature and other areas of popular culture since the early days of the United States. Formal academic study of African American speech took off in the twentieth century, led, not surprisingly, by dialectologists (e.g. McDavid and McDavid, 1951). The rise of sociolinguistics in the 1960s brought renewed interest in the speech patterns as well as broader issues related to African American language.

Labels for this distinctive variety of English have evolved along with those for the people associated with it. The term "Nonstandard Negro English" that appeared in early studies gave way to "Black English Vernacular" (or "Black Vernacular English") in the 1970s and 1980s. Eventually that too gave way to "African American Vernacular English" or AAVE.[1] Many scholars today prefer "African American English," as a general label. Labov sees the latter as appropriate for referencing the "wide range of grammatical and phonological features" in the speech of African Americans, but he uses "African American Vernacular English" to designate "the geographically uniform grammar found in low-income areas of high residential segregation" (2010, p. 348).[2] This usage is in keeping with his theories on stylistic variation where "vernacular" describes a particular variety that occupies the end of a continuum opposite the standard language (see Chapter Five). I will use "African American Vernacular English" or AAVE throughout this chapter since that term predominates in Labov's writing on the subject.

Definitionally, AAVE clearly constitutes a social dialect of American English. It has received more scholarly attention than any other social dialect in the US, and for good reason. While AAVE shares many phonological and grammatical features with other dialects, most notably with southern white speech, it also involves usages that are more exclusive. For example, in many dialects of English around the world, *ain't* is used in contexts where Standard English would use a negated form of *have* or *be* (e.g. *We ain't seen him.* ~ *We haven't seen him*; *He ain't here.* ~ *He isn't here.*). These usages appear in AAVE as well, but speakers of this dialect may also use *ain't* where others would use *didn't* (e.g. *We ain't go.* ~ *We didn't go.*), something not found in most other varieties.

Linguists have documented a long list of features found in AAVE. Among those that Labov has investigated or frequently references are the following:

- Reduction of final consonant clusters: When two or more consonants appear at the end of a word, one might be dropped. This occurs in all varieties of English, but appears to follow somewhat different rules in AAVE (e.g. *wes' side*; *wes' end*).

- Copula deletion: the absence of *is* or *are* when functioning as a linking verb or auxiliary (e.g. *He hungry now*; *We working late*).

- Habitual *be*: the verb *be*, in its uninflected form, may mark an event or situation that occurs regularly (e.g. *We be working late.* This usage denotes a regular situation that might be conveyed by Standard English *We are always working late.*)

- Verbal *–s* absence: the suffix *–s* may be omitted on present-tense verbs (e.g. *She walk*).

- Plural and possessive *–s* absence: the *–s* suffix marking the plural or possessive forms of nouns may also be omitted (e.g. *two girl*; *Mary house*).

Fuller descriptions of these and many other AAVE characteristics are available from Rickford (1999, chapter 1) or Green (2002).[3]

Simply listing features like these carries a danger of misrepresenting the speech of African Americans. We must remember that phonological and grammatical features such as those mentioned here function as sociolinguistic variables. No individual uses any feature of AAVE categorically. As we find in all nonstandard dialects, usage varies by stylistic context (e.g. casual vs. careful speech) and according to social factors such as class and gender. Moreover, we should recognize that despite the label, AAVE features are not used by all or by only African Americans.

The principle of error correction

It's no secret that nonstandard dialects carry tremendous stigma in mainstream culture. This represents the flipside of the overt prestige of standard varieties. Moreover, the negative evaluations often extend beyond the speech patterns to the character and capabilities of the speakers. Thus, someone who uses nonstandard grammar or phonology can be taken to be morally or mentally deficient and called "lazy" or "stupid." In the case of AAVE, the legacy of racism adds fuel to the fire that powers these attitudes.

As prevalent as such perceptions are today, they were even more widely held when Labov entered the field in the 1960s. Such willingness to assume the worst of people based on their speech had come to shape scholarly approaches to real social problems especially those related to poverty and education. At the time many children, African Americans and others, from low-income neighborhoods struggled in school and performed poorly on standardized tests and other academic measures. This shameful situation continues to plague American education today, but back then efforts to remedy it operated under linguistic assumptions that few scholars would endorse today.

In the 1960s educational reform on behalf of poor children was often guided by the notion of cultural deprivation. Educational psychologists and other researchers located the source of these children's academic struggles in the culture of their home environments, which were thought to deprive the children of the experiences they needed to succeed in school and life. Language played a central role in this argument as many problems seemed to stem from inferior linguistic habits. The problems were felt to be especially acute in the case of African American children, owing to the breadth of the grammatical divide between AAVE and Standard English and to the researchers' ignorance of relevant linguistic facts.

We get a sense of the dominant views of that time from comments by Carl Bereiter, a psychologist who advocated for radically redesigned preschool programs to address the cultural deprivation of poor, African American children.[4] For Bereiter, a child's language offers a direct reflection of thinking. More specifically, mastery of "the formal, structural aspects of language," including the grammatical rules, stands as a prerequisite for logical reasoning. Based on apparent evidence of linguistic deficits, Bereiter and his colleagues conclude that "culturally deprived children do not just think at an immature level: many of them do not think at all" (1966, p. 107). The fault, the psychologists believe, lies with the native speech patterns that these children acquire. It is "not merely an underdeveloped version of standard English, but is a basically non-logical mode of expressive behavior which lacks the formal properties necessary for the organization of thought" (1966, pp. 112–13).

What evidence could warrant such strong conclusions about the cognitive abilities of these children? Here we need to consider the nature of the evaluation procedures. Bereiter and his collaborators remark on how little many of the children spoke in the early phases of their project, noting that they communicated "by gesture . . . by single words . . . or a series of badly connected words or phrases" (1966, p. 114). The possibility that this behavior may have reflected the children's shyness, or the anxiety produced in them by the unfamiliar environment, seems to not have occurred to the researchers. Recall that these were African American four-year-olds being forced to interact with white adult strangers in a new school. Nor, apparently, did the researchers seem to recognize the cultural assumptions inherent in their procedures. They deduce that the children lacked the capacity to answer simple questions, but this comes from the children's unsure reaction in situations like the teacher placing a book on the table and asking "Is the book on the table?" Outside of particular social settings such as the classroom, people do not normally ask questions that they already know the answers to. How is a child unfamiliar with this cultural pattern to know how to respond in such a pragmatically odd interaction?

Labov took on this thinking in his influential essay "The logic of nonstandard English," which first appeared in 1969 and was later reprinted in his 1972 collection *Language in the Inner City*.[5] He effectively dismantles the premise that poor African Americans grow up in an environment of language deprivation by exposing the fallacies on which the psychologists' interpretations rest. Drawing on his Harlem research (Labov et al., 1968), he argues that the limited verbalness observed by Bereiter's team reflected the testing situation rather than the children's linguistic capabilities. The Harlem project found that even a skilled African American interviewer, who is a member of the community, can have trouble eliciting extended conversation in the context of a one-on-one interview. In fact this difficulty led the researchers to use group sessions for recording (see Chapter Five). An eight-year-old who gave only minimal responses to direct questions in an interview engaged excitedly in a fast-flowing conversation when one of his friends joined the mix. More broadly, Labov questions how anyone familiar with African American culture could arrive at the notion that it acts as a source of verbal deprivation. He notes that many common speech events in African American communities rely on displays of verbal skill – he has written on the tradition of ritual insults known as "sounding" or "playing the dozens" (1972a, chapter 8). Language is clearly something of value in these communities and children raised there are "bathed in verbal stimulation from morning to night" (1972a, p. 212).

Labov weaves together various strands of evidence to dispute the suggestion that speakers of AAVE lack the ability to reason logically. He quotes from a memorable theological discussion with Larry H., one of the adolescents interviewed in the Harlem research. Asked about the existence of God, Larry observes:

> You know, like some people say if you're good an' shit, your spirit goin' t'heaven 'n' if you bad, your spirit goin' to hell. Well, bullshit! Your spirit goin' to hell anyway, good or bad ... I'll tell you why. 'Cause, you see, doesn' nobody really know that it's a God, y'know, 'cause I mean I have seen black gods, pink gods, white gods, all color gods, and don't nobody know it's really a God. An' when they be sayin' if you good, you goin' t'heaven, tha's bullshit, 'cause you ain't goin' to no heaven, 'cause it ain't no heaven for you to go to. (1972a, pp. 214–15)

Larry illustrates that speaking AAVE is not incompatible with logical argumentation. As Labov summarizes Larry's reasoning, he puts

forward a thesis (your spirit is not going to heaven), and supports it
with a series of deductions (Nobody knows whether there is really
a God, and if there's no God, there can't be any heaven).

In an even more pointed illustration that AAVE does not serve as
a barrier to logic, Labov reports on a test employed in the Harlem
project. The interviewer spoke a sentence in Standard English and
asked the adolescents to repeat it back verbatim. They found that
often their subjects proved unable to do this. What's interesting,
however, is how they "failed" at the task. They frequently responded
with translations of the sentence into AAVE. For example, the
standard "Nobody ever sat at any of those desks, anyhow" might
be rendered "Nobody never sat in none of those desses anyhow"
(1972a, p. 227). These reworkings clearly demonstrate that the
subjects grasped the meaning of the Standard English versions –
they understood the grammatical logic of the original – but they
simply did not attend closely to the surface form in which that
meaning was couched.

Ultimately the claim of verbal deprivation collapses under scrutiny
because it rests on a fundamental misunderstanding of the nature
of nonstandard dialects like AAVE. Bereiter and those of his ilk
confuse the grammar of Standard English with grammar in general.
They assume that anyone who fails to follow the grammatical rules
of the standard language lacks any structured linguistic system.
We see this in their use of "badly connected words or phrases" to
describe usages like "They mine" (Bereiter et al., 1966, p. 114).
This example illustrates the grammatical feature of copula deletion
mentioned earlier (cf. "They are mine"). It does not represent an
idiosyncratic usage of an individual child, but instead functions as a
regular part of AAVE grammar. The idea that nonstandard varieties
might be as rule-governed and structured as Standard English did
not penetrate the worldview of those advocating verbal deprivation
theories.

Linguists have the knowledge and evidence to dispel such
misconceptions. Indeed, Labov argues that we have a duty to do so.
He formulates this as the "principle of error correction":

> A scientist who becomes aware of a widespread idea or social
> practice with important consequences that is invalidated by his
> own data is obligated to bring this error to the attention of the
> widest possible audience. (1982b, p. 172)

"The logic of non-standard English," which was written with general readers in mind (and reprinted in *The Atlantic Monthly*), stands as one illustration of how Labov has tried to live up to this principle, but it is far from the only way, as we'll see below.

AAVE in schools: Ann Arbor and Oakland

Labov's response to educational psychologists like Bereiter forms part of a larger debate between those who view AAVE as a deficit to be overcome and those who see it as an alternative to be maintained in one's linguistic repertoire. This deficit versus difference debate comes to a head in the educational system where teaching children to read and write (and perhaps also to speak) the standard dialect stands as a fundamental objective. Both sides in this debate agree that success in school requires some competence in Standard English. What they disagree about is how to achieve that goal.

Naturally, the approach advocated by those endorsing a deficit model calls for the eradication of children's native speech patterns. Bereiter and his colleagues are quite explicit in noting that their goal "could be seen as not that of improving the child's language but rather that of teaching him a different language which would hopefully replace the first one" (1966, p. 113). They adopted methods from foreign language instruction such as having children repeat basic statements like "This block is big" and eliciting simple observations by demanding "Tell me about the block." Imagine what this must have been like for the child. I suspect that one lesson many of these four-year-olds took from this experience was that school is a place where people make you do boring things and treat you like you're stupid.

As Labov points out, the deficit model has real consequences for the classroom. It adds an imprimatur of scientific scholarship to linguistic prejudice. Like the majority of the population, most teachers operate with a prescriptivist bias that sees Standard English as superior to other dialects. Out of respect for cultural diversity or simple politeness, however, they might temper their stigmatization of AAVE and other non-standard dialects in the classroom. But deficit theorists tell them that these other varieties have harmful effects on children's ability to think. This message might not only lead them to act more freely in "stamping out" nonstandard dialects, but may also affect their views of those students who use those dialects. The danger stems from the fact that a teacher's expectations and attitudes can have a significant effect on a child's success or failure (Labov, 1972a, p. 230).

These issues came to the fore in a legal case that began in 1977 when several African American parents filed suit against school officials in Ann Arbor, Michigan.[6] These parents were concerned by the treatment their children received at their school where the student population was overwhelmingly white (80 percent). The school, Martin Luther King Jr Elementary, had acted to label the African American children as educational failures in various ways, judging them as having behavioral problems, learning disabilities, mental retardation, and so forth. (Labov, 1982b, p. 167). The parents alleged that the school had failed to take into account the children's cultural background in ways that would allow them to succeed academically. As the case progressed, the argument narrowed to the role of language as an element of that cultural background. Federal law prohibits an educational agency from discriminating against people by failing "to take appropriate action to overcome linguistic barriers that impede equal participation by its students in its instructional programs" (quoted by Labov, 1982b, p. 169). Thus, the case hinged on whether the differences between AAVE and Standard English functioned as a linguistic barrier that the school should recognize and address.

The parents' legal team benefited from the support of several linguists, most importantly Geneva Smitherman, an experienced AAVE researcher who analyzed the speech of the children in the case. Labov and others played supporting roles, appearing as expert witnesses. The testimony the linguists provided demonstrated the breadth of the linguistic gulf between AAVE and Standard English. Labov, for example, drew the court's attention to features like "habitual *be*" (e.g. *The dog be hungry*), which highlight the distinctiveness of the AAVE grammatical system. In fact an example like this, which is not equivalent to Standard English *The dog is hungry*, underscores the complexities of the AAVE tense and aspect system. AAVE verb forms can convey subtle differences of meaning that can't be translated directly by the more limited grammar of Standard English.[7]

With the help of linguistic experts, the plaintiffs also succeeded in demonstrating that teachers and others at the school lacked knowledge of the structure of AAVE and that this ignorance led them to misjudge the children. One of the more straightforward illustrations of this tendency appears in the tests used to diagnose students as learning disabled. Some students showed apparent deficiencies in auditory processing based on their inability to hear certain differences of sound. But closer examination revealed that the standardized test used relied on phonological distinctions that did not hold in AAVE. For example, AAVE and southern dialects typically have no difference between the vowels /ɛ/ and /ɪ/ when they appear before nasal consonants, resulting in a well-documented pattern known as the "*pen/pin* merger." Yet pairs like *ten* ~ *ten* and *hem* ~ *him* appear on auditory tests. An AAVE-speaker who doesn't produce or perceive a difference between such pairs does not represent someone with a learning disability, but rather someone who has learned his or her native phonology well.

The evidence at trial also established that teachers and other school officials held general attitudes about AAVE that led to disadvantages for the children. As Labov summarizes the judge's opinion:

> [T]here were no barriers to communication in the classroom. According to [Judge Joiner's] observations, teachers could understand children and children could understand children.[8] Rather, he believed that the language barrier that did exist was in the form of unconscious negative attitudes formed by teachers towards children who spoke Black English, and the reactions of children to these attitudes. (1982b, p. 193)

Overcoming this kind of linguistic discrimination presents a challenge much greater than the one related to removing obvious biases in standardized tests.

The judge ruled for the plaintiffs and ordered the school to develop a plan for working with AAVE-speaking children. The goal was to educate teachers about the grammatical and phonological patterns of the dialect and provide them with strategies to implement this knowledge to help students gain better proficiency in Standard English.

We can find implicit in this approach a rejection of the deficit model. The native AAVE of the children is treated not as a destructive force to be removed, but rather as a different linguistic system, one that is equally rule-governed and structured as Standard English. The goal becomes one of "bidialectalism" where the children have mastery of both AAVE and Standard English and know how to switch between the two as the situation demands.

The issues at the heart of the Ann Arbor case again rose to public prominence at the end of 1996 when the school board of Oakland, California, passed what came to be known as its "Ebonics resolution." The board acted out of concern over the poor academic performance of many of their African American students, as had been well-documented by grades, standardized tests, graduation rates, and so on. They recognized the centrality of language to learning and formulated a plan to improve the teaching of linguistic skills necessary for educational success. While comprising a number of specific strategies, this plan boils down to two main components: (1) Recognize the phonological and grammatical patterns that govern AAVE, and (2) Use knowledge of AAVE to devise effective pedagogies for teaching proficiency in Standard English.

Unfortunately, the Oakland school board made some missteps in communicating their goals and their plan for achieving those goals. The details lie outside the scope of our discussion here, but accessible treatments are available from Baugh (2000) and Rickford (1997). One point that does merit clarification relates to the term "Ebonics." This label was coined by psychologist Robert Williams in 1973 as a cover term for the languages of the African diaspora created by the slave trade. Thus it encompassed West African languages, Caribbean Creoles, and dialects of English like AAVE, spoken by the descendants of slaves (Baugh, 2000, pp. 15–16). The term did not catch on among sociolinguists working on AAVE. When the Oakland resolution introduced "Ebonics" into public discourse, it quickly came to function as a synonym for AAVE, despite its originally broader scope.

Oakland's Ebonics resolution raised important issues about the relationship between language and race, and in a telling display of the power of those issues to inflame emotions, an enormous public uproar ignited. The media certainly added fuel to the fire by misrepresenting the Oakland position and the underlying issues. The common misinterpretation of what the school board was proposing held that Standard English would be abandoned and AAVE would serve as the medium of instruction. Running throughout the overwhelming backlash against the Oakland proposal was a familiar mischaracterization of AAVE as street slang expressed through random grammar errors.

Early in 1997, the Linguistic Society of America (LSA), the scholarly organization for the profession in the US, adopted a resolution in support of the Oakland board. Labov's former student John Rickford drafted the language of the statement and led the effort for its endorsement. Naturally, the LSA resolution notes that AAVE "is systematic and rule-governed like all natural speech varieties" and that labels such as "'slang,' 'mutant,' 'lazy,' 'defective,' 'ungrammatical,' or 'broken English' are incorrect and demeaning."[9] It also acknowledged that vernacular speech varieties have value for their users and that recognizing that value can lead to a more productive pedagogy for mastering other dialects like Standard English.

Labov came to play an active role in the controversy when the US Senate held hearings on the matter. As he had some 20 years earlier, Labov gave testimony as an expert witness. He appeared on a panel with other scholars including Robert Williams, the coiner of "Ebonics." Labov outlined the consensus view of AAVE within the field and reviewed the key observations from the decades of research on the dialect. Like his co-panelists, he commended the Oakland school board on their courage to explore new approaches to the problems facing poor African American children in schools.

Perhaps out of a feeling that every issue must have two sides, another panel of speakers testified in opposition to the Oakland resolution. This panel consisted of a minister and a radio talk-show host, both African American. I continue to be struck by this juxtaposition. On the one hand we have Labov and other scholars who have been engaged in scientific study of the issues for over 30 years, and on the other we see two people who have no special training or expertise in linguistics or education but whose professions would seem to demand certain language skills. To my mind, the situation is comparable to holding a government hearing on the potential of wind power as an energy source and inviting testimony from climatologists and engineers on one side and sailing enthusiasts and kite-hobbyists on the other. Perhaps it's fortunate, therefore, that nothing concrete came of the Senate hearings. No laws emerged, and politicians seemed to lose interest as the issue gradually disappeared from the media reports.

While the Ebonics controversy revealed that ignorance about AAVE was as profound and widespread in 1996 as it was in 1977 and earlier, in one way this story does illustrate how at least one aspect of the issues had changed. While the school officials in Ann Arbor operated under a deficit model, those in Oakland represented the "difference" side of that long-standing debate. Thus, the efforts that Labov and many others had taken to correct errors about AAVE seem to have paid off. The good news from the linguist's perspective is that at least this message has made in-roads among educational policymakers.

AAVE and reading research

The Oakland proposal and Judge Joiner's ruling in the Ann Arbor case rest on the premise that arming teachers with knowledge of nonstandard dialects – how AAVE and other varieties work – will improve their ability to teach speakers of those dialects. Learning the details of complexities such as those seen in verb forms (e.g. habitual *be*), as well as just the basic fact that AAVE actually has rules, can inspire greater respect for the dialect. For teachers, knowledge about the grammatical and phonological patterns of AAVE can also apply directly to their curriculum. We see evidence of this in research on the teaching of reading.

Labov has been interested in the relationship between non-standard dialects and reading throughout his career. The project he directed in south Harlem sought to address this issue specifically (Labov et al., 1968). Then (as now) evidence of lower levels of educational achievement among poor children of color could be found in abundance. Labov's focus on reading makes sense given the acknowledged fact that reading stands as a cornerstone to success in school. Of course, because reading is a linguistic process, it also makes sense that spoken-language patterns would play a role in the acquisition of this skill.

One recurrent challenge in reading pedagogy stems from the need to distinguish reading errors from vernacular pronunciations. When children are learning to read, teachers commonly chart their progress by having them read aloud. A true error occurs when the reader misidentifies a word in the text; for example, when the reader processes the written *car* as *cat*. Such errors would usually be clear to the teacher from the pronunciation. However, sometimes the reader's pronunciation may give less clear indications of how they've understood the text.

We can illustrate the challenge by considering how ambiguities might arise from a regular phonological process like consonant cluster reduction. When a cluster of two consonants appears at the end of a word, all speakers of English tend to simplify the pronunciations by dropping the second consonant. Thus, *best picture* becomes *bes' picture* and *ground game* becomes *groun' game*. The rules governing this process vary by dialect, but many sociolinguistic studies have shown it to apply quite frequently in AAVE (e.g. Labov et al., 1968). It's easy to see how cluster reduction might contribute to ambiguous pronunciations when we realize that the regular past tense suffix *–ed* often creates clusters. When someone pronounces *passed* [pæst] without the final [t] or *teased* [tizd] without the final [d], their pronunciations are identical to those of the corresponding base forms of the verbs, *pass* and *tease*.

And herein lies the difficulty for the reading teacher. When a child reading aloud pronounces *passed* as [pæs], we don't know whether the child has processed the intended word correctly and simply reduced the consonant cluster or whether a true error has occurred. Distinguishing between these alternative interpretations is crucial. As Labov explains:

> We have two distinct cases to consider. In one case, the deviation in reading may be only a difference in pronunciation on the part of a child who has a different set of homonyms [e.g. *passed* = *pass*] from the teacher. Here, correction might be quite unnecessary. In the second case, we may be dealing with a boy who has no concept of *–ed* as a past tense marker, who considers the *–ed* a meaningless set of silent letters. Obviously the correct teaching strategy would involve distinguishing these two cases and treating them quite differently. (1972a, pp. 33–4)

Determining which case applies for a given student, while no trivial matter, can be facilitated with the application of findings from studies of nonstandard dialects. In AAVE, for example, consonant cluster reduction applies with much lower frequency when the following word begins with a vowel. Thus, *passed* is more likely to sound like *pass* in a phrase like *passed by* than one like *passed over*.

A child who doesn't pronounce the *-ed* consistently before vowels is more likely to be having difficulty with the "concept of *-ed* as a past tense marker" than one who only omits the [t] or [d] before other consonants.[10]

In a number of empirical studies, Labov has explored the issue of how children's native speech patterns affect their reading performance. In one early project, he designed a rather ingenious method for testing the extent to which AAVE-speaking children rely on the *-ed* suffix as a signal of past tense (see Labov, 1972a, pp. 30–2). The children read aloud a series of sentences that included the verb *read*. By itself, of course, the spelling *read* represents both the present and past tense forms that we distinguish in pronunciation ([rid] vs. [rɛd]). Labov's test sentences included elements that clarified which tense applied to *read* but did so in two different ways. Sometimes the meaning was indicated by adverbial expressions (e.g. *Last month I read five books*) and other times by a subordinate clause with a past tense verb with *-ed* (e.g. *When I passed by, I read the posters*). Labov could tell whether the child had correctly interpreted the sentence based on the pronunciation of *read*. The results revealed that the readers arrived at the correct interpretation of *read* much more frequently when the time information came in adverbials. When the interpretation of tense relied on the *-ed* verbs in the prior clause, the children produced the correct form at a rate of about 40 percent. Moreover, Labov had access to standardized test data for these children which allowed him to explore whether performance in his experiment correlated with overall reading ability. He discovered a dramatic difference in these comparisons. While the scores on the standardized test did correlate with performance on Labov's *read* task for those cases involving adverbial markers of tense, no such correlation appeared for the other cases. That is, the tendency to interpret *-ed* as a tense marker was no greater for good readers in this sample than for struggling ones.

In more recent explorations of these issues, Labov has expanded the scale and scope of his inquiry. He has also adopted more sophisticated statistical techniques. In studies like those reported by Labov and Baker (2010), a more nuanced picture emerges. We see that some features of AAVE seem to have a more significant impact on reading errors than others. For example, absence of verbal *-s* (e.g. *he walk*) appears to serve as a greater stumbling block for

AAVE-speakers learning to read than does absence of the plural –*s* on nouns (e.g. *two dog*) (Labov and Baker, 2010). Findings like these can aid teachers and others involved in reading pedagogy by identifying priorities and offering strategies for tackling the complex task of helping struggling readers.

As we noted earlier, when Labov spoke out to decry the injustice he saw in the notion of verbal deprivation, his action reflected a commitment to what he called the principle of error correction. Certainly the research that Labov has conducted on reading errors as well as his more public participation in the Ann Arbor trial and in the Senate hearing on Ebonics also demonstrate a commitment to attacking misconceptions about AAVE and other nonstandard dialects. We understand better the motivations behind Labov's work when we place it in the context of another of his guiding principles, the principle of debt incurred:

> An investigator who has obtained linguistic data from members of a speech community has an obligation to use the knowledge based on that data for benefit of the community, when it has need of it. (1982b, p. 173)

The debt arises from the research in the community. Labov acknowledges that his career has benefited greatly from the willingness of hundreds, and by now thousands, of people to talk with him and allow him to record their speech. In the case of those members of the AAVE speech community, Labov has worked to repay this debt by bringing his insights to bear on various discussions of educational policy from the courthouse to the halls of Congress to the teachers' lounge.

The past, present, and future of AAVE

While Labov's engagement with AAVE has always included an element of public outreach, this line of research has also addressed important theoretical questions of primary interest to other linguists. I mentioned earlier that the complicated facts related to copula deletion played a central role in Labov's development of the notion of variable rules. That work highlights the broader linguistic lessons that AAVE informs, and exploring the intricacies of the phonological and grammatical features of AAVE has occupied Labov and many other sociolinguists for decades.

Much of what makes AAVE so interesting and valuable to scholars pertains to its distinctiveness. Here we find a number of patterns that set AAVE apart not only from mainstream American speech, but also from other marked varieties like southern regional dialects. These facts have led Labov and others to questions of how to conceptualize AAVE grammar in relation to other varieties.

On one hand, no linguist would argue that AAVE constitutes a separate language from English. The usual standard for differentiating languages rests on mutual intelligibility. If speakers of two varieties can understand each other, then we say they speak dialects of the same language. If they can't understand each other, they're speaking two separate languages. By this criterion, AAVE functions as a dialect of English.

On the other hand, certain dimensions of AAVE structure seem to operate by principles not found in most (or any) other dialects of English. So, we might consider a more abstract inquiry into the status of AAVE in the mind of its speakers. Perhaps the model of bilingualism is apt. Someone who is bilingual in, say, Spanish and English, has access to two distinct mental grammars and chooses between them in constructing sentences.[11] In this case we can view Spanish and English as co-existing in the bilingual's mind. Does AAVE function as a separate grammatical system in this same sense?

Glossing over many finer theoretical points, I would summarize Labov's view as arguing that AAVE does involve co-existent systems, though not exactly in the same way as in the bilingual case (1998, pp. 117–18). Essentially, the mental grammar of an AAVE speaker involves two elements: the "General English" component and the "African-American" component. The General English component represents a kind of grammatical core of English. Crucially, this is not synonymous with Standard English, but rather describes a more general set of structures operant in all standard and nonstandard varieties. The African American component stands as "a subset of grammatical and lexical forms that are used in combination with much but not all of the grammatical inventory of [General English]" (1998, p. 118). The forms that Labov has in mind include habitual *be*, copula deletion, and others related to the distinctive treatment of verbs in AAVE. For Labov, such features give evidence of a system governed by principles independent of those at work in other forms of English.

The theoretical issues regarding the relationship between AAVE and other varieties of English beg historical questions about AAVE's origins. Whether they hold that certain AAVE usages illustrate a separate layer of grammatical structure or not, linguists still acknowledge the distinctive character of the dialect and want to understand how AAVE came to have such a varied set of phonological and grammatical features. This subject has generated a long-standing and occasionally heated debate in the field.[12]

We might assume that any search into the origins of AAVE features would naturally look to Africa. Perhaps forms heard in AAVE today represent a legacy of the languages spoken by the African ancestors stolen into slavery centuries ago. For various reasons this suggestion has not played a significant role in the linguistic exploration of the issue. Part of the challenge is methodological. The African slaves sent to America and the Caribbean represented hundreds of languages with very different structures, and it's hard to argue convincingly that a particular AAVE feature stems from any one source.

Many linguists have stressed the connections between elements of AAVE and comparable usages in other dialects of English. Of course we know that many features of AAVE – phonological features like final consonant cluster reduction (e.g. *las' year*) and grammatical features like "double modals"[13] (e.g. *he might could go*) – appear in southern white speech and other varieties. Some researchers have sought the origins of even the more distinctive features of AAVE in dialects outside the US. For example, we find in Irish English a grammatical construction quite similar to the habitual *be* of AAVE. The enormous number of Irish immigrants to America and the fact that they often occupied a social position that might have put them in contact with African Americans lend some credence to the possibility of a Hiberno-English influence on AAVE.[14]

Labov has generally emphasized a different perspective, one that connects AAVE historically to the creole languages of the Caribbean. Creoles like Jamaican Patois or Haitian Creole, arise within a particular sociolinguistic setting. First a group of people who speak several different languages come together (or are forcibly placed together). Because they have no common language, they construct one by combining various elements and simplifying structures. Linguists call this product a "pidgin." Over time, children are raised to speak that pidgin as their first language. To serve as a primary language of a community, a pidgin must evolve by adding vocabulary and developing a more elaborate grammatical structure. The result is a creole. The vocabulary of a creole language often comes from the language of the socially dominant group, but the grammar differs significantly from that language. Thus, creoles spoken in places like Jamaica and Barbados bear a superficial resemblance to English but stand as separate languages and not simply as dialects of English.

Advocating what has come to be known as the "Creolist" position, Labov and others seek the origins of several aspects of AAVE grammar in this creole history. We can get a flavor for how such explorations proceed by considering the evidence on copula deletion. Labov presented a detailed analysis of the sociolinguistic variation associated with this feature based on the Harlem research (Labov et al., 1968; Labov, 1969, 1972a). This variable involves three alternative forms related to the use of *is* and *are* as linking verbs or auxiliaries:

Full: *He is hungry. They are working.*
Contracted: *He's hungry. They're working.*
Deleted: *He hungry. They working.*

The full and contracted forms appear is all varieties of English while deletion seldom occurs outside AAVE. We might suspect, therefore, that copula deletion represents a distinct historical development, perhaps a creole transfer, since similar constructions appear in many creole languages.

In his early explorations of this feature, however, Labov highlights the parallels between contraction and deletion. Specifically, he points out that both processes seem to respond to similar grammatical conditioning; that is, the grammatical contexts that favor one seem also to favor the other. The most striking illustration of this comes with Labov's observation that the same contexts that disallow contraction in Standard English also disallow deletion in AAVE. Consider these examples:

How beautiful you *are*!
He's as nice as he says he *is*.
Who *is* it? [responding to a knock on the door]
He wasn't planning to go, but he *is* now.

The italicized verbs must appear in their full forms in these sentences. They cannot be contracted (e.g. *How beautiful you're!*) in any dialect of English, and they cannot be deleted (e.g. *How beautiful you ___!*) in AAVE. Such similarities suggest that contraction and deletion represent the same basic pattern and differ only on a more superficial level of how much phonological material is removed. In other words, deletion seems to represent contraction taken to its logical extreme.

As more studies of copula deletion appeared, Labov came to modify his thinking on the issue. Work by John Baugh, a former student of Labov's, identified an important wrinkle in the grammatical patterning of copula deletion. Specifically, Baugh (1980) found that the deletion occurs at unexpectedly low rates when the copula functions to mark a location (e.g. *He is at home*; *They are not here*). The significance of this observation stems from the existence of a similar pattern in Caribbean creoles. Languages like Jamaican Creole, for example, do not use a linking verb in most of the grammatical contexts where AAVE allows for *is* or *are* to be deleted. But when the sentence describes a location, Jamaican Creole includes its equivalent of English *is/are*. Baugh as well as Labov and others take this parallel as suggesting a creole connection in AAVE's history. This stands as one of many such strands of evidence that have, in Labov's view, brought the field to consensus around the creolist hypothesis as at least a partial explanation for the development of AAVE grammar (e.g. Labov, 1982b, 1995).

We find markedly less consensus on the question of current trajectory of AAVE, especially with regard to other nonstandard dialects. This issue erupted in the 1980s as a debate about whether the structure of AAVE was becoming more or less similar to white vernaculars. On one hand, the creolist hypothesis might imply a general trend of convergence. After all, it assumes that AAVE has roots in a creole language that, by definition, represented a linguistic system distinct from English. Given that today AAVE clearly stands as a dialect of English, supporters of the creolist view suggest that a process of gradual assimilation ("decreolization") has taken place over centuries of contact with English. While sympathetic to aspects of this scenario as a historical trend, Labov has argued that today African American and white varieties are diverging (see, e.g. 1987, 1995).

He links this divergence to changes from both sides. For example, many sound changes in progress – including local developments like (au) fronting in Philadelphia (Chapter Six) and broader regional trends like the Northern Cities Shift (Chapter Seven) – affect only white speech. African Americans often do not participate in such changes. On the other hand, AAVE does not remain totally stable. Labov finds evidence of various changes underway in the grammar of AAVE. He cites, for example, apparent-time data suggesting that features like habitual *be* appear more frequently today than in the past. We also see indications of younger AAVE-speakers using established features in new ways and developing wholly new structures.

Labov's views on this matter have met with strong challenges from other scholars (see, e.g. Vaughn-Cooke, 1987). Much of the criticism of his divergence hypothesis centers upon the problems of discerning historical trends from the limited evidence. Real-time data on how AAVE may have changed in the last century or so is rather sparse. If we observe AAVE-speakers using some feature today that was not reported in the past, we shouldn't assume that it represents a new development. It might simply have escaped the notice of previous researchers. Moreover, the scarcity of historical material has meant that Labov and other researchers must rely more on apparent-time evidence. But, as we noted in Chapter Seven, this approach carries the risk of mistaking a pattern of age-grading for a change in progress. Younger people might use AAVE features at higher rates than older generations as a way of marking their position in vernacular culture, a common finding with stable age-graded variables.

Labov's views on the divergence of AAVE and other varieties are certainly provocative within the field, but they also carry broader implications about race relations in the US. Indeed, Labov is quite explicit in noting that "There is no doubt that the divergence that we have witnessed on the linguistic front is symptomatic of a split between the black and white portions of our society" (1987, p. 10). Certainly the persistent patterns of residential segregation in many urban centers play a significant role here, with physical separation contributing to linguistic separation. But we might also consider how ideological factors might reinforce differences as use of AAVE functions as a marker of identity. As Wolfram and Thomas (2002) demonstrate, for example, younger African Americans in rural communities often abandon the traditional regional speech of their parents and grandparents in favor of the

AAVE patterns associated with urban dwellers. Such findings highlight the work that cultural identity does in shaping linguistic behavior.

Conclusion

African American English has served as a font of intellectual inspiration for countless linguists. We can find testimony of the fruitfulness of this line of research in the bibliographic record. Nearly 20 years ago, Edgar Schneider surveyed this record and found that the number of scholarly publications on African American English greatly exceeded those related to any other variety of American English – the closest competitor for research attention, Mexican-American English, had roughly one-fifth as many studies devoted to it (1996, p. 3). In the last two decades this interest in African American English has continued to grow.

Labov pioneered the sociolinguistic study of African American speech, and he remains a prominent voice in this scholarly conversation. As we've seen in this chapter, his work in this area has pursued two goals. He has sought to understand the complexities of AAVE structure as well as the broader sociolinguistic context in which the dialect lives. The lessons learned from these pursuits have been many and the field's knowledge has been greatly enriched. But from the beginning, a different kind of goal has also motivated Labov's work. He believed then, and he does now, that linguists have something valuable to offer, that they "can make a contribution to the urgent social problems of our time" (1973, p. 98). He worked to apply his insights to the difficulties that many poor African Americans experience in school, giving special attention to the teaching of reading. These lessons reflect Labov's commitment to repaying the debts that researchers owe to the speech communities we study.

How should we assess Labov's performance in achieving his goals? Without question his worked has enhanced knowledge of AAVE within the field of linguistics. On the other hand, his efforts to effect broader societal changes have met with mixed success. Early on in his career, Labov suggested that the main challenge for researchers hoping to address the problems faced by AAVE-speakers in school stemmed from attitudes rather than from differences of linguistic structure: "[T]he major causes of reading failure are political and cultural conflicts in the classroom, and dialect differences are important because they are symbols of this conflict" (1972a, p. xiv). He and many other linguists have worked tirelessly to address this issue. Yet Labov's assessment some 35 years later highlights the challenges that remain:

> There has been a certain amount of change at the higher levels of instruction, at the university level, but if you get down to local schools, in Philadelphia certainly, we find that the negative reactions to the use of AAVE are pretty constant. There are broad general principles controlling people's reaction to everyday language, and the struggle to change them should not be confused with the struggle to improve the reading and writing of the children you're dealing with. Those are two separate enterprises. I don't want to engage in a quixotic effort to change the attitudes of teachers and parents about something that they believe as fundamentally as anything else in their lives. Rather, we're going to use our knowledge of African American English to improve the teaching of reading. (quoted in Gordon, 2006, p. 343)

Despite the rather pessimistic tone, Labov's comments do give some evidence of the progress made since his work began. Specialists in reading pedagogy can and do draw on knowledge of AAVE structure to design strategies for more effective teaching. Moreover, this knowledge is becoming increasingly available to a wider audience in popular books such as Rickford and Rickford (2000) and Baugh (2000), on the internet, and elsewhere.

In my experience, such knowledge can change attitudes. I talk about issues related to AAVE and other stigmatized varieties every semester, and what I have found gives me hope. Most students I encounter have never thought critically about such questions and certainly have little sense that nonstandard dialects operate by rules just like Standard English. When their assumptions are challenged by such facts, they quickly recognize the flimsy basis for their linguistic prejudices. I'm not naïve enough to believe that they all emerge from my class in a state of linguistic enlightenment that frees them from all dialect bias; but even a little critical awareness seems to go a long way when it comes to fighting the ideology of Standard English.

Thus, as Labov and other linguists continue to share the lessons learned from their research, we will see attitudes change, though perhaps at a frustratingly slow pace.

Notes

1   In an interesting demonstration of practicing what you preach, sociolinguists vary in their pronunciation of the abbreviated form, AAVE. Some use [ɑveɪ] (like *Ave Maria*) and others [æv] (like *have* without the [h]).

2   Labov's emphasis on the speech of urban, working class African Americans has drawn criticism by scholars concerned about the rather limited perspective this approach offers (see, e.g. Wolfram, 2007).

3   Nonspecialist readers may also wish to consult Rickford and Rickford (2000) and Baugh (1999, 2000).

4   I quote Bereiter here as he seems to have inspired Labov's early statements (e.g. 1972a, chapter 5), but in fairness we should note that Bereiter represents widely held views of that period.

5   Labov published a condensed version of this piece as "Academic ignorance and black intelligence" in the *Atlantic Monthly* in 1972.

6   My summary of the case comes from Labov (1982b). Another valuable insider perspective on the case is provided by Smitherman (1998).

7   I don't wish to overstate the separateness of AAVE grammar. While it does feature several distinctive usages, the bulk of its structure is shared with other dialects of English.

8   It's unclear whether this is an editorial mistake and Labov meant to write that "children understood teachers."

9   The full text of the resolution is available from the Linguistic Society of America's website: <http://www.lsadc.org/info/lsa-res-ebonics. cfm>.

10   Labov offers a broad range of advice for teachers and others interested in how sociolinguistic research can benefit reading instruction in a 1995 essay.

11   This characterization oversimplifies the process. Code-switching, which involves the mixing of elements from both languages, occurs commonly in bilingual speech, even within sentences.

12 Wolfram and Schilling-Estes (2006) and Rickford (1997) provide accessible overviews of this debate.

13 Modals represent a subclass of auxiliaries or helping verbs that convey notions like permission or possibility.

14 John Rickford offers a thorough examination of this proposal with regard to habitual *be* (see 1999, chapter 8).

CHAPTER NINE

The revolution at 50

In the fall of 1961, Labov took his first steps in linguistic research when he disembarked from a ferry onto Martha's Vineyard. Though eager to make his mark in a field he had just begun to study formally only months earlier, he could not have envisioned that his work on that island would launch a revolution in linguistics. Or could he? He may in fact have entertained such thoughts; after all, he entered graduate study with revolutionary goals in mind. He sought to position the study of language on a firmer empirical footing, one accountable to the evidence of everyday speech from a broad range of people. The research he carried out on Martha's Vineyard, and a few years later in New York City, broke new ground by demonstrating the insights to be drawn from this approach to language. Soon other scholars followed his lead and the revolution gained momentum, eventually growing into a major subfield of linguistics with thousands of practitioners across the globe.

Decades later, Labov continues to preside over this subfield of variationist sociolinguistics. His works remain essential reading for students, and the research literature teems with citations of his publications. Now in his 80s, he maintains an active research agenda, publishing in prestigious venues and presenting his work at professional meetings around the world. Remarkably, he also continues to teach courses at the University of Pennsylvania and to supervise several graduate students in their research.

While Labov's prominence in the field remains indisputable, it's also clear that the boundaries of variationist sociolinguistics are not isomorphic with those circumscribing his work. Scholarship in the variationist paradigm today includes, but is not limited to, the pursuit of questions that have occupied the founder of this paradigm. This fact in no way diminishes Labov's contribution; indeed it testifies to the fruitfulness of the seeds he has planted. A field that fails to expand beyond the ideas that gave birth to it has no future. This is not the case here. Variationist sociolinguistics thrives today and has a bright future.

In this final chapter we survey the landscape of sociolinguistics with an eye to assessing Labov's legacy. We will see that many of the trails he blazed continue to be well traveled. Indeed, extending the metaphor, some of those trails have undergone tremendous improvements and currently stand as multi-lane super-highways. On the other hand, the map of the field today covers territories that Labov has explored very little, or not at all. In fact, some recent developments arose in part from a frustration with traditional variationist approaches. Labov, the revolutionary, has in some ways become the establishment. Still, even this work challenging established approaches represents an expansion rather than a rejection of the framework Labov assembled some 50 years ago.

Variationists united

Variationists continue to subscribe to the fundamental principles that set this approach apart from mainstream linguistics as well as from other flavors of sociolinguistics. As discussed in Chapter Four, these principles include a rejection of the axiom of categoricity that governs thinking in many areas of linguistic theory. Language structure does not depend on rules that operate with perfect regularity. Instead, many rules apply variably with their output shaped by a range of factors. Thus, for example, we cannot divide English speakers neatly into those who pronounce *park* without the [r] and those who pronounce it with the [r], nor into those who use "double negatives" (e.g. *I don't know nothing*) and those who use only one negative element in a clause (e.g. *I don't know anything/I know nothing*). In a given community, indeed in a given speaker, we can find variable application of the phonological and grammatical rules involved in these cases.

The crucial observation that informs all work in the Labovian tradition is that linguistic variation in the community and the individual is not random, but rather patterned. Language functions by means of orderly heterogeneity, and patterns in the variation reflect the influence of linguistic and social factors. The challenge for the researcher comes in attempting to reveal those sociolinguistic patterns amid the apparent chaos of variable usage. Labov and those following in the variationist paradigm take up this challenge by turning to quantitative techniques. The orderliness of the heterogeneity comes into much sharper focus when usages are measured and compared on the basis of precise counting rather than informal estimates.

In the mainstream of linguistic research, heterogeneity in language structure ranks as much less of a concern. In part this lack of interest stems from their commitment to the axiom of categoricity. Variation muddies the waters when one seeks the uniformity that is presumed to underlie the linguistic system. This view reflects adherence to Chomsky's delineation of performance and competence and predecessors like Saussure's notions of *parole* and *langue*. Accordingly, a diverse set of "irrelevant" factors affect actual use of language (performance/*parole*), and what linguists really want to study is the more perfect grammatical knowledge that exists in the mind (competence/*langue*). We see a significant methodological consequence of this thinking in many linguists' reliance on intuitions about what can be said rather than empirical evidence of what actually was said.

On this score, variationists join sociolinguists of all stripes in rejecting the mainstream approach and embracing a study of language produced in (more or less) authentic contexts. This commitment to observing language in use carries with it an acknowledgment of the relevance of the social dimension of that use. Labov's general approach to this social dimension sees linguistic variation as embedded in the social structure of a speech community. Accounting for that variation demands a "socially realistic linguistics" that surveys the distribution of speech variables across social parameters like age, gender, and class. While some variationists might question the particulars of Labov's social analysis, a broad consensus still holds with regard to the larger issue: Language exists in a social context, and attending to that context enriches our understanding of how language works.

This review of general principles reminds us of the common ground on which all variationists tread. The core framework pioneered by Labov and given its theoretical fleshing-out by Weinreich et al. (1968) continues to guide research today. This is a useful reminder as we turn to a survey of current variationist research.[1] While much of this work builds fairly directly on the model established by Labov, other research bears less obvious similarities to that model.

Variationist study of language change

Understanding how and why linguistic changes proceed has occupied a top slot in Labov's research priorities throughout his career. He has explored changes active in small communities like Martha's Vineyard, and in large metropolitan areas like Philadelphia, as well as those shaping broad regional patterns like the Northern Cities Shift (see Chapter Seven). The model that Labov established has been enormously influential, and this line of research remains a central pillar of variationist sociolinguistics as a whole.

Variationist work on language change operates with a range of goals in mind. As discussed in Chapter Seven, Weinreich et al. (1968) framed the issues in terms of central "problems" to address. Thus, for example, researchers might concentrate on the "transition problem" by seeking to detail how a language moves from one stage to another or on the "embedding problem" by examining how innovations attain their distributions in the linguistic matrix (the grammatical or phonological system) and the social structure of the speech community. The variationist approach offers great advantages over traditional methods for scholars pursuing these questions because it opens the investigation to active changes. Exploring changes while they are in progress produces a picture of the process that is much higher in resolution. Labov has drawn on this enhanced perspective for insights into the linguistic and social dimensions of language change. For example, weighing in on a long-standing debate about how innovations proceed through the structure of the language, he demonstrated that some changes spread with the regularity envisioned by the Neogrammarians while others rely on lexical diffusion. On the social front, he identified several patterns related to which groups lead change, including the curvilinear class distribution, which reflects the role of people on the interior of the economic scale (e.g. the upper working class) as drivers of change.

Building on this foundation, variationists continue to explore language change in progress in ever more speech communities and languages. In recent years, *Language Variation and Change*, an academic journal dedicated exclusively to variationist research, has featured studies of change in dialects of English around the world from the UK to North America and New Zealand. We also find studies of change in an impressive diversity of languages including Spanish, French, Swedish, Australian Sign Language, and Guaraní (an indigenous language of Paraguay). Each of these projects pursues its own set of particular questions, though together they contribute to a broader mosaic of the change process. Comparing findings from a wide range of cases ultimately serves the goal that has motivated Labov from the start of identifying general principles shaping language change.

Closer to Labov's home turf we find an expanding body of research with more direct connections to his work. Labov has focused his attention on the study of sound change in English, and this topic remains a bountiful font of sociolinguistic research. Labov's work in New York City and Philadelphia inspired several similarly large-scale projects in the early decades of the field, and some recent studies continue in these footsteps. For example, Maciej Baranowski, a former student of Labov's, carried out an ambitious investigation of phonological variation in the city of Charleston, South Carolina (2007). With a sample of 100 speakers, stratified by age and class, Baranowski traces the progress of several sound changes in Charleston, a speech community with a traditionally distinctive accent. Much like Labov did in Martha's Vineyard and New York City, Baranowski anchors his study in real time by looking at the dialectologists' descriptions of Charleston speech from the middle of the twentieth century. He finds that many of the local features that traditionally distinguished Charleston from surrounding dialects are in decline and broader regional patterns are increasingly adopted. Interestingly, the trend with some of these changes represents a counterexample to Labov's curvilinear pattern as the innovations seem to be led by upper class Charlestonians. Such findings lead Baranowski to a fascinating exploration of the social dynamics in the speech community. The broader lesson we can draw from Baranowski's study relates to the enduring relevance of his mentor's model. The Charleston study reminds us that such an approach to language change – one that surveys a large community and draws correlations across social parameters like age, gender, and class – not only remains viable, but actually produces new insights that enrich and refine our understanding of the change process.

We find similar evidence of Labov's influence in the mountains of research investigating sound changes that he "discovered." Over the course of his career, Labov has identified a number of linguistically interesting patterns of change, including several that affect large territories. The Northern Cities Shift certainly fits this bill. While some components of this change were noted by another sociolinguist, Ralph Fasold, in the late 1960s, a fuller description of the Northern Cities Shift appeared in Labov et al.'s (1972) study. Labov also drew on this case in his formulation of general principles of chain shifting (e.g. 1994). I speak from experience when I note that Labov's research inspired others to explore the Shift. My dissertation project was designed to complement the picture that Labov had sketched (see Gordon, 2001). Whereas his work on these changes had surveyed urban speakers from places like Chicago and Detroit, I turned to smaller communities lying between the cities. Other researchers have built on Labov's groundwork in different dimensions. Corinne McCarthy (2011), for example, examined the Shift in Chicago, drawing on a sample of 36 speakers stratified by age, sex, and education. Labov's studies of the Northern Cities Shift had looked at the speech of a smaller number of Chicagoans and concentrated on young people (see Labov et al., 1972). Thus, McCarthy's work added much-needed depth to the picture of the Northern Cities Shift in this city of over 2.5 million people. Both McCarthy and I have found that while much of Labov's description of the Shift held in the places we investigated, the picture was not exactly as he proposed. My results, for example, led me to question Labov's chronology of the changes in the Shift, and McCarthy's findings indicate that some of those changes may be reversing course.

Studies like McCarthy's and mine certainly contribute to filling in the picture of the Northern Cities Shift sketched by Labov, but they also have relevance for broader questions about the process of chain shifting described in Chapter Seven. The ordering of the individual changes in the Shift, for example, determines whether it constitutes a push or drag chain. In the ways that McCarthy and I explore such issues, we again see Labov's influence. The general principles he laid out provide a critical point of comparison for all researchers investigating changes like the Northern Cities Shift. For those of us who focus on phonological change in American English, Labov's *Atlas of North American English* has greatly facilitated such comparison. The *Atlas* sketches the dialect topography of the continent, tracing the broad outlines of regional patterns in a way that highlights areas where more in-depth study seems most fruitful.[2] With the publication of the *Atlas* in 2006, researchers have only just begun to build on this achievement – certainly Baranowski (2007) and McCarthy (2011) illustrate this trend – and a detailed phonological picture of American dialects will continue to develop for many years. As we've seen in other areas, even though Labov's work on sound change is voluminous and rich in insights about particular changes and the process in general, it is not intended to serve as the final word but rather as a spark for a lively scholarly conversation.

The methods for studying sound change have evolved significantly since Labov's earliest projects. We see this particularly with regard to how phonological variation is measured. While auditory coding – where researchers listen to recordings in order to judge which variants a speaker uses – dominated variationist approaches for decades, sociolinguists today rely much more heavily on instrumental acoustic analysis. The development of software allowing this kind of analysis to be performed on personal computers has no doubt fueled this switch. Equipment costs no longer serve as a barrier to entry in this area. Indeed, one of the most popular programs for acoustic analysis, Praat, is available free of charge online.[3] Moreover, the power and accuracy of the current tools for acoustic measurement far exceed those of decades ago.

In the last several years a new subfield of "Sociophonetics" has developed, marking the strengthening ties between sociolinguistics and laboratory phonetics. Each side in this former academic divide has learned from the other. Many phoneticians have become more aware of the value of taking sociolinguistic variation into account in their research. Sociolinguists, in turn, have become more sophisticated in their adoption of theory and tools from phonetics. In the study of vowels, for example, some sociolinguists have come to recognize the limited picture provided by F1 and F2 alone, especially when measurements of these formant values are taken at a single point in time. Often speakers do not hold constant the sound of a vowel as they pronounce it; the tongue may glide across the oral cavity during the articulation of the vowel. This is most obvious in the case of recognized diphthongs, but it commonly occurs even with those vowels we normally categorize as monophthongs. If the researcher only measures the vowel at a single point in time, then none of that movement is captured. Taking multiple measurements across the duration of each vowel results in a more detailed view that may reveal patterns of sociolinguistic relevance as seen, for example, in studies like Thomas (2001) and Majors (2005).

While Labov was an early adopter of acoustic technology, having drawn on these methods in his Martha's Vineyard study, he has tended to rely on fairly tried-and-true techniques. In *The Atlas of North American English*, for example, the presentation draws on data stemming from measurements of F1 and F2 frequencies taken at a single point in a vowel's duration. This is essentially the same technique as that used by Labov et al. (1972), the study that first demonstrated the usefulness of acoustic analysis for studying vowel shifts and other sound changes. These measurements provide a convenient means of exploring vowels in a two-dimensional space parallel to the traditional articulatory parameters of height and frontness, and Labov has shown the usefulness of this view for tracking changes like vowel shifts and mergers. Still, these F1 and F2 values represent a tiny sliver of the information available in the speech signal. Since speakers may exploit any part of that signal for their sociolinguistic needs, it only makes sense for researchers to consider casting a wider net in seeking to account for phonological variation.[4]

The study of sound change in progress is not the only area where technological advances have altered the research landscape in recent years. We also find a steady rise over the last 15 years or so in the application of variationist theory and methods to the exploration of historical changes. Fueling this research has been the development of electronic corpora – digitized collections of texts – that contain documents illustrating how English was written across its 1,500-year history. Such collections have long served as valuable resources for language historians and literary scholars, but their translation to the digital realm has greatly increased their utility. Now it's possible to search for particular usages in a database of millions of words within a few seconds.

For researchers interested in the sociolinguistic dimensions of language change, the most useful corpora are those containing less formal writings instead of or in addition to published works. The Corpus of Early English Correspondence (CEEC) illustrates this principle. It was developed in the 1990s by Terttu Nevalainen and

Helena Raumolin-Brunberg of the University of Helsinki and collects letters from 777 English writers spanning the years 1417–1681.[5] Personal letters offer key advantages over more formal writings for the study of language change. From a stylistic perspective, especially one like Labov's which posits a continuum from standard to vernacular, letters between friends and family generally occupy a space nearer the informal end and thus closer to everyday spoken language. Moreover, they don't reflect the editorial oversight of published works. This means that the language used can be more readily connected to an individual, the letter writer. It also reduces the normative influence of Standard English. As a result, for example, researchers may look to the variable spelling in letters for evidence of sound changes.

The CEEC design responds to Labov's call for a socially realistic linguistics by attempting to represent the widest possible range of people. A corpus of written materials has obvious limitations in this regard. Researchers clearly have no control over what letters have survived the centuries, and the high illiteracy rates of earlier periods mean that the majority of the English population remains completely unrepresented in the sample. Still, the Helsinki researchers took care to include in the CEEC writers from a variety of social ranks and from many different regions. They also gathered correspondence from both men and women writers.

Studies drawing on the CEEC material have revealed some interesting parallels with Labov's work. For example, Nevalainen (2000) traced several grammatical changes over the period covered by the CEEC with special attention given to their social embedding. One of those changes was the replacement of multiple negation (e.g. *I can't see nothing*) with the pattern of Standard English today (e.g. *I can't see anything/I can see nothing*). The CEEC evidence suggests that this change was led by members of the merchant class rather than by the nobility (above them in status) or the non-gentry (below them in status). In other words, the drivers of this change come from the interior of the social scale, creating a curvilinear pattern much like Labov finds with many innovations today.

As this discussion suggests, the study of linguistic change remains a major focus of research in the variationist mold. The models pioneered by Labov continue to bear fruit, and his insights have inspired countless explorations of change in speech communities and languages around the world. Moreover, recent developments in sociophonetics and corpus linguistics have opened up new avenues of investigation and demonstrate the vitality of sociolinguistic research into language change.

Perceptual aspects of variation

We've noted in various places how language stands as a topic that people often have strong feelings about. Indeed, the ending of the previous sentence in a preposition might incite such feelings in some readers. When we notice linguistic variation, we rarely remain neutral on the choice between competing usages. We tend to view some forms as better than others, and we judge people based on which forms they use, sometimes with damaging consequences (see Chapter Eight).

Labov has long recognized the significance of this subjective dimension of language variation. Weinreich et al. (1968) included "evaluation" among the central problems to consider in accounting for language change, and Labov incorporated methods of examining this dimension directly in his research protocols in the New York City study. For example, he elicited responses to various New York accents, asking participants to rank the speakers in terms of their suitability for different kinds of jobs. He also explored participants' senses of their own speech – which pronunciations they claimed to use, how secure they were in the correctness of their usage, and so on – as well as general attitudes toward the New York dialect.

Despite Labov's apparent enthusiasm for investigating the evaluation problem early in his career, it has not featured prominently in his subsequent work. Nonetheless, the topic has not wanted for attention from the field more generally. Indeed an impressive body of research has grown up around the questions of how attitudes and perceptions shape sociolinguistic variation and change.

Much of the work on these questions proceeds under the banner of "folk linguistics," an approach championed by Dennis Preston.[6] As the name suggests, research in this area pursues an account of folk beliefs about language, seeking to understand what regular people (as opposed to those with specialist training in linguistics) think about how language works. Preston has devoted particular attention to the issue of perceptual dialectology, exploring beliefs about regional and social variation. Among his best-known techniques in this pursuit is a mapping task in which he presents subjects with a blank map of the country or some particular area and asks them to draw where the significant dialect boundaries fall. The results often show that perceptions of dialect differences stand at odds with the evidence from linguistic studies of actual speech. What should we make of such discrepancies or of these findings more generally?

Some linguists might dismiss such folk perceptions out of hand, arguing that they reflect cultural stereotypes with little connection to real speech patterns. To be sure, we do find ample evidence of regional typecasting in the results from a mapping task when, for example, California is labeled as the home of surfers and valley girls. Still, cultural stereotypes often have a linguistic component, as is certainly the case for the California example. In this way, studies in perceptual dialectology serve to document the salience of dialect features, revealing what people notice in the speech of other people and what they don't notice. These insights contribute to our understanding of broader questions about the forces underlying language variation and change. For example, they connect with Labov's theories on the life cycle of linguistic change and how a variable might develop from an indicator to a marker to a stereotype as it acquires increasing degrees of social awareness (see Chapter Seven).

Other work on language attitudes and perceptions has proceeded in a more experimental mode.[7] Using techniques similar to those Labov employed in New York City, researchers have investigated how listeners react when listening to recordings of different speech patterns. These studies often incorporate a "matched guise" design in which the same speaker is recorded using two different languages or dialects. This approach reduces the potential for things like tone of voice to influence listeners' judgments. The recordings are played for listeners who evaluate the speaker(s) on a number of characteristics, such as how friendly or intelligent they seem. The social psychologist Wallace Lambert pioneered the matched guise technique to investigate reactions to French and English among Canadians (see Lambert et al., 1960). This work revealed that the same voice is evaluated differently when speaking French than when speaking English. Comparable differences in evaluation have been found in matched guise studies involving dialects of the same language. Thus, Britons judge voices differently when they use an upper-class "Received Pronunciation" accent from when they adopt a regional accent (see, e.g. Giles, 1971).

In addition to investigating attitudes and social judgments about particular language varieties, this general experimental approach can examine perceptions of a very different sort by testing what listeners hear and how their hearing might be shaped by sociolinguistic factors. Researchers investigating phonological mergers, for example, commonly use perception tests to determine the status of a phonemic distinction. Thus, to see whether someone has adopted the *cot/caught* merger (see Chapter Seven), they might be asked to listen to several examples of each word pronounced by someone who does distinguish the vowels and to identify which word they hear. Someone with this merger normally not only fails to distinguish the vowels in his or her own pronunciation, but also cannot reliably hear the difference in someone else's.[8] Labov has incorporated this kind of test into his investigations of merger, and he has used a similar technique to investigate how sound changes might lead to problems of cross-dialect comprehension. Thus, for example, a word like *bus* spoken by someone with the Northern Cities Shift might sound like *boss* to someone from outside that region. He reports on several experiments in this vein in the final volume of his *Principles of Linguistic Change* (2010).

Several researchers have taken this style of perceptual study in new directions by adding social variables to the mix. Nancy Niedzielski (1999), for example, offers a clever demonstration of how dialect stereotypes shape speech perception. She recorded a speaker from Detroit, Michigan, and excerpted several examples of that person's pronunciation of the /au/ diphthong in words like *about* and *house*. In many North American dialects, the pronunciation of this vowel varies in terms of the height of the nucleus (the first element in the diphthong). Just as Labov found on Martha's Vineyard, Niedzielski's Detroiter often pronounced this vowel with a raised/ centralized nucleus. This pronunciation is actually quite common in the northern US, including Michigan, but such raised diphthongs act as a stereotype of Canadian English. Niedzielski found that this stereotype had a powerful effect on perceptions of the vowels. She assembled a group of listeners, all natives of Michigan, and presented them with a set of different forms of /au/ as models. The nuclei in these model forms ranged from extremely low to extremely high. For the experiment, subjects listened to several recordings of sentences containing a word with /au/, and they were asked to match what they heard with one of the models. The recordings all came from the same speaker, the Detroiter, but half of the listeners were told that the person whose speech they were evaluating was Canadian and half were told that person was American. This difference led to very different categorizations. The listeners were much more likely to hear the raised diphthong that the Detroiter actually used, and thus to match the recorded pronunciation to one of the models with a raised vowel, when they thought they were listening to a Canadian. In this way, when the aural input fit with their stereotype, they judged it more accurately; but when that input conflicted with their expectation, they opted to side with the latter, and they matched the raised pronunciation used with a model representing a more standard form.

Studies like Niedzielski's underscore complexities in the seemingly straightforward process of speech perception. We already knew that people have sociolinguistic expectations about which kind of people speak one way or another, but this line of research demonstrates that such preconceived notions operate even in an artificial social context like a laboratory experiment. This work, in its methodology and theoretical underpinnings, also illustrates how the disciplinary bridge represented by sociophonetics extends beyond the study of language change and has opened up investigations into a wide variety of interesting questions.

Variation and social meaning

We round out this survey of some recent trends in variationist sociolinguistics by turning to an issue that lies at the heart of the field: the relationship between language and social structure. What do sociolinguistic variables mean and how do they take on those meanings? These questions have spurred a lively debate in recent years and have opened up fruitful avenues of investigation.

As you might expect of a field practiced for five decades, variationists have explored a range of approaches to the issue of the social meaning of linguistic variation. Penelope Eckert, a former student of Labov's, has put forward an influential categorization of the various approaches in terms of waves of research.[9] These waves appeared chronologically, though Eckert notes, "No wave supersedes the previous, but each represents a quite distinct way of thinking about variation and a distinct methodological and analytic practice, each of which grew out of the findings of the previous wave" (2012).

The first wave is characterized by large-scale studies mostly of urban communities. This "survey era," as Eckert dubs it, began with Labov's dissertation project in New York City. Research in this model explores the social side of the sociolinguistic equation by correlating linguistic usages with broad demographic characteristics like age, sex, ethnicity, and class. In this way linguistic variables mark an individual's place in the wider social structure; they give his or her "social address." In New York, for example, a 40-something, lower middle class woman pronounces /r/ in words like *fourth floor* at a different rate from a 20-year-old, working class man due to the differences in these speakers' positions in structure of the speech community.

The survey approach produces a macro-level sketch of the speech community as a whole that Eckert likens to a map. A study like Labov's charts the major dimensions of the sociolinguistic structure of New York City in the same way that a map represents the streets. But a map doesn't indicate what it's like to live in a certain neighborhood, and a survey approach offers a limited perspective on the social dynamics at work in the construction of variation at a more local level. When the analysis relies on broad social categories (e.g. men vs. women), any explanations for the observed patterns must rely on generalizations about those groups. If the question becomes "what is it about women or the lower middle class that leads them to do X?" then no answer can satisfy because there is as much distinguishing the members of these groups as there is uniting them.

An interest in exploring how variation functions from a local perspective led to the second wave, which Eckert labels the "ethnographic era." Borrowing from anthropology, researchers in this ethnographic mode seek to understand a community on its own terms. Thus, rather than adopting presupposed analytical lenses like those of the first wave, the emphasis lies with uncovering social distinctions with local relevance.

Eckert's study (2000) of a suburban Detroit high school stands as a model case in this regard. Taking on a participant-observer role, Eckert immersed herself in the culture of the high school for two years. She discovered a population separated into two main camps: the Jocks and the Burnouts. These groups differ in a great number of ways from how they dress to how they spend their free time to what they plan to do after graduation. Of course they also differ sociolinguistically, and Eckert examines variation in this community in relation to several linguistic features including the sound changes of the Northern Cities Shift (see Chapter Seven).

The differences between an ethnographic approach like Eckert's and the familiar survey approach come into focus when we consider the Jock-Burnout divide in terms of class. The opposition of Jocks and Burnouts represents one of the ways that class divisions in the wider community play out in the school. Jocks represent a middle class orientation and Burnouts a working class orientation in terms of their relationship to the corporate culture of the school, their projected career paths, and their family backgrounds. Most Jocks come from middle class homes and most Burnouts from working class homes, but there are exceptions. In a traditional community survey, adolescents might be categorized according to their parents' class status. For a working class child who affiliates with the Jocks or a middle class one who affiliates with the Burnouts, the survey approach would misrepresent who they are. Moreover, a survey methodology would not provide the rich picture of the social dynamics underpinning the Jock-Burnout divide. When Eckert turns to explain the sociolinguistic patterns she documents, she draws on a deep understanding of the social setting. She can point to particular practices that might account not only for differences between Jocks and Burnouts, but also within each group.[10] Still, the ethnographic approach relies primarily on linking linguistic features to social categories. Those categories are uncovered through observation rather than presupposed, and they represent a more localized perspective, but are still generally treated as part of the existing social structure.

Enter the third wave of variationist research, which challenges this view of social structure as given, and in so doing marks a substantial departure from tradition. Many of the ideas associated with the third wave have circulated for decades though research in this paradigm has gained tremendous momentum in the last five to ten years. Third-wave scholars frame their investigations in terms of social action rather than social structure. They ask "how we create and fill out our 'sociality' (our sense and experience of being social actors in social situations) through our social actions and therefore through our language use" (Coupland and Jaworski, 2009, p. 10).

In this view, social meaning does not reside in static categories but rather is continually created through interactions. As a result, greater emphasis is placed on speaker agency. Individuals do not passively inherit speech patterns reflecting their social addresses, but rather they actively construct social identities by drawing on a range of linguistic and nonlinguistic resources. In this way the social meaning of a particular linguistic form is complex and fluid.

The third-wave focus on how social meaning is made has prompted renewed interest in the intra-speaker variation that sociolinguists traditionally label "style." As described in Chapter Five, Labov explores style in rather narrow terms. In his work, stylistic variation operates in a single dimension of formality, and speaking styles represent points on a continuum from standard to vernacular.[11] Third-wave researchers conceive of style in much broader terms. Indeed, style involves more than just language and encompasses a range of social behaviors. Styles are central to how we make sense of our environments, as Eckert explains:

> Speaking in the social world involves a continual analysis and interpretation of categories, groups, types, and personae and of the differences in the ways they talk . . . These emerge as we come to notice differences, to make distinctions, and to attribute meaning to them. Thus we construct a social landscape through the segmentation of the social terrain, and we construct a linguistic landscape through a segmentation of the linguistic practices in that terrain. The level of social practice that corresponds to distinctions in the terrain in which we study variation is style. In all areas of art, style is what characterizes schools, periods, and individuals. Style has a similar function in everyday language, picking out locations in the social landscape such as Valley girls, cholos, cowboys, jocks, burnouts, Italian hoods. (2008, pp. 455–6)

This view of style as social practice emphasizes the performative nature of even everyday language use. In each interaction we enact some ways of being, including some ways of talking (or writing).

By foregrounding style, third-wave theorists also bring a new perspective on linguistic variables. For the most part, this research still investigates the traditional kinds of phonological and grammatical variables discussed throughout this book as these variables serve as components of linguistic styles. But a given style may incorporate a range of linguistic variables, and a given variable may operate in a range of styles. Interpreting the meaning of linguistic variables, therefore, demands attention to their stylistic context. The same form might convey one sense when combined with components of one particular style and convey a very different sense when combined with components of another style.

We see a simple illustration of this with the familiar (ing) variable. This variable codes the alternation between the velar [ŋ] and alveolar [n] nasal consonants in the *–ing* suffix (e.g. *fishing* vs. *fishin'*). As noted in Chapter Five, Labov treats this variation as operating on a vernacular-standard continuum though it hardly seems to function like other variables that occupy this territory, such as (dh) (e.g. *these* and *dese*). The (ing) variation seems to often code differences of formality. As Eckert (2008) notes, however, formality might be interpreted in different ways. Thus, someone using the alveolar form (e.g. *fishin'*) might be read in a positive light as relaxed and easygoing or in a negative light as inarticulate and lazy. Likewise, someone using the velar form (e.g. *fishing*) might come off as well-mannered or as pretentious. Context determines the social meaning contributed by (ing), and context includes the setting of the speech event (e.g. lecturing in class, chatting over a coffee, etc.) as well as the accompanying components of the speaker's style. Thus, use of the velar form of (ing) by someone speaking with an identifiable regional accent might contribute to an impression of pretentiousness or insincerity since listeners expect the "informal" variant from such a person.[12] By the same token, use of the alveolar form might seem just as contextually inappropriate when used by someone speaking Standard English, including markedly formal elements (e.g. *It is he about whom we have been conversin'*). In this way we see that not only can the same linguistic form activate quite distinct social meanings, but, moreover, the same social meaning can be activated by different linguistic forms.

As this brief description conveys, third-wave variationist research adopts a substantially different perspective from the one that has guided most of the work in the field since its beginnings. Still, to describe the third wave as a break with the Labovian roots would overstate the case. Without a doubt this work challenges some fundamental ways of thinking about sociolinguistic variation. Still, third-wave researchers are variationists; they gather speech data through empirical methods (that is, by examining actual usage) and rely on quantitative analyses to uncover the order beneath the heterogeneity. Nevertheless, the kinds of questions they pursue do suggest a different set of priorities from those guiding work in other waves including Labov's. The third-wave reframing of the sociolinguistic investigation on social action recalls issues debated at the founding of modern sociolinguistics in the 1960s (see Chapter One). Labov voiced his view then that sociolinguistics stands as a branch of linguistics, and his research agenda has stayed true to this position. The object of Labov's study remains language. Fundamentally, he studies linguistic variation and change for what it reveals about the nature of language. By contrast, other sociolinguists focus more on what language does, on its social and cultural functioning. Coupland and Jaworski represent this perspective when they describe sociolinguistics as "studying social worlds through language" (2009, p. 1). Much of the work in the third wave proceeds from this perspective as it explores questions of how social meaning is constructed from linguistic resources.

The fact that research in variationist and other branches of sociolinguistics goes on today with varying degrees of emphasis on either the socio or linguistic sides testifies to the health of the field. Studies done in each of Eckert's three waves complement work in the others. Community-level surveys provide an essential wider context for understanding the sociolinguistic moves an individual might make in a particular interaction investigated through a micro-level study. The variationist tent has gotten bigger in recent years, and we should celebrate this growth. After all, there is no shortage of variation to investigate. More ways of approaching that variation can only lead to a fuller appreciation of the complex functioning of language in society.

Concluding remarks

In the 1960s a diverse group of language researchers launched a scholarly conversation, or rather a series of conversations, that laid the groundwork for new ways of studying language. Though this work came to flourish under different academic labels such as the sociology of language, ethnography of communication, and sociolinguistics, the practitioners of these disciplines were (and remain) united in the belief that we have much to gain from exploring language as a social phenomenon and not just as a set of phonological and grammatical structures in the mind. Labov and others who were working within the disciplinary walls of linguistics sought to expand the scope of inquiry in the field and to change accepted practices by placing research on a firmer empirical footing.

Several decades later, the landscape within linguistics certainly has changed though we remain far from the point where "sociolinguistics" might be considered a redundant term, where it would be inconceivable to practice linguistics without attending to the social dimension of language. In many branches of the field, social considerations do no enter into the conversation. Indeed, following Chomsky, many who work in "theoretical" linguistics view such considerations as irrelevant. In this paradigm, the fact that people speak differently in different situations, for example, is a matter of mere performance when what really matters is the underlying knowledge of language, a person's linguistic competence.

At the same time, linguists in a range of subfields have come to acknowledge the value of gathering empirical support for proposed theories. In phonology today, experimental evidence frequently informs thinking about the principles governing sound systems. The growth in corpus linguistics has opened up new arenas for generating and testing ideas related to syntax, semantics, and a wide range of other dimensions of language. Even in the realm of grammatical theory, where Chomsky's influence has dominated, we find challenges to the traditional reliance on intuitions as evidence and calls to raise the evidentiary bar (see, e.g. Schütze, 1996; Wasow and Arnold, 2005).

To what extent (if any) have such developments been inspired by work in sociolinguistics or Labov's efforts in particular? It's difficult to answer such a question, but it is clear that the field of linguistics has evolved dramatically in the last 50 years, and the rise of sociolinguistics has contributed to these transformations by broadening the scope of linguistic inquiry. Even though many linguists choose not to pursue questions related to the social aspects of language, no one denies that such questions have a legitimate place in linguistics. This was not necessarily the case for previous generations of linguists.

In the US and the UK, no individual has contributed more to this expanded sense of what linguistics should care about than Labov.

He taught the field new ways of examining language. The theoretical underpinning of Labov's approach begins with a rejection of the traditional dogma that linguistic structure relies on invariance and categorical rules. His exploration of the orderly heterogeneity of speech blazed new methodological trails and demonstrated the wealth of insight to be gained from careful observation of the language used by a diverse range of people across a variety of social settings.

The approach that Labov pioneered has evolved greatly over the decades and continues to stretch in new directions, reaching out to neighboring disciplines and re-exploring familiar territory from fresh perspectives. Variationist research today addresses a spectacular array of engaging questions with an equally impressive diversity of methods. The excitement and energy that suffuse variationist sociolinguistics today offer a powerful testimony to Labov's legacy. The field has expanded to become much more than the eponymous label "Labovian sociolinguistics" implies, but Labov's influence continues to be felt in ways great and small. Understanding what contemporary sociolinguistics is all about begins with appreciating the foundations Labov laid and his many contributions over the years. My goal in this book has been to bring to light the main strands of Labov's work and to convey, especially to nonspecialists, a sense of his significance. Ultimately, I hope this discussion will motivate readers to engage further with Labov's work and with sociolinguistics more broadly. Exploring the relationship between language and society brings new perspectives on both and leads us to a deeper appreciation of the complex sociolinguistic behaviors at work every time we start a conversation.

Notes

1   While I highlight several key trends in variationist research, I do not pretend to offer a complete survey of this work and certainly not of sociolinguistics in general. Readers seeking a wider view of the state of sociolinguistics might consult recent collections like Coupland and Jaworski (2009) or Wodak et al. (2011). Chambers and Schilling (2013) offer a fuller account of variationist research. For the most up-to-date perspective, one might consult programs from recent New Ways of Analyzing Variation conferences. At these annual gatherings, variationists present findings from their current research.

2 I have borrowed the phrase "dialect topography" from J. K. Chambers, who uses it to describe a similar kind of survey research he conducted on Canadian English.

3 Praat was designed by Paul Boersma and David Weenink of the University of Amsterdam and is available at their site: <http://www. fon.hum.uva.nl/praat/>. Bartek Plichta developed a package called Akustyk to work with Praat by facilitating the kinds of analysis that variationists frequently carry out. It is also available at no cost online at <http://bartus.org/akustyk/>.

4 Thomas (2011) provides an overview of these issues as well as an accessible description of methods in sociophonetics.

5 The team at Helsinki continue to expand this project. Updates on the work can be found at their website: <http://www.helsinki.fi/varieng/index.html>.

6 See Niedzielski and Preston (2003) or Preston (1989) for overviews of this research.

7 Thomas (2002) and Hay and Drager (2007) provide helpful reviews of decades of research in this area.

8 As it happens, Labov discovered that in some cases a perception test reveals that a person fails to hear a distinction even when a close examination of their actual pronunciation indicates that they make a consistent difference in pronouncing the sounds in question. He labels this interesting case a "near-merger" (see Labov, 1994 for further details).

9 I base my discussion on a pre-publication version of Eckert's (2012) paper.

10 For example, some burnouts engage in "cruising" (driving up and down certain streets and occasionally stopping to hang out), which connects these suburban teenagers to the larger urban community. This practice might facilitate the spread of linguistic features associated with Detroit proper such as the Northern Cities Shift.

11 Recall that Labov does not claim that his approach represents a full treatment of style. Indeed, he is clear that his model, which is based on attention paid to speech, is designed to account for the stylistic variation found in sociolinguistic interviews (see Chapter Five).

12 Campbell-Kibler (2007) explores this very question through a matched-guise study.

BIBLIOGRAPHY

Baranowski, M. (2007). *Phonological Variation and Change in the Dialect of Charleston, South Carolina*, (Publications of the American Dialect Society, 92). Durham, NC: Duke University Press.

Baugh, J. (1980). "A re-examination of the Black English copula." In W. Labov (ed.), *Locating Language in Time and Space* (pp. 83–106). New York: Academic Press.

—(1999). *Out of the Mouths of Slaves: African American Language and Educational Malpractice*. Austin: University of Texas Press.

—(2000). *Beyond Ebonics: Linguistic Pride and Racial Prejudice*. Oxford: Oxford University Press.

Bell, A. (1984). "Language style as audience design." *Language in Society*, 13, 145–204.

Bereiter, C., Engelman, S., Osborn, J., and Reidford, P. A. (1966). "An academically oriented pre-school for culturally deprived children." In F. M. Hechinger (ed.), *Pre-school Education Today* (pp. 105–36). Garden City, NY: Doubleday.

Bloomfield, L. (1984). *Language*. Chicago: University of Chicago Press. (Original work published in 1933).

Bright, W. (ed.) (1966). *Sociolinguistics: Proceedings of the UCLA Sociolinguistics Conference, 1964*. The Hague: Mouton.

Campbell-Kibler, K. (2007). "Accent, (ING), and the social logic of listener perceptions." *American Speech*, 82, 32–64.

Cedergren, H. and Sankoff, D. (1974). "Variable rules: Performance as a statistical reflection of competence." *Language*, 50, 333–55.

Chambers, J. K. (2008). *Sociolinguistic Theory* (3rd edn). Malden, MA: Wiley-Blackwell.

Chambers, J. K. and Schilling, N. (eds). (2013). *Handbook of Language Variation and Change* (2nd edn). Malden, MA: Wiley-Blackwell.

Chambers, J. K. and Trudgill, P. (1998). *Dialectology* (2nd edn). Cambridge: Cambridge University Press.

Chambers, J. K., Trudgill, P., and Schilling-Estes, N. (eds). (2002). *Handbook of Language Variation and Change*. Malden, MA: Blackwell.

Chomsky, N. (1965). *Aspects of the Theory of Syntax*. Cambridge, MA: MIT Press.

Coupland, N. (2007). *Style: Language Variation and Identity*. Cambridge: Cambridge University Press.

Coupland, N. and Jaworski, A. (2009). *The New Sociolinguistics Reader*. New York: Palgrave Macmillan.

Curzan, A. and Adams, M. (2011). *How English Works: A Linguistic Introduction* (3rd edn). New York: Pearson-Longman.

Duranti, A. (1997). *Linguistic Anthropology*. Cambridge: Cambridge University Press.

—(2001). "Linguistic anthropology: History, ideas, and issues." In A. Duranti (ed.), *Linguistic Anthropology: A Reader* (pp. 1–38). Malden, MA: Blackwell.

Eckert, P. (1997). "Age as a sociolinguistic variable." In. F. Coulmas (ed.), *The Handbook of Sociolinguistics* (pp. 151–67). Malden, MA: Blackwell.

—(2000). *Linguistic Variation as Social Practice*. Malden, MA: Blackwell.

—(2001). "Style and social meaning." In P. Eckert and J. R. Rickford (eds), *Style and Sociolinguistic Variation* (pp. 119–26). Cambridge: Cambridge University Press.

—(2008). "Variation and the indexical field." *Journal of Sociolinguistics*, 12, 453–76.

—(2012). "Three waves of variation study: The emergence of meaning in the study of sociolinguistic variation." *Annual Review of Anthropology*, 41 (forthcoming).

Eckert, P. and McConnell-Ginet, S. (1992). "Think practically and look locally: Language and gender as community-based practice." *Annual Review of Anthropology*, 21, 461–90.

Eckert, P. and Rickford, J. R. (eds). (2001). *Style and Sociolinguistic Variation*. Cambridge: Cambridge University Press.

Fasold, R. (1984). *The Sociolinguistics of Society*. Oxford: Blackwell.

—(1991). "The quiet demise of variable rules." *American Speech*, 66, 3–21.

Finegan, E. (2011). *Language: Its Structure and Use* (6th edn). Boston: Wadsworth.

Fischer, J. L. (1958). "Social influences on the choice of a linguistic variant." *Word*, 14, 47–56.

Fought, C. (2006). "Talkin' with mi gente (Chicano English)." In W. Wolfram and B. Ward, *American Voices: How Dialects Differ from Coast to Coast* (pp. 233–7). Malden, MA: Blackwell. (Also available at <http://www.pbs.org/speak/seatosea/americanvarieties/chicano/>).

Giles, H. (1971). "Patterns of evaluation to R. P., South Welsh and Somerset accented speech." *British Journal of Social & Clinical Psychology*, 10, 280–1.

Gordon, C. (2011). "Gumperz and interactional sociolinguistics." In R. Wodak, B. Johnstone, and P. Kerswill (eds), *The Sage Handbook of Sociolinguistics* (pp. 67–84). Los Angeles: Sage.

Gordon, M. J. (2001). *Small-Town Values and Big-City Vowels: A Study of the Northern Cities Shift in Michigan* (Publications of the American Dialect Society, 84). Durham, NC: Duke University Press.

—(2006). "Interview with William Labov." *Journal of English Linguistics*, 34, 332–51.

Green, L. (2002). *African American English: A Linguistic Introduction.* Cambridge: Cambridge University Press.

Gumperz, J. J. and Hymes, D. (eds). (1964). *The Ethnography of Communication.* (Special publication, *American Anthropologist* 66 [6], part 2). Washington, DC: American Anthropological Association.

—(1972). *Directions in Sociolinguistics: The Ethnography of Communication.* New York: Hold, Rinehart and Winston.

Guy, G. (1993). "The quantitative analysis of linguistic variation." In D. R. Preston (ed.), *American Dialect Research* (pp. 223–49). Amsterdam/ Philadelphia: John Benjamins.

Harris, Z. (1951). *Structural Linguistics.* Chicago: University of Chicago Press.

Hay, J. and Drager, K. (2007). "Sociophonetics." *Annual Review of Anthropology*, 36, 89–103.

Hubbell, A. F. (1950). *The Pronunciation of English in New York City: Consonants and Vowels.* New York: King's Crown Press, Columbia University.

Hymes, D. (1964). "Introduction: Toward ethnographies of communication." In J. J. Gumperz and D. Hymes (eds), *The Ethnography of Communication* (pp. 1–34). (Special publication, *American Anthropologist* 66 [6], part 2). Washington, DC: American Anthropological Association.

—(1972). "On communicative competence." In J. B. Pride and J. Holmes (eds), *Sociolinguistics* (pp. 269–93). Harmondsworth: Penguin. Reprinted in A. Duranti. (ed.), (2001). *Linguistic Anthropology: A Reader* (pp. 53–73). Malden, MA: Blackwell.

—(1974). *Foundations in Sociolinguistics: An Ethnographic Approach.* Philadelphia: University of Pennsylvania Press.

Ivinson, G. (2011). "Bernstein: Codes and social class." In R. Wodak, B. Johnstone, and P. Kerswill (eds), *The Sage Handbook of Sociolinguistics* (pp. 40–56). Los Angeles: Sage.

Kenyon, J. (1948). "Cultural levels and functional varieties of English." *College English*, 10, 31–6.

Kepser, S. and Reis, M. (2005). *Linguistic Evidence: Empirical, Theoretical and Computational Perspectives.* Berlin: Mouton de Gruyter.

Koerner, K. (1991). "Towards a history of modern sociolinguistics." *American Speech*, 66, 57–70.

Kretzschmar, W. A. Jr, McDavid, V. G., Lerud, T. K., and Johnson, E. (1994). *Handbook of the Linguistic Atlas of the Middle and South Atlantic States.* Chicago: University of Chicago Press.

Kroch, A. (1978). "Toward a theory of social dialect variation." *Language in Society*, 7, 17–36.

Kurath, H. (1949). *Word Geography of Eastern United States.* Ann Arbor: University of Michigan Press.

Kurath, H. and McDavid, R. I. (1961). *The Pronunciation of English in the Atlantic States.* Ann Arbor: University of Michigan Press.

Labov, W. (1963). "The social motivation of a sound change." *Word*, 19, 273–309. Reprinted in W. Labov (1972b).

—(1966a). "Hypercorrection by the lower middle class as a factor in linguistic change." In W. Bright (ed.), *Sociolinguistics: Proceedings of the UCLA Sociolinguistics Conference* (pp. 84–102), The Hague: Mouton.

—(1966b). "The effect of social mobility on linguistic behavior." *Sociological Inquiry*, 36, 186–203.

—(1969). "Contraction, deletion, and the inherent variability of the English copula." *Language*, 45, 715–62.

—(1972a). *Language in the Inner City: Studies in the Black English Vernacular.* Philadelphia: University of Pennsylvania Press.

—(1972b). *Sociolinguistic Patterns.* Philadelphia: University of Pennsylvania Press.

—(1972c). "Some principles of linguistic methodology." *Language in Society*, 1, 97–120.

—(1973). "The place of linguistic research in American society." In E. P. Hamp (ed.), *Themes in Linguistics: The 1970s* (pp. 97–129). The Hague: Mouton.

—(1975). *What is a Linguistic Fact?* Lisse: Peter de Ridder Press.

—(1978). "Sociolinguistics." In W. O. Dingwall (ed.), *A Survey of Linguistic Science* (2nd edn) (pp. 339–72). Stamford, CT: Greylock.

—(1981). "Resolving the Neogrammarian controversy." *Language*, 57, 267–308.

—(1982a). "Building on empirical foundations." In W. P. Lehmann and Y. Malkiel (eds), *Perspectives on Historical Linguistics* (pp. 17–92). Amsterdam/Philadelphia: John Benjamins.

—(1982b). "Objectivity and commitment in linguistic science." *Language in Society*, 11, 165–201.

—(1982c). "Speech actions and reactions in personal narrative." In D. Tannen (ed.), *Analyzing Discourse: Text and Talk* (pp. 219–47). Washington, DC: Georgetown University Press.

——(1984). "Field methods of the project on linguistic change and variation." In J. Baugh and J. Sherzer (eds), *Language in Use: Readings in Sociolinguistics* (pp. 28–53). Englewood Cliffs, NJ: Prentice-Hall.

——(1987). "Are black and white vernaculars diverging? Papers from the NWAVE XIV panel discussion." *American Speech*, 62, 5–12.

——(1990). "The intersection of sex and social class in the course of linguistic change." *Language Variation and Change*, 2, 205–54.

——(1994). *Principles of Linguistic Change* (*Vol. 1: Internal Factors*). Oxford: Blackwell.

——(1995). "Can reading failure be reversed?" In V. Gadsden and D. Wagner (eds), *Literacy among African-American Youth* (pp. 39–68). Cresskill, NJ: Hampton Press.

——(1997a). "How I got into linguistics and what I got out of it." Retrieved from <http://www.ling.upenn.edu/~wlabov/HowIgot.html>.

——(1997b). "Some further steps in narrative analysis." *Journal of Narrative and Life History*, 7, 395–415.

——(1998). "Co-existent systems in African-American vernacular English." In S. S. Mufwene, J. R. Rickford, G. Bailey, and J. Baugh (eds), *African-American English: Structure, History and Use* (pp. 85–109). London: Routledge.

——(2001a). "The anatomy of style-shifting." In P. Eckert and J. R. Rickford (eds), *Style and Sociolinguistic Variation* (pp. 85–108). Cambridge: Cambridge University Press.

——(2001b). *Principles of Linguistic Change* (*Vol. 2: Social Factors*). Malden, MA: Blackwell.

——(2006). *The Social Stratification of English in New York City* (2nd edn). Cambridge: Cambridge University Press.

——(2007). "Transmission and diffusion." *Language*, 83, 344–87.

——(2010). *Principles of Linguistic Change* (*Vol. 3: Cognitive and Cultural Factors*). Malden, MA: Wiley-Blackwell.

Labov, W., Ash, S., and Boberg, C. (2006). *The Atlas of North American English: Phonology and Sound Change*. Berlin: Mouton de Gruyter.

Labov, W. and Baker, B. (2010). "What is a reading error?" *Applied Psycholinguistics*, 31, 735–57.

Labov, W., Cohen, P., Robins, C., and Lewis, J. (1968). "A study of the non-standard English of Negro and Puerto Rican speakers in New York City." Report on Co-operative Research Project 3288. New York: Columbia University.

Labov, W. and Fanshel, D. (1977). *Therapeutic Discourse: Psychotherapy as Conversation*. New York: Academic Press.

Labov, W. and Waletzky, J. (1967). "Narrative analysis: Oral versions of personal experience." In J. Helm (ed.), *Essays on the Verbal and Visual Arts* (pp. 12–44). Seattle: University of Washington Press. Reprinted in *Journal of Narrative and Life History*, 7 (1997), 3–38.

Labov, W., Yaeger, M., and Steiner, R. (1972). *A Quantitative Study of Sound Change in Progress*. Philadelphia: US Regional Survey.

Lambert, W. E., Hodgson, R. C., Gardner, R. C., and Fillenbaum, S. (1960). "Evaluational reactions to spoken languages." *Journal of Abnormal and Social Psychology*, 60, 44–51.

Lavandera, B. R. (1978). "Where does the sociolinguistic variable stop?" *Language in Society*, 7, 171–82.

— (1988). "The study of language in its socio-cultural context." In F. J. Newmeyer (ed.), *Linguistics: The Cambridge Survey, Volume IV: Language: The Socio-cultural Context* (pp. 1–13). Cambridge: Cambridge University Press.

Majors, T. (2005). "Low back vowel merger in Missouri speech: Acoustic description and explanation." *American Speech*, 80, 165–79.

Martinet, A. (1952). "Function, structure, and sound change." *Word*, 8, 1–32.

McCarthy, C. (2011). "The Northern Cities Shift in Chicago." *Journal of English Linguistics*, 39, 166–87.

McDavid, R. I. Jr and McDavid, V. (1951). "The relationship of the speech of American negroes to the speech of whites." *American Speech*, 26, 3–17.

Milroy, J. (1992). *Linguistic Variation and Change*. Oxford: Blackwell.

Milroy, J. and Milroy, L. (1985). "Linguistic change, social network and speaker innovation." *Journal of Linguistics*, 21, 339–84.

Milroy, L. (1987). *Language and Social Networks* (2nd edn). Oxford: Blackwell.

Milroy, L. and Gordon, M. (2003). *Sociolinguistics: Method and Interpretation*. Oxford: Blackwell.

Milroy, L. and Milroy, J. (1992). "Social network and social class: Towards an integrated sociolinguistic model." *Language in Society*, 21, 1–26.

Mishler, E. G. (1997). "A matter of time: When, since, and after Labov and Waletzky." *Journal of Narrative and Life History*, 7, 69–74.

Nevalainen, T. (2000). "Gender differences in the evolution of Standard English: Evidence from the Corpus of Early English Correspondence." *Journal of English Linguistics*, 28, 38–59.

Niedzielski, N. (1999). "The effect of social information on the perception of sociolinguistic variables." *Journal of Language and Social Psychology*, 18, 62–85.

Niedzielski, N. A. and Preston, D. R. (2003). *Folk Linguistics*. Berlin: de Gruyter.

Pederson, L. (1965). *The Pronunciation of English in Metropolitan Chicago*. (Publications of the American Dialect Society, 44). Tuscaloosa, AL: University of Alabama Press.

Pew Research Center (2008). *Inside the Middle Class: Bad Times Hit the Good Life*. Washington, DC: Pew Research Center. Retrieved from <http://www.pewsocialtrends.org/2008/04/09/inside-the-middle-class-bad-times-hit-the-good-life/>

Preston, D. R. (1989). *Perceptual Dialectology: Nonlinguists' Views of Areal Linguistics*. Dordrecht: Foris.

Rickford, J. R. (1986). "The need for new approaches to social class analysis in sociolinguistics." *Language and Communication*, 6, 215–21.

—(1997). "Suite for ebony and phonics." *Discover*, 18 (12), 82–8. Reprinted in J. R. Rickford (1999), pp. 320–8.

—(1999). *African American Vernacular English*. Malden, MA: Blackwell.

Rickford, J. R. and Rickford, R. J. (2000). *Spoken Soul: The Story of Black English*. New York: Wiley.

Rousseau, P. and Sankoff, D. (1978). "Advances in variable rule methodology." In D. Sankoff (ed.), *Linguistic Variation: Models and Methods* (pp. 57–69). New York: Academic.

Russell, R. L. (1979). "Speech acts, conversational sequencing, and rules" (Review of the book *Therapeutic Discourse*, by W. Labov and D. Fanshel). *Contemporary Sociology*, 8, 176–9.

Sankoff, D. and Labov, W. (1978). "On the use of variable rules." *Language in Society*, 8, 189–222.

Sankoff, G. and Blondeau, H. (2007). "Language change across the lifespan: /r/ in Montreal French." *Language*, 83, 560–88.

Sapir, E. (1921). *Language: An Introduction to the Study of Speech*. San Diego, CA: Harcourt Brace Jovanovich.

Saussure, F. de. (1959). *Course in General Linguistics* (W. Baskin, Trans.). New York: McGraw-Hill. (Original work published in 1916).

Schegloff, E. (1997). "'Narrative analysis' thirty years later." *Journal of Narrative and Life History*, 7, 97–106.

Schilling, N. (2013). "Investigating stylistic variation." In J. K. Chambers and N. Schilling (eds), *Handbook of Language Variation and Change* (2nd edn). (forthcoming). Malden, MA: Wiley-Blackwell.

Schneider, E. (1996). "Introduction: Research trends in the study of American English." In E. Schneider (ed.), *Focus on the USA* (pp. 1–12). Amsterdam/Philadelphia: John Benjamins.

Schütze, C. T. (1996). *The Empirical Base of Linguistics: Grammaticality Judgments and Linguistic Methodology*. Chicago: University of Chicago Press.

Seuren, P. A. M. (1998). *Western Linguistics: An Historical Introduction*. Oxford: Blackwell.

Shuy, R. W. (1990). "A brief history of American sociolinguistics, 1949–1989." *Historiographia Linguistica*, 17, 183–209. Reprinted in C. B. Paulston and G. R. Tucker. (eds), (2003). *Sociolinguistics: The Essential Readings* (pp. 4–16). Malden, MA: Blackwell.

Shuy, R. W. (ed.). (1965). *Social Dialects and Language Learning*. Champaign, IL: NCTE.

Shuy, R., Wolfram, W., and Riley, W. K. (1967). *A Study of Social Dialects in Detroit*. Final Report, Project 6-1347. Washington, DC: Office of Education.

Smitherman, G. (1998). "'What go round come round': King in perspective." In T. Perry and L. Delpit (eds), *The Real Ebonics Debate: Power, Language, and the Education of African-American Children* (pp. 163–71). Boston: Beacon.

Tagliamonte, S. (2006). *Analysing Sociolinguistic Variation*. Cambridge: Cambridge University Press.

Thomas, E. R. (2001). *An Acoustic Analysis of Vowel Variation in New World English* (Publications of the American Dialect Society, 85). Durham, NC: Duke University Press.

— (2002). "Sociophonetic applications of speech perception experiments." *American Speech*, 77, 115–47.

— (2011). *Sociophonetics: An Introduction*. New York: Palgrave Macmillan.

Trudgill, P. (1972). "Sex, covert prestige, and linguistic change in the urban British English of Norwich." *Language in Society*, 1, 179–95.

— (1974). *The Social Differentiation of English in Norwich*. Cambridge: Cambridge University Press.

— (1978). "Introduction: Sociolinguistics and sociolinguistics." In P. Trudgill (ed.), *Sociolinguistic Patterns in British English* (pp. 1–18). London: Arnold.

Vaughn-Cooke, F. B. (1987). "Are black and white vernaculars diverging? Papers from the NWAVE XIV panel discussion." *American Speech*, 62, 12–32.

Wasow, T. and Arnold, J. (2005). "Intuitions in linguistic argumentation." *Lingua*, 115, 1481–96.

Weiner, E. J. and Labov, W. (1983). "Constraints on the agentless passive." *Journal of Linguistics*, 19, 29–58.

Weinreich, U., Labov, W., and Herzog, M. (1968). "Empirical foundations for a theory of language change." In W. Lehmann and Y. Malkiel (eds), *Directions for Historical Linguistics* (pp. 95–188). Austin: University of Texas Press.

Wodak, R., Johnstone, B., and Kerswill, P. (2011). *The Sage Handbook of Sociolinguistics*. Los Angeles: Sage.

Wolfram, W. (1991). "The linguistic variable: Fact and fantasy." *American Speech*, 66, 22–32.

— (1993). "Identifying and interpreting variables." In D. R. Preston (ed.), *American Dialect Research* (pp. 193–221). Amsterdam/Philadelphia: John Benjamins.

— (2007). "Sociolinguistic folklore in the study of African American English." *Language and Linguistic Compass*, 1, 292–313.

Wolfram, W. and Schilling-Estes, N. (2006). *American English* (2nd edn). Malden, MA: Blackwell.

Wolfram, W. and Thomas, E. R. (2002). *The Development of African American English*. Oxford: Blackwell.

Wolfson, N. (1976). "Speech events and natural speech: Some implications for sociolinguistic methodology." *Language in Society*, 5, 189–209.

Woolard, K. (1985). "Language variation and cultural hegemony: Towards an integration of linguistic and social theory." *American Ethnologist*, 12, 738–48.

INDEX